P9-CJV-802

PS
3509
L43
Z7854
1987

121689

N. L. TERTELING LIBRARY
THE COLLEGE OF IDAHO
CALDWELL, IDAHO

Discovering Modernism

Discovering Modernism

T. S. Eliot and His Context

Louis Menand

New York   Oxford
OXFORD UNIVERSITY PRESS
1987

PS 3509
L43
Z 7854
1987

Oxford University Press

Oxford New York Toronto
Delhi Bombay Calcutta Madras Karachi
Petaling Jaya Singapore Hong Kong Tokyo
Nairobi Dar es Salaam Cape Town
Melbourne Auckland

and associated companies in
Beirut Berlin Ibadan Nicosia

Copyright © 1987 by Oxford University Press, Inc.

Published by Oxford University Press, Inc.,
200 Madison Avenue, New York, New York 10016

Oxford is a registered trademark of Oxford University Press.

All rights reserved. No part of this publication may be reproduced,
stored in a retrieval system, or transmitted, in any form or by any means,
electronic, mechanical, photocopying, recording, or otherwise,
without the prior permission of Oxford University Press.

Library of Congress Cataloging-in-Publication Data
Menand, Louis.
Discovering modernism.
Bibliography: p. Includes index.
1. Eliot, T. S. (Thomas Stearns), 1888–1965—
Criticism and interpretation. 2. Modernism (Literature)
I. Title.
PS3059.L43Z7854 1986   821'.912   86-8646
ISBN 0-19-504069-4 (alk. paper)

Acknowledgment is made to the following for permission to reprint
copyrighted material:

The Huntington Library, San Marino, California, for a letter from
Martin Donisthorpe Armstrong to Conrad Potter Aiken, 11 October
1914 (AIK 47).

Faber and Faber Ltd., London, England, and Harcourt Brace Jovanovich,
Inc., for *Collected Poems 1909–1962,* by T. S. Eliot, copyright 1936
by Harcourt Brace Jovanovich, Inc., copyright © 1963, 1964
by T. S. Eliot.

The Ezra Pound Literary Property Trust and Faber and Faber Ltd.,
London, England, and New Directions Publishing Corp., agents,
for a previously unpublished letter by Ezra Pound, copyright © 1986
by the trustees of the Ezra Pound Literary Property Trust.

Raritan: A Quarterly Review, for material in *Raritan,* vol. V,
no. 3 (Winter 1986).

9 8 7 6 5 4 3 2 1

Printed in the United States of America
on acid-free paper

121689

To Emmy

Nie wird es zu hoch besungen
Retterin des Gatten sein.

N. L. TERTELING LIBRARY
THE COLLEGE OF IDAHO
CALDWELL, IDAHO

Contents

Discovering Modernism

Introduction

This is a book about some of the things that happened to the reputation of literature in the early years of this century—about why some writers found it necessary to try to preserve literature's values by transforming them, and about the ironies of that enterprise. More particularly, it is an account of the way in which one writer, T. S. Eliot, took advantage of a moment of cultural change, and of some of the consequences of his opportunism.

How does literature change without ceasing to be literature? Philosophically, the question belongs to a famous class of unanswerables. But like many problems of identity—as when we wish to become better persons by being more true to ourselves—it is no less consequential for being metaphysically indeterminable; and at certain moments in literary history, the problem of how to make literature different without losing all the advantages conferred by the title of "literature" seems to present itself to a whole generation of writers as a matter of genuine practical urgency. These moments are naturally of special interest to the cultural historian, since they promise to tell us something about the mechanisms by which art adapts itself to circumstance.

T. S. Eliot began his career at a time when it appeared to many of his contemporaries that literary values had somehow lost their authority, that literature had become the victim of its own reputation. To those writers who imagined themselves to be its fomenters, this crisis no doubt seemed in the beginning only the sort of calculated disruption that is likely to attend any major turn of literary generation. The modernists engaged in a good deal of shouting against the nineteenth century and, as we have become increasingly aware, at the same time did their best in various ways to live up to the nineteenth century's cultural standards. But the crisis was not a controlled one. The cultural values the modernists hoped would in the last event give them direction were discovered to have lost their powers—and not by modernism's doing—beyond repairing. Eliot was an avant-gardist, but he was also a critic of avant-garde aspirations, and he grasped the particular fatality of modernism's predicament with (to borrow one of his own praise words) a clairvoyance that is even now a little disquieting.

After having enjoyed for many years a starring role in most versions of the story of twentieth-century culture—even when he played the villain, his intentions seemed unambiguous—Eliot has become something of a tough case for the literary historian. The more carefully his career is looked at these days, the more uncertain it is just where his importance lies. Part of the problem is that now that Eliot's own "tradition" has—as all self-proclaimed and self-justifying traditions eventually must—come to seem factitious, it is hard to know to what cultural genealogy he might in fact plausibly be said to belong. He had (as it is now common to point out) a problematic relation, not at all purely antagonistic, to the cultural values of the nineteenth century; but he had a problematic relation, not at all perfectly sympathetic, to many of the values of twentieth-century modernism as well.[1] It is often impossible to tell which direction he is pointing in; he seems at some moments to be the conservator of a certain tradition of literary values and at others to be the analyst of their exhaustion—a confusion exacerbated by his habit of portraying himself in his poetry as history's victim and then prescribing his own cure in his criticism.

There are many ways of trying to account for Eliot's ambivalence; it is my suggestion that we learn something about how literature preserves its identity, and how literary fortune is made, if we think of that ambivalence as deliberate. The genius of Eliot's literary strategy might be characterized as the genius of a weak pragmatism. Eliot first established his authority as a cultural figure not by an exertion of personal will, but by borrowing strength from the very forces that militated against him. He turned a crisis in the reputation of literature to literature's advantage. In describing this strategy in operation, I hope

I have been able to capture something of the complexity of its motivation and the ambiguity of its consequences. Eliot reinscribed the received set of literary values with a modernist surface; and one of the interests his writing therefore has for us is that the nineteenth-century cultural values he made such a show of discrediting can be read, so to speak, beneath the modernist ones he made a show of declaring. But it was also characteristic of Eliot's temperament that he was drawn to ideas and devices whose authority had become suspect, and it was not a small part of his achievement to have made of the anachronistic and the disreputable a kind of fashion.

The Eliot of my book is the poet and critic, and his problems are cultural ones. Eliot the man has become, since the publication of Valerie Eliot's edition of *The Waste Land* in 1971, a valuable ingredient in our revised understanding of the work, and it has seemed important to try to get to know him.[2] I have tried to get to know him and have been helped in doing so by recent biographically informed studies; but though I have not prohibited him from making an occasional appearance in my discussion, I have tried to avoid giving Eliot the man much explanatory work to do.

This is not simply because of a feeling which anyone who has attempted to analyze Eliot's writings for his character will know—the feeling that the moment you think you have psyched Eliot out is likely to be the moment Eliot has succeeded in psyching you out. Nor is it because, as even many of his contemporaries felt, Eliot's personality was a tissue of deliberate disguise: "when you steal up & try to catch hold of him," a casual acquaintance wrote after meeting Eliot in London in 1914, "off he goes like a sand-eel & begins twirling again a few yards further on."[3] For personality is like that, and Eliot's was not, I think, uniquely inscrutable; it only made inscrutability a feature of its surface. Nor is my approach dictated in any way by the doctrine of impersonality, since I understand that doctrine to have derived from a common nineteenth-century way of claiming for one's work sincerity of a particularly exalted kind. It is guided by the assumption that to the extent that Eliot did want to reveal his inner life in his work, he could only have done so by using the literary conventions that indicated to readers of his day that he was being sincere; and it is in part the circumstance that when Eliot entered the literary scene those conventions were in the process of being reformulated that gives his writings their special interest. My argument, in short, is that when Eliot the man—now that our revised conception has helped to give him an identity distinct from the movement with which he was for so long associated—is put back into his historical moment, we can discover for Eliot the writer a new sort of consequentiality.

Arguments about Eliot's proper place in the scheme of literary history tend to turn on the way his irony is read. Though it is now often taken to have been of the self-lacerating kind, the symptom of a belated Romanticism-in-spite-of-itself, Eliot's irony was, of course, to an earlier generation the sign of his "classicism" and "maturity." In trying to rescue Eliot from a certain style of biographical revisionism, I have not wanted to resurrect the exponent of an unremitting high-mindedness. Nor have I wanted to propose some new kind of theoretical coherence for Eliot's work. The Eliot who figured for many years as the champion of high culture can certainly be shown to exist; he has been put together many times. If in my discussion this Eliot seems somewhat neglected, it is in part because I do not quite believe in him. But it is also in part because as soon as Eliot is shown to have had a program for literature, he is transformed from a writer whose peculiar mix of skepticism and opportunism gives to much of his work the look of an indirect but implacable critique of literary values, into another conventional apologist for poetry, proposing aesthetic "solutions" to metaphysical "problems." Eliot's irony seems to me to have been, in his early years and within the limits of what irony alone is capable of, an instrument of wonderful lucidity and force, and always at the service of the interests of the moment. When Eliot built a poem from a series of literary allusions, or when he maintained that the artist must be a professional, or when he proposed to consider poetry as poetry and not another thing, or even when he championed the virtues of tradition, he was not, in my view, formulating a coherent cultural program; he was exploiting a contemporary cultural condition. And if we want to understand what the poetic figure of allusion, or the idea of tradition, or the motto "poetry as poetry" meant to Eliot, and why his readers found the use he made of those things persuasive, we need to understand them not as they make sense to us, but historically. We cannot, that is, explain what made modernism work by looking at modernist writing solely in the context of a literary ideology created by modernism itself. Insofar as Eliot can be said in the first phase of his career to help us to understand the nature of literary change in the modernist period, it is because we have not burdened him with the requirement of consistency that goes with having a prescriptive system. When such a system begins to emerge, as of course it does dramatically in the later years, Eliot's irony takes on a rather different complexion.

At the same time, I have tried to resist the temptation to make the younger Eliot into our contemporary. The traditional defense of literature as a special way of knowing has been displaced in our time by its defense as a subverter of established forms of knowledge, a kind of writing that, without imposing a new normative structure on us, disrupts conventional habits of perception and the ideological assumptions those habits are understood to enforce. We like to dwell on this destabilizing property of literary writing as though it were in itself enough to explain literature's value to us, and as though it did not carry with it ideological baggage of its own. In emphasizing the skeptical side of Eliot's relation to a certain tradition of literary values, I do not mean to ascribe to him such a postmodernist ethic. I like to imagine that it would have seemed to him, in one of his moods at any rate, only another way for culture to insinuate itself into our confidence, to encourage our belief that art is on our side against the paradigms of organized thought. But Eliot had other moods, too, and it is not the least valuable lesson of his career that having a keener and more unforgiving sense of irony than any of his contemporaries did not save him from committing himself, on many literary and extraliterary matters, to judgments that seem to ratify the socializing aspects of culture's authority in some of their most self-aggrandizing forms.

This study is organized around a series of issues that seem to me especially illustrative of the difficulties modernism faced in the period 1910–1922, and especially revealing of Eliot's characteristic manner of responding to those difficulties. I have tried, in the case of each issue discussed, to locate a point in literary history where the cultural solutions of the nineteenth century can be observed becoming the cultural problems of the twentieth, a point where some feature of the received reputation of literature seemed to require rehabilitation. And I have made an effort, in describing these areas of trouble, to distinguish between the problems modernist writers invented their aesthetic solutions for and the problems they invented to explain their solutions—that is, to tell the story of the modernist episode in literary history without relying entirely on modernism's own account of what makes it interesting.

My argument generally is that if some of the familiar features of literary modernism are viewed against the background of certain aesthetic and social issues whose relevance is not usually made explicit in the writings of the modernists themselves, we may find it worthwhile at least to qualify some of our conventional ways of characterizing modernism. In particular, it seems to me that the habit of talking about modernist poetics as an effort to achieve some sort of transcendental epistemology—to "break through" to the object—misses, to the extent that it induces us to try to evaluate the success of that enterprise, some of the interesting features of modernist writing by getting caught up in a discussion whose terms are essentially without meaningful reference. It is certainly true that talk of, for instance, a "language of intuition that would hand over sensations bodily" (T. E. Hulme's phrase) was a part of the announced program of various avant-garde movements in the modernist period. But this was hardly a new ambition for writers to proclaim, and therefore hardly definitive of modernism. And, as I hope I have been able to demonstrate in the chapters that make up the first part of this book, it is certainly not an ambition with which it makes sense to associate Eliot.

It has also been customary to speak of (and often to denigrate) literary modernism as a formalist ideology, one whose distinctive features can be explained as reactive against, rather than reflective of, the "modern world" and its values. This responds, to be sure, to a notable aspect of modernist rhetoric; but again, I think it is a habit of thinking that has become lazy. It is often said, for purposes of explaining modernist formalism, that the modern world is "chaotic" or "formless" or "without values"—characterizations one still hears today in defenses of high-culture art. These are not terms that, even as part of a background generalization, seem to me to explain very much. The early twentieth century was a period, particularly in England, of social change which, because it involved a long-deferred coming to terms with economic realities, was of an unusually unsettling kind. But it was therefore not a period *without* values so much as a period with *too many* values. In some respects, modernism can be seen as an effort to adapt the vocabulary used to describe literature to changing ways of measuring the social value and prestige of different kinds of work, and to do so without at the same time losing the advantages literature enjoyed as a "traditional" field of endeavor. I have tried to suggest, in the second part of this book, how this strategy of adaptation, which did indeed produce an aesthetically formalist ideology, might be understood as a reflection of "worldly" values.

Eliot is the protagonist of the story I have tried to tell, but because this is not only a story about Eliot, its treatment of his work is selective. And while each chapter offers a completed argument, the discussions recall and (though not inconsistently, I hope) rewrite each other at various points. What I have been most interested in is how Eliot did it—how he managed, on the basis of only a few poems and critical essays and in a relatively short amount of time, to capture the central ideological ground of an entire literary period—and I have therefore wanted to suggest that certain devices in Eliot's poetry and certain formulations in his criticism were particularly effective because they managed to respond to a number of different problems simultaneously.

There is, finally, a kind of distortion which I think is unavoidable in a study of this kind but which is worth mentioning here at the start. Literary history, as I conceive it, is an effort to say reasonable things about relations among writers in the face of the fact that for the writers involved the relations were never merely reasonable. Writers are compelled to deal not with their predecessors, but with their predecessors' reputations, which is a very different thing, and much more difficult for us to describe. If in the pages that follow the nineteenth century tends to figure as a kind of ghost, taking on an exaggerated authority and uttering impossible demands, it is not because that is how I imagine the nineteenth century to have been, but because that is the way ghosts are, and the way the nineteenth century must have appeared to Eliot when he set out in 1910 or so to confront the idea of literature.

I

The Literary Object

1

Literary Honesty

On what authority does art make its claim on the emotions of its audience? Many people today are likely to think this question not worth asking, for the simple reason that it seems unanswerable. But it is, of course, one of the leading questions in a long line of aesthetic theory-making—a very long line if we think of Plato as its originator—and that succeeding generations of artists and critics have agreed that the question was a useful one to ask and disagreed about what the right answer might look like is one of the reasons art has a history. For the question is not merely academic; each time it is answered differently every work of art presents a new face. What had been trusted begins to seem fickle or ingratiating, and what had been avoided as affected or perverse is suddenly valued for its authenticity.

To say that good art is good because it offers a just representation of general nature, or because it imitates the universal process of being, or because it preserves the best that has been thought and said, is to suggest a distinction between art that is legitimate and art that is not. We may feel that we are better off without such a distinction; but having no agreed upon criterion for a judgment of this kind makes the business of explaining why the art we value should be worth more to anyone but ourselves than the art we despise especially problematic. The task of finding respectable reasons for the legitimacy of a certain kind of art—or, for the matter can be put the other way around, the task of making an art better suited to contemporary notions of the

legitimate—was one writers in the modernist period thought it important to undertake. For it seemed to them that many of the traditional
arguments for the legitimacy of good art were no longer adequate and
that much of the art conventionally thought good was founded on a
specious authority. The modernist effort to establish a better kind of
theory for a better kind of art involved, for reasons this book attempts
to make clear, difficulties of an especially aggravated kind. It was
T. S. Eliot's characteristic practice as a poet to find ways of transforming
some of those difficulties into literary opportunities.

Any effort begun in the realm of theory to establish the basis for
art's authority runs into difficulties as soon as it reaches the realm of
practice, and none of the theoretical arguments offered by the nineteenth century generated more intricate textual ironies than the argument that a work of art exerts a claim on its audience to the extent
that it is the genuine and uncompromised expression of the inner life
of the artist who produced it. "What the audience demands of the
artist—really demands, in its unconscious desire—and what the artist
thinks it ought to be given turns out to be the same thing . . . the
sentiment of being," is the way Lionel Trilling puts it in his brief
history of two of the argument's key terms, *Sincerity and Authenticity*.[1]
In Trilling's account, this notion gradually achieves, in the course of
its evolution since the late eighteenth century, a crippling hegemony
over the concept of aesthetic value, and ultimately over the concept of
the subject itself; and twentieth-century applications of the standard
of truth-to-self often are expressed in terms of severe moral astrin-
gency. Thus, for instance, Harold Rosenberg on Abstract Expressionism, which Rosenberg called Action Painting and which operated out
of one of the most stridently individualistic sets of artistic conventions
ever devised: "Art as action rests on the enormous assumption that the
artist accepts as real only that which he is in the process of creating.
. . . The test of any of the new paintings is its seriousness—and the
test of its seriousness is the degree to which the act on the canvas is
an extension of the artist's total effort to make over his experience."[2]
The postmodernist will want to know just how sincerity of this order is to be measured, and how the genuine act of self-expression is
to be distinguished from the factitious one. The critical issue is, of
course, deeply embedded in the tradition of Romanticism. It is fully
present in Longinus's treatise: if sublimity is the echo of a great soul,

how is it that one can learn techniques for creating it? Or, to look at the matter from the point of view of the audience, how are we to recognize a work of art without some received notion of the artistic? The case of Abstract Expressionism, coming late in the history of Romanticism, poses the issue rather bluntly and, so to speak, nonnegotiably; but the literature of the nineteenth century provides many subtler instances of the contradictions inherent in the standard of sincerity, and the emergence of a feeling that some of those contradictions could no longer be tolerated is part of the background of Eliot's early poetry.

Though he later learned he had been mistaken, Tennyson thought that the stanza form he used for *In Memoriam* was his own invention.[3] An octosyllabic quatrain with an a-b-b-a rhyme scheme is not an obvious choice for an elegy running to over three thousand lines, but Tennyson no doubt had many reasons for thinking it a good one. He may have felt that it exerted a desirable restriction on moods that threatened to run first to emotional and later to meditative excess; he may have thought of its repetitiveness as a formal echo of the repetitiveness of the poem's memories and memories of memories; he may have considered the form congenial because of its suitability to his particular stylistic strengths, because of the close work it called for with meter and rhyme. But the stanza's originality must have been important to Tennyson for a different sort of reason: it was to be the signature on his memorial to his friend, the emblem of the poem's private significance and the pledge of the poet's sincerity. A conventional form would imply conventional feelings; it might suggest what Tennyson was surely anxious (for the success of his poem depended on it) never to suggest—that Hallam's death was not an event in the history of Tennyson's soul but the occasion for a successful poem.

It was a characteristic practice of T. S. Eliot to sign his poems with traces of the signatures of other writers, which is one among many reasons why it is not surprising to find an echo of the *In Memoriam* stanza in the first of the series of urban landscape poems Eliot began to write in the fall of 1909. "First Caprice in North Cambridge" opens with an a-b-b-a quatrain reminiscent of Tennyson's, though Eliot added a foot to the line, which has the effect of slackening the pace slightly. The poem describes a street scene: a street-piano, frail and garrulous; the evening light, colored a decadent yellow; the distant cries of children's voices.[4]

Like most of the echoes Eliot worked into his poetry, the allusion to Tennyson's poem performs several ingeniously incompatible functions at once. As it would for most poets, of course, the reminder of an earlier poem borrows a mood and announces a debt. If Eliot's lines do put us in mind of *In Memoriam,* we will understand immediately that these images have been collected not for what might be found in them but for what will be discovered to be missing from them; and we will expect the poet's own voice soon to intervene, its tone divided between pity for itself over what has been lost and pity for the world for having lost it. At the same time, as it would for many poets who shared Eliot's kind of ambivalence toward an influence felt to be in danger of becoming an obsession, the echo of *In Memoriam* hints at a revision of the older poem by filling the familiar form with a slightly ill-fitting content: we can anticipate that at some point in the poem the Tennysonian mold will be broken so that Eliot's voice can be heard. And as they would for other poets who, like Eliot, were beginning to think of themselves as avant-gardists, the lines offer a little lesson in the sociology of art by reminding us that the form Tennyson invented to avoid conventionality had by its success become a convention.

But what is most typical of Eliot's poetic practice is the way the allusion disposes of the very problem that led Tennyson to invent his quatrain in the first place: it answers the question of sincerity by referring it back to an anterior authority. This tactic has the curious effect of establishing Eliot's own sincerity, since we cannot accuse him of manufacturing a literary emotion when he has declared his poem's literariness in advance. To put it another way, we cannot ask whether or not Eliot is sincere without asking whether or not Tennyson was sincere, and that question will get us nowhere because the quatrain does not belong to Tennyson any longer; it belongs to literature. The distinction the criterion of sincerity wants us to make between a private feeling and its public expression—the distinction that enables us to judge the degree of their congruence—is no longer of any use, since the poet has chosen to regard his own feelings from the outside, as it were. He seems to suggest, in fact, not that the form for his feeling is artificial or inadequate (a perfectly conventional literary decorum), but that the feeling itself is as much a public thing, a construct, as its literary form.

If we wanted to propose a biographical explanation for this technique, we might suggest that few poets can have mistrusted their own feelings as thoroughly as Eliot seems to have mistrusted his in the poetry he wrote before his religious conversion, and that the strategy of putting feelings he suspected of being factitious in the literary quotation marks of imitation and allusion was one of the methods he discovered for neutralizing that mistrust. This is why the issue of dishonesty—which might arise naturally enough in a discussion of a poem like *In Memoriam,* since *In Memoriam* is a poem in which the distinction between private feeling and public form is still treated as something it makes sense to argue about—seems meaningless in a discussion of Eliot's early poetry. And it is why the notes to *The Waste Land,* sometimes dismissed as the padding Eliot hastily provided to fill out the Boni and Liveright edition of the poem,[5] might plausibly be thought of as the label Eliot wrote, in the period of exhaustion and despondency he went through after his poem was finished, to certify that the product was genuinely synthetic. Whenever we begin to grow skeptical of the authenticity of the feelings we encounter in Eliot's early poetry, we invariably find that Eliot has gotten there ahead of us and is pointing silently to those feelings as though they were objects as puzzling to him as they are to us.

That this is indeed the situation in the "First Caprice" is made clear by the rest of the poem: three rhymed couplets, describing more details of the street—broken glass and barrows, birds delving in the gutter—and ending with an abrupt exclamation at the triviality of the entire experience. The final shrug of dismissal is a habitual gesture of Eliot's—we meet with it everywhere in the poems of this early period—and it is a miniature instance of what would always be his favorite kind of ambiguity. It is impossible to tell whether the contempt is directed at the world for providing such rubbishly material for the imagination to work with, or at the self for being betrayed into such shabby feelings by its incurable habit of trying to manufacture significance from second-rate objects like these. At the same time, the sense that a pathos of special intensity lurks behind these scraps of landscape is somehow heightened by the confession that the poet cannot quite connect himself up to it—the suggestion that the feelings that attach to these images are someone else's.

The same little drama of mistaken identity is enacted in "Portrait of a Lady," which Eliot began a few months after writing the "First Caprice." Here the street-piano is no longer garrulous and frail, like an old man, but mechanical and tired, like a bad poem, and the chance

to let the landscape articulate an emotion is passed up on the explicit
grounds that its images speak to others, but not to the poet:

> I keep my countenance,
> I remain self-possessed
> Except when a street-piano, mechanical and tired
> Reiterates some worn-out common song
> With the smell of hyacinths across the garden
> Recalling things other people have desired.
> Are these ideas right or wrong?[6]

The affectation of affectlessness—who can know the feelings of those
incapable of ordinary feelings?—is, of course, one of the outward signs
of the curse of overcultivation, the subject of many of these poems;
but the situation the lines describe is easily recognized by anyone who
has caught himself gazing at an ordinary landscape in the vague hope
of discovering a grammar for converting a fuzzy emotion into a meaningful one. The significance turns out to be the one conventionally
invested there, and the landscape becomes a familiar text expressing a
commonplace sentiment.

But it will not do to leave the matter here, with the suggestion that
Eliot's early poems are about the problematics of self-expression. For
those poems were successful precisely because they seemed to many
readers expressive not only of a recognizable set of feelings, but of a
personality that is distinctively Eliot's. Eliot's failure (there is a struggle, to be sure, but it seems to be conducted with only half a heart) to
keep his feelings from becoming literary clichés amounts, in other words,
to a literary technique. To understand some of the reasons for the
effectiveness of that technique is to understand, as Eliot seems to have
understood it, something about the limits of literary possibility in 1910,
and something about the cultural distance that separated Eliot's poems
from Tennyson's.

"First Caprice in North Cambridge" is evidently not a finished piece
of work; something seems to have gone wrong with the syntax in the
second stanza. It survives in a notebook Eliot kept for recording drafts
of the poems he wrote between the fall of 1909, when he began work
toward an M.A. in English literature at Harvard, and the fall of 1911,
his first term as a doctoral student in philosophy. A number of the
poems were written in Europe: Eliot spent the academic year 1910–11

in Paris, where he attended Henri Bergson's celebrated lecture course
at the Collège de France and where he became friends with that somewhat obscure figure, Jean Verdenal, who was killed in the First World
War and to whose memory the poems in the notebook—and later those
in *Prufrock and Other Observations* (1917) and *Poems* (1920)—were
eventually dedicated.

"First Caprice" is the first entry in the notebook. It is dated November 1909, and it inaugurates a series of short lyrics describing encoun-
ters with various common urban scenes: a "Second Caprice in North
Cambridge," dated the same month; "Silence," dated June 1910; two
"Preludes in Roxbury," dated October 1910 (the first originally "Prelude in Dorchester"; these were to become the first two "Preludes");
"Fourth Caprice in Montparnasse," October 1910 (originally "Fourth
Caprice in North Cambridge"; if Eliot wrote a "Third Caprice," he
did not preserve it in the notebook); "Interlude: in a Bar," February
1911; "Interlude in London," April 1911; the third "Prelude," here
titled "(Morgendämmerung) Prelude in Roxbury" and dated July 1911;
and a poem Eliot inserted into the notebook on a loose sheet and left
undated called "Abenddämmerung," the poem that became the fourth
"Prelude." Considered as a sequence, these poems seem to act out the
hint given in the "First Caprice": they constitute a kind of abbreviated
In Memoriam, in which a fastidious but mildly neurasthenic consciousness insists on taking the imperturbability of the quotidian for a sign
of its own estrangement. But Eliot's poems stand to Tennyson's elegy
somewhat as Browning's "Childe Roland" stands to the traditional quest-
romance: the protagonist finds himself in a situation he recognizes
structurally as an inquiry into significance, but he is no longer sure
what he is supposed to be looking for. Eliot's sequence is an *In Memoriam* without a Hallam; if it has a drama, it is the drama of much
modernist writing, performed with unrelenting irony by Joyce and
wearisome bravado by Hemingway—the drama of a style in search of
a subject.

The four "Preludes" were the only poems in this series that Eliot
chose to publish; they appeared in July 1915, nearly four years after
they had been composed, in the second and final number of Wyndham
Lewis's *Blast*. There is much about them, of course, that could hardly
be called Tennysonian. There are the traces of *Bubu de Montparnasse*
and *Marie Donadieu*—Grover Smith has pointed out the passages in
Charles-Louis Phillipe's naturalistic novels of Parisian low life, which

seem to have held a peculiar fascination for Eliot, from which the
scene in the third "Prelude" and a few lines of the fourth were drawn.[7]
There is the evidence of Eliot's familiarity with Baudelaire's "Tab-
leaux Parisiens"; there is the Bergsonian talk of "images" in the third
and fourth "Preludes"; and there is Laforgue. No one, I think, has
remarked on the rather exact echoes in the first two "Preludes" of the
opening lines of Laforgue's "Crépuscule." In William Jay Smith's prose
translation:

> Twilight . . . From the houses I pass come the smell of cooking
> and the rattle of plates. People are preparing to dine and then go to
> bed or to the theater . . . Ah, too long have I hardened myself against
> tears; I can be a terrific coward now in the face of the stars!
> And all this is without end, without end.
> Beaten-down horses drag their heavy carts along the streets—women
> wander by—gentlemen greet one another with polite smiles . . . And
> the earth whirls on.[8]

The mise en scène of the urban landscape poem puts the poet face
to face with material that is traditionally "unpoetic," and it therefore
seems to promise an occasion for sincerity: since the poet has placed
himself out of conventional literary bounds, he will not be betrayed
into the expression of a merely literary emotion. But by 1910, of course,
the urban landscape poem had become an established literary genre; it
had a tradition of its own. In the case of Eliot's "Preludes," the variety
of literary sources and their contribution not merely to the mood but
to the details of the poems arouse, as though deliberately, the suspicion that they were composed not in the field, so to speak, but at the
poet's desk, where his favorite books were propped open before him.
And if this is figuratively so, it is easy to imagine that when Eliot came
to write the last poem of the series, one of those books was opened to
the seventh section of *In Memoriam:*

> Dark house, by which once more I stand
>   Here in the long unlovely street,
>   Doors, where my heart was used to beat
> So quickly, waiting for a hand,
>
> A hand that can be clasped no more—
>   Behold me, for I cannot sleep,
>   And like a guilty thing I creep
> At earliest morning to the door.

> He is not here; but far away
> The noise of life begins again,
> And ghastly through the drizzling rain
> On the bald street breaks the blank day.[9]

Eliot's admiration for this poem is well known. He quotes all of it in both of his critical pieces on Tennyson—the "In Memoriam" essay of 1936 and his 1942 radio talk, " 'The Voice of His Time' "—and a number of commentators, encouraged by these citations, have pointed to Tennyson's stanzas as the kind of thing Eliot must have been aiming for when he wrote the "Preludes."[10] The relationship is not simply generic. The fourth "Prelude" seems to have borrowed its plot from the "Dark house" episode: it too is a sort of ghost story, in which the speaker, nearly a ghost himself, feels for a moment the almost palpable presence of something that is not there, only to have his intuition evaporate and to find himself confronting the spectacle of existence without entelechy—the desolate street and the revolving day:

> His soul stretched tight across the skies
> That fade behind a city block,
> Or trampled by insistent feet
> At four and five and six o'clock;
> And short square fingers stuffing pipes,
> And evening newspapers, and eyes
> Assured of certain certainties,
> The conscience of a blackened street
> Impatient to assume the world.

> I am moved by fancies that are curled
> Around these images, and cling:
> The notion of some infinitely gentle
> Infinitely suffering thing.

> Wipe your hand across your mouth, and laugh;
> The worlds revolve like ancient women
> Gathering fuel in vacant lots.

"He can never take anything in stride," Richard Poirier has written of the author of this poem; "he moves, falteringly, toward the formation of images and concepts which dissolve as soon as he has reached them."[11] And one of the concepts that does not cohere, we might add, is the concept of a poem; the ghost fails to appear because the machine has broken down. After the manner of the other entries in this sequence, the fourth "Prelude" assembles materials that have worked before—for Tennyson, for Baudelaire and Laforgue—but finds it impossible to do anything satisfactory with them. The magical arithmetic of Symbolism, whereby the sum of ordinary images is made to yield what Arthur Symons called "the finer sense of things unseen, the deeper meaning of things evident,"[12] is discovered to be a sleight of hand: the poet can solve the equation any way he chooses. That the poem's naturalist or tough-minded solution—"The worlds revolve like ancient women"—is felt by the poet to be as contrived as its metaphysical, tender-minded solution is made clear in the notebook version by a final couplet that in effect apologizes for both by ascribing the poem's strange opinions to the kinds of thoughts that enter one's head at four o'clock in the morning.

It is the official policy of any symbolist poetics to maintain that the successful poem runs on the natural energy of its images, which are themselves simply sensations veridically transcribed. "Sincerity, and the impression of the moment followed to the letter," was Verlaine's way of putting it;[13] "a number of impressions, too multiplied, too minute, and too diversified to allow of our tracing them to their causes, because just such was the effect . . . produced on [the poets'] imaginations by the real appearance of Nature," was Arthur Hallam's.[14] The aesthetic ideology served by this policy is easily unmasked, of course. A post-Kantian will point to Verlaine's "to the letter" and Hallam's "real appearance" (a redundancy or an oxymoron?) as contradictions that give the game away: just what is it whose power is being transferred through the medium of the poet's special consciousness? If we pass up the invitation to look for the sanction of the poem's effectiveness in some extratextual source like the nature of the objects being represented or the structure of the mind representing them, we are likely to feel that while the poem's images (insofar as they are isolable from the linguistic mass of the poem) retain a kind of titular authority, the real work is done by various unauthorized agents.

One such agent is the allusion. By the standards of sincerity, an allusion is an operative of questionable legitimacy, since its energy derives not from anything that might be pointed to in the poet's experience but from the fact of its already having enjoyed an aesthetic success: it works because it has worked before. But its effectiveness, like the effectiveness of any literary figure, will depend on its cultural sta-

tus. "[W]hen he should have been broken-hearted, he had many reminiscences," Verlaine complained about the author of *In Memoriam,* a
poem he told Yeats he had tried but was unable to translate.[15] If we
ask why Verlaine was ever tempted to translate a poem whose spirit
he evidently considered unsympathetic, the answer must be that his
dissatisfaction became apparent to him only after he had actually set
about the business of rendering *In Memoriam* into French. For "reminiscence" was a late-nineteenth-century term for poetic borrowing, and
Verlaine's trouble began when he found himself attempting to reproduce in French phrases that owed their resonance to the memory they
evoked of some English original. The difficulty of translation must
eventually have converted itself into a difficulty of sympathy: that Tennyson could have allowed his effects to be derived from books instead
of the nature of his own grief seemed to Verlaine a state of mind too
alien to imitate.

The late nineteenth century was much interested in the psychology
of reminiscence,[16] for a number of questions about literary values turned
on it: If the poet was unconscious of the obligation, was the integrity
of the poem compromised, and more or less than if he knew what he
was echoing? If the reader was ignorant of the original, had he been
tricked into a spurious response by mistaking the sincerity of what he
had read? The connotations of the term tell us something about the
status of the phenomenon it names. A reminiscence is a pleasant memory, and one deliberately recalled; as a literary term, it has the air of
giving a look of respectability to matters of potential embarrassment.
It suggests something more honorable than a borrowing of effects, which
points in the direction of plagiarism, but less violent than a poetic
figure, which, by treating the original as a quarry for new edifices,
points toward literary rivalry, a deed done to the predecessor's authority.

Verlaine's complaint about Tennyson was not, when he made it to
Yeats in the 1890s, a new one, or even a French one. We find Tennyson being defended by his admirers as early as 1873 against the
suggestion that his habit of repeating his own more successful lines in
later poems cheated on the requirements of sincerity.[17] And in 1880,
John Churton Collins, an ambitious young scholar who had impressed
and entertained his Oxford tutors with the capacity of his memory for
poetry, began a series of articles in the *Cornhill* devoted to the enu-
meration of Tennyson's "obligations to his predecessors." The tone

was reverential—the borrowings were said to be testimony to Tennyson's "wondrous assimilative skill, his tact, his taste, his learning"—but the massive display of evidence had something slightly scandalous about it, and the Laureate, though impressed, was decidedly not entertained.[18] The general issue was alive enough in 1901 for A. C. Bradley to think it necessary to devote several pages of his well-known *Commentary* on *In Memoriam* to a discussion of what he too called Tennyson's "reminiscences" or "unconscious reproductions." "Unconscious" was Bradley's way of surmounting the difficulty: Tennyson may not have been the most inventive of our poets, he allowed, but this should "not . . . cast doubts on his originality. . . . [I]f ever a poet were a master of phrasing he was so, and the fact that he was so is quite unaffected by the further fact that he was sometimes unconsciously indebted to his predecessors."[19]

But though *In Memoriam* is strewn with borrowed phrases whose provenance Tennyson no doubt did not reflect on when they occurred to him, the poem holds many echoes for which it seems likely that "unconscious" describes not the nature of the poet's recollections but what he intended the nature of the reader's to be. If, to take one of the echoes Bradley identifies,[20] the phrase "guilty thing" in the second of the "Dark house" stanzas puts us vaguely in mind of the predawn ghost watch in the opening act of *Hamlet,* Tennyson has successfully traded some of the spontaneity of his poem for a bit of useful ambience from someone else's; if we recall more specifically that the words appear in Horatio's description of the ghost—"And then it started, like a guilty thing" (I, i, 148)—we may simply wonder what they are doing in Tennyson's stanzas being applied to the ghost-watcher. The "once more" in "Dark house, by which once more I stand" may, as a reminder of the first line of Milton's elegy for *his* Cambridge friend, seem an unobtrusive striking of the proper generic note; but if we recall that Tennyson will spend most of *In Memoriam* IX through XIX imagining Hallam's body lost at sea, it may appear that a piece of literary rivalry is being prepared that has little to do with the immediate poetic occasion. And the reader who notices, as John Rosenberg has, that the ninth line of *In Memoriam* VII has an authoritative ring because it is borrowed from the angel at the empty sepulchre who informs the two Marys that "He is not here, for he has risen,"[21] will perhaps feel that this is stealing an effect from a ghost story off limits to even the most devoted admirer of Arthur Hallam.

But if *In Memoriam* is riddled with allusions that seemed to later readers to compromise the sincerity of the poet's grief, why did the poem seem to its original audience such an extraordinary success? Not, we can assume, because the borrowing in most cases went unnoticed, but because an allusion is not a figure of balance: it is often most useful when it outweighs its occasion, and in the case of a poem like *In Memoriam* it is likely to be wanted precisely for its extravagance. The illegitimacy of the echo of the Gospels—nothing in the scene of Hallam's old house, or in Tennyson's feelings for Hallam, or in Hallam's spiritual significance for the nineteenth century can possibly authorize it—is, as far as the poem's emotional effect is concerned, the most important thing about it. It is a risky gesture because *In Memoriam* is an exercise in the management of a dangerous emotion. The man who stands in the street outside his dead friend's house is a "guilty thing": he fears that his feelings are somehow other than what they ought to be. And Tennyson's nineteenth-century readers, fascinated as they were by the economics of mourning, must have taken much of his poem's drama to lie in its handling of the question of what kind of excess would be the wrong kind of excess. That the poet's grief might become, even by the standards of Victorian society, abnormal—too self-indulgent, too close to homoeroticism—is a danger deliberately flirted with throughout the poem; at the same time, the emotion must always be shown to run slightly ahead of what is socially desirable, or what would be the point of having a decorum in these matters? The formal constraints of a poem like *In Memoriam* impress us if we have the sense that there is something there that needs constraining, and since that sense can only come from the poem itself, the poet sometimes has to cheat against his own form to give it to us. Insofar as it is a poem that depends on the principle of sincerity according to which the poet's feelings may not be artificially enhanced in their expression, those moments when that principle seems to be in jeopardy are important to *In Memoriam*'s success. An allusion is likely to be such a moment; but its effectiveness is a function of what is happening at the margin of the aesthetically permissible—of the degree to which the audience recognizes an allusion as a device that takes the measure of the limits of sincerity but does not, finally, exceed them. What tested the bounds of literary honesty in 1850 transgressed them in 1910; and it was precisely the aura of insincerity that was eventually understood to cling to the allusion that enabled Eliot to convert it, as we have begun to see, into such a spectacular trope.

But an allusion is only one of the more blatant trespasses against the requirement of sincerity. For what *would* qualify, under a strict application of the standard, as an unadulterated impression? Tennyson's sensations of Hallam's house are in fact a tissue of rhetorical figures: the house is not observed; it is apostrophized, and the situation is reduced to a transaction among emotionally charged objects—a door, a heart, a hand—by the process of synecdoche. The whole poem might be described as a literary figure for a literal one: the street is not "bald" because that is the way the street looked but because "bald" is the word that transforms the entire landscape into an actualization of the metaphor latent in the image of the house—it describes the head of a corpse. The pieces of anatomy that are scattered like the limbs of Osiris around the poem belong, it turns out, to the body of Arthur Hallam. If the poem works, the machinery remains submerged as the ghost silently appears.

This is the equipment the author of the fourth "Prelude" feels obliged to demonstrate his ineptitude with. In his hands, conceits become riddles (how are "the worlds" like the women—only in their revolving?); the rhyme scheme is disheveled; pronouns displace one another without any apparent narrative authorization. His first stanza is a syntactical cul-de-sac: it cannot seem to decide whether to become a sentence or not, and what looks like synecdoche—the feet, fingers, and eyes—turns out to be fragmentation, parts without wholes. The text itself becomes a sign for what nothing in the text can quite manage to signify: the trouble with the form is a trope for trouble with the emotion. The trouble with the emotion is that it cannot discover whether it is sincere, and not a hallucinatory four-o'clock-in-the-morning thought, because all the objects on which it seeks to ground itself threaten to turn into figures of speech. The trouble with the form is that without a figure of speech to give the objects a grammatical field in which to play, no emotion will be recognizable. It is the problem posed by a poetic that has declared what is merely literary to be illegitimate: where everything must be genuine, everything will end up looking artificial.

But just as there are effects associated with literary forms of various kinds, there is an effect associated with form-breaking, and Eliot's poem does not aspire to inconsequence. It is often maintained that what looks like broken form in modernist writing is really a more perfect kind of form, form that brings us closer to the object. Thus the long line of arguments that Eliot in the Cubistic style of the "Preludes" simply found a way to produce a fuller impression than Tennyson was able to produce with the more primitive Symbolist techniques at his disposal.[22] This is, of course, one way of claiming an advance in knowledge: the transformational devices in the predecessor's language are treated as walls, and those in the successor's are treated as windows. Tennyson's manner of representation produces wordiness; Eliot's produces thinginess. But insofar as readers of Eliot's early poetry experience a sense of thinginess, feel that this is the way the city really is for a particular consciousness at a certain pitch of *aboulie,* it is perhaps the consequence not of the creation of a new form but of the shattering of an old one, and, if so, it is important to the effect that the damaged vessel not be mistaken for a new and more adequate container—just as it is important for poems that break cultural artifacts into bits such as *The Waste Land* and Pound's *Cantos* that some of the shards be too small to identify. The ghost in the fourth "Prelude" is the soul of the world, and the rationale behind the poem's method seems to be the sort that would be articulated by Heidegger in *Being and Time* (1927): the thereness of the world suddenly reveals itself at the moment the tool breaks down. Or to put it another way, a poem that professes to find in the received forms of literary language only the means for the production of secondhand sentiments will rely on its objects becoming real to its readers by the mechanism that makes a person seem most real to us when we are searching for the words to describe him.

Tennyson was, of course, careful not to pretend that his forms were adequate to his feelings; in *In Memoriam* an embarrassment over the fact of his poem is one aspect of the poet's "guilt." And Tennyson did not need Bradley to excuse him on this count, for he took the precaution early in his poem (section V) of making a self-consciousness about the epiphenomenal character of literary expression an attribute of his sincerity:

> I sometimes hold it half a sin
> > To put in words the grief I feel;
> > For words, like Nature, half reveal
> And half conceal the Soul within.

But to a twentieth-century modernist Tennyson would have seemed rather too sure of his arithmetic in this passage, and the appeal by analogy to "Nature" would have looked like an attempt to authorize a

Tennysonian kind of poetic language all over again: the last two lines
of the stanza suggest that the soul actually *is* most honestly—most
naturally—revealed when it is, as in the figurative language of poetry,
partly concealed. The equipment Tennyson undertook to legitimate by
this argument and which he used to generate the emotion in his poem
the twentieth century would lump under the category of "the poetical," and it was the ambition of a certain strain of modernism to see
if one could have such a thing as poetry without it. One of the notable
things about the fourth "Prelude" is that it seems to take a dim view
of the prospects of this enterprise even before the main effort had
begun.

2

Problems About Objects

The doctrine of the image presents the literary historian with an odd sort of problem: the more fully its genealogy is explored, the more it seems to touch on everything. The persuasive power of the term "image" is so great that it sometimes seems as though every critic from the late seventeenth century to the mid-twentieth has wanted to claim it for his* theory; and thus being used to underwrite nearly everything, it ends up explaining almost nothing. Like "value" in the history of economic theory and "object" in the history of psychology, "image" refers to a fiction every literary theory that uses the term tries to make real; but since what it denotes can never be settled on to anyone's complete satisfaction, its meaning is determined not so much by the particular set of practices it is intended to describe as by the particular set of errors its user has enlisted it in reaction against. Whenever "image" or one of its allied terms—such as "impression," "sensation," or "symbol" in its nineteenth-century usage—has made an appearance in prescriptive writing about poetry since the seventeenth century, it has invariably been accompanied by a counterterm—"rhetoric," "ornament," "thought" or "idea," "allegory." And these sets of terms have a way of changing places like partners in a dance through the history of literary theory.

---

* When gender is unspecified, the pronouns *he, him, his,* etc., should be understood throughout as abbreviations for *he or she, him or her, his or her,* etc.

Thus we find "image" being recruited on behalf of the Restoration demand for "perspicuity" and against the highly figured contrivances of the school of Donne, and then on behalf of the associative structure of descriptive poetry in the later eighteenth century and against the discursiveness of the Augustans.[1] When Wordsworth, in turn, charged the eighteenth century with the manufacture and dissemination of "arbitrary and fickle habits of expression," he argued that properly understood "Poetry is the image of man and nature," and that no poet would therefore want to violate "the sanctity and truth of his pictures by transitory and accidental ornaments."[2] And when, in his persona of neoclassical disciplinarian, the young Matthew Arnold complained that critics under the influence of Romantic standards were encouraging mere "bursts of fine writing" by permitting the poet "to leave their poetical sense ungratified, provided that he gratifies their rhetorical sense," he was careful to recommend the Aristotelian standard of unified action in the language of sensation by calling for attention to the poem's "total-impression."[3]

The appeal of this sort of language is easily appreciated: there is no arguing with sensations, and if readers can be persuaded that a certain kind of writing owes its effects not to the artificial stimulus of rhetoric but to its having managed to reproduce the feel of experience, an imposing authority for that poetry's claim on the emotions of the audience has been established, for those claims are now understood to be backed by the full faith and credit of the world's objects themselves. We have already seen some of the practical difficulties this line of theorizing can entail (and some of the opportunities those difficulties have made available to poets willing to exploit them), but the argument is complicated still further by the circumstance of its having borrowed its vocabulary and its model of the mind from the very philosophy whose skeptical view of the imagination it was traditionally expected to refute. For "image" derives from Hobbes, who had no very high opinion of poetry, and the distinction between "impressions"—sensations of the first order, fresh from the object—and "ideas"—impressions that have decayed in the unreliable storage cellar of the mind— is Hume's.[4] Since, on the view of empiricism, all we know of the world is the data transmitted to the mind by the senses, and since we have nothing but those data to measure our ideas of the world against, the closer to the sensations themselves and the farther from the analysis of those sensations we get ("Not the fruit of experience, but expe-

rience itself," in the outstanding aestheticist rendition of this view),
the less distortion is likely to have occurred. Forever separated by what
Pater called "the thick wall of personality"[5] from objects in all their
thinghood, the poet presses the surface of his poem up against the
bricks. Though it is often supposed to be the epistemological foundation for the methods of modern science (but if the scientist did not
have a prior idea of what he was looking for, how would he know
which of his sense data mattered?), empiricism is in fact one of the
sponsors of modern aesthetic theory. It is not an eccentricity that Pater's thought is characterized by both an overzealous acceptance of the
materialist implications of Locke and Darwin and a carefully cultivated
nostalgia for the essential "unworldliness"[6] of Plato: if empiricism is,
as A. D. Nuttall suggests, a materialist's Platonism,[7] sharing Plato's
suspicion of the artist, then modern aesthetic theory is a secularist's
neo-Platonism, rushing to promote art into the gap empiricism leaves
between experience and knowledge.

As frequently as it has been presented, this is an argument every
generation of poets has wanted to invent for itself, for it offers a convenient theoretical authorization for the practical business of making
the poetry of the previous generation obsolete. It has seemed natural
to want to place Eliot within this critical tradition by giving his aesthetic prescriptions a theoretical shape of their own, and it has consequently seemed like a good idea to look for the place where that
shape might be discovered to have been adumbrated. Eliot's dissertation for the Harvard philosophy department has seemed to many commentators an obvious candidate, but when we examine it we find that
it is not so useful. Or, rather, we are likely to feel that it is useful for
a different reason entirely; for it seems to suggest not only that Eliot
had no consistent theory of poetry, but that he had good theoretical
reasons for not wanting one.

1

The history of the Imagist movement is a tale made fairly indecipher-
able at points by the bad feelings of its participants, whose recollections are largely taken up with disputes over the issue of priority. Richard
Aldington, who was not always overly generous in these matters, was
willing to give most of the credit for the movement to Pound; Pound,

who sometimes was overly generous, gave it to Ford. F. S. Flint informed Pound that Ford "was one of the generals of division in an army composed of many divisions. No doubt his operations seemed of paramount importance to you because you were enrolled under him," and cited (in addition to his own articles on French poetry) Hulme's Poets' Club and Edward Storer's 1908 *Mirrors of Illusion*. Robert Frost, who had been in England at the time, thought all the credit belonged to Flint.[8] It seems reasonable to conclude that a movement whose principles were vague enough to attract, during the brief period of its serious vogue, writers of such different ambitions as Ford, Pound, and Amy Lowell (who, after an attempted merger with Pound had been rebuffed, made the question of ownership academic by buying out the entire enterprise in 1915) owed most of those principles to the atmosphere of the time. But no doubt, too, that atmosphere was thickened appreciably by the writings of Bergson.

Distinctive as it was in many respects, Bergsonism shared with a number of contemporary philosophical undertakings a purpose and a strategy: it proposed to disprove the mechanistic conclusions of traditional empiricist epistemology, and to do so by elevating the subject, which nineteenth-century science had made into the toy of matter, to an equal status in the definition of reality with the world. "[M]aterialism will always fail of universal adoption," was the way William James put it in *The Will to Believe* (1897); ". . . For [it] denies reality to the objects of almost all the impulses which we most cherish."

> . . . The monstrously lopsided equation of the universe and its knower, which we postulate as the ideal of cognition, is perfectly paralleled by the no less lopsided equation of the universe and the *doer*. We demand in it a character for which our emotions and active propensities shall be a match. Small as we are, minute as is the point by which the cosmos impinges upon each one of us, each one desires to feel that his reaction at that point is congruous with the demands of the vast whole,— that he balances the latter, so to speak, and is able to do what it expects of him.[9]

Bergson's *"durée réelle"* is an ally to James's "pure experience," and to F. H. Bradley's "immediate experience" and Alfred North Whitehead's "event" (a concept that provided Edmund Wilson with the definition of a symbol for his history of modernism, *Axel's Castle* [1931]), in postulating a strong subject side to the equation of the mind and the world. But though each of these terms arises out of and issues in very different philosophical tendencies, to the extent that they are intended as a basis for assessing the validity of beliefs they are epistemological, and to the extent that they are backed by an appeal to the feel of experience they are empiricist. Thus Richard Rorty is right when he notes the "spirit of playfulness which seemed about to enter philosophy around 1900," but he is not, I think, quite right when he appears to include Bergson, Bradley, and the James of radical empiricism with Nietzsche, Dilthey, Dewey, and the James of pragmatism in his suggestion that philosophy was threatening at that moment to "turn away once and for all from epistemology, from the quest for certainty."[10] To say that the universe is like a fountain and not like a clock, as Bergson did, or that reality does not lie inert but blooms and buzzes, as James did, may license a broader ethical scope and a more imaginative style for philosophical writing, and may provide metaphors with a greater value for, say, the writing of poetry, but insofar as those descriptions claim to give more accurate pictures of the world, they suggest that a new vocabulary might privilege itself as the right way for talking about things as they really are.

Which is how the matter seems to have presented itself to T. E. Hulme when he began to read Bergson around 1907. Hulme described the effect of Bergson's *Essai sur les donnés immédiates de la conscience* (1889) in the language of conversion: "It gave one the sense of giddiness that comes with a sudden lifting up to a great height. . . . I had been released from a nightmare which had long troubled my mind." But as with the most effective sorts of conversions, Hulme's was successful not because Bergson had invented a new and original philosophy—Hulme was quite emphatic about this, wishing above all "to avoid any suspicion of romanticism"—but because he had brought a familiar problem to a more satisfactory solution. The paradigm of consciousness that had become the prison-house of mechanism was not broken; its terms were simply rearranged.

> It was not simply a case of an intolerable state being changed into a pleasanter one; it was not merely that one state changed into its opposite. On the contrary, there was a certain resemblance between the initial state and the final stages. There was a certain continuity between them. The first state might even be considered as a very rough

> microcosm of part, at any rate, of the second. . . . [T]he key with
> which this prison door was opened corresponded to the type of key
> which I had always imagined would open it.[11]

In insisting on this point, Hulme was only following the lead of his
master, for the *Essai* opens with the promise that what looks like a
problem in the empiricist model of the mind can be shown to be merely
a problem with the way that model had conventionally been described:

> . . . [I]t may be asked whether . . . by merely getting rid of the
> clumsy symbols round which we are fighting, we might not bring the
> fight to an end. . . . What I attempt to prove is that all discussion
> between the determinists and their opponents implies a previous con-
> fusion of duration with extensity, of succession with simultaneity, of
> quality with quantity: this confusion once dispelled, we may perhaps
> witness the disappearance of the objections raised against free will, of
> the definitions given of it, and, in a certain sense, of the problem of
> free will itself.[12]

The great appeal of Bergson's philosophy was that without essentially
damaging the paradigms of nineteenth-century science—of empiricist
psychology in the *Essai* and in *Matière et mémoire* (1896), of Darwinism
in *L'Évolution créatrice* (1907)—it refurbished those paradigms to provide spiritual comfort to a generation that was, in the decade before
the First World War, suspicious of the pretensions of science and at
the same time anxious not to appear unscientific.

It is no surprise, then, to find in Bergson's *Essai* the customary
distinction between what is felt and what is thought, here described
as a distinction between two selves: one that is like a body, experiencing without analyzing, and one that is like a brain, analyzing without
feeling. We have been misled into neglecting the true testimony of the
first self—Bergson calls it "the real and concrete self"[13]—because we
have been cowed by the factitious authority of the second. At this
point, the argument runs into a contradiction common in theories of
this sort, for it seems that we are to go about recovering "this fundamental self" by "a vigorous effort of analysis"[14]—by the exertions,
that is, of the unreliable second self. But Bergson does not even break
stride at this obstacle, for he has a greater one in view: standing in
the path of our analysis, and the agent of our alienation, is language.

> We instinctively tend to solidify our impressions in order to express
> them in language. Hence we confuse the feeling itself, which is in a

perpetual state of becoming, with its permanent external object, and especially with the word which expresses this object. . . . Not only does language make us believe in the unchangeableness of our sensations, but it will sometimes deceive us as to the nature of the sensation felt. . . . In short, the word with well-defined outlines, the rough and ready word, which stores up the stable, common, and consequently impersonal element in the impressions of mankind, overwhelms or at least covers over the delicate and fugitive impressions of our individual consciousness. To maintain the struggle on equal terms, the latter ought to express themselves in precise words; but these words, as soon as they were formed, would turn against the sensation which gave birth to them, and, invented to show that the sensation is unstable, they would impose on it their own stability.[15]

But the suggestion that language is always a lock and never a key is not quite credible—after all, had not Bergson performed his miracle with determinism by substituting good words for bad ones?—and Hulme must have been quick to read in passages like this an invitation to invent a new mode of discourse. In Bergson's "Introduction à la métaphysique" (1903), he discovered what language might look like.

The "Introduction" is more careful than the *Essai* about ruling "analysis" out of court. The inner life, the "Introduction" explains, is accessible only to "intuition"; it is—and here the invariable feature of what was for Plato "up there" and for Locke "out there" is transposed to the "in here"—unrepresentable. But what cannot be described can be pointed to, and though with "concepts," the tools of intellect, we can only "move round the object," "images" can direct us "into it":

the image has at least this advantage, that it keeps us in the concrete. No image can replace the intuition of duration, but many diverse images, borrowed from very different orders of things, may, by the convergence of their action, direct consciousness to the precise point where there is a certain intuition to be seized.[16]

The image is an arrow, aimed at a target only intuition can pierce. An "image" plus an "intuition" sounds like an etymology for "imagination," and at the end of his essay Bergson makes this hint explicit by comparing, in Coleridgean fashion, a metaphysics of intuition to the process of literary composition. Thus provided with a term and the guidelines for a method, Hulme began around 1908 to put together his "Notes on Language and Style"—"Each *word* must be an image *seen*, not a counter"[17]—and in 1909 announced in *The New Age,* in a series

called "Searchers after Reality," that poetry "is not a counter language, but a visual concrete one. It is a compromise for a language of
intuition which would hand over sensations bodily. . . . Images in
verse are not mere decoration, but the very essence of an intuitive
language."[18]

Pound had no patience for "crap like Bergson,"[19] and Ford thought
that poetry should be more, not less, like prose; but their prescriptions
for good writing were founded on the same argument that supported
Hulme's: since our sensations are more immediate than the ideas we
derive from those sensations, words that describe what can be grasped
by the senses are to be trusted more than words that describe what
can only be thought about. But any argument that bases itself on the
primacy of sensation quickly reaches the end of its tether, since it is,
after all, trying to prove the importance of things whose virtues are
not immediately apparent to the senses of everyone; and a theory that
has had to rewrite itself as many times as the theory of the image will
contain the elements of its own critique within it. The extreme version of the imagist formula that Pound finally produced is perfectly
expressive of the contradictions inherent in every edition of the doctrine over the history of the enterprise.

Pound and Ford did not need to read Bergson or (though Pound
surely did) to attend to Hulme, for they were both students of Pater,
in whose essay on "Style" (1888) most of the recurrent themes of their
prescriptive writings can be discovered. "Style" is one of those curious
performances of Pater's later career in which he seems determined to
make whatever is subversive in his cultural program appear perfectly
conventional, and thus guided by this spirit of conciliation his argument springs loose terms which, when they turn up later in the critical literature of Imagism, mark the points where that theory had to
compromise with its own implications.

Pater's argument turns on a distinction between the literature of
fact and the literature of what he calls "the sense of fact." The distinction would ordinarily be unexceptionable, and it has a significant
history—Pater cites De Quincey's "the literature of knowledge and the
literature of power," and Hazlitt's essays stand in the background[20]—
but it is hard to see what it could have meant to the author of the
"Conclusion" to *The Renaissance* (1873). The model of the mind presented there allows for nothing *but* "the sense of fact":

> At first sight experience seems to bury us under a flood of external
> objects, pressing upon us with a sharp and importunate reality, calling
> us out of ourselves in a thousand forms of action. But when reflexion
> begins to play upon those objects they are dissipated under its influ-
> ence; the cohesive force seems suspended like some trick of magic;
> each object is loosed into a group of impressions—colour, odour, tex-
> ture—in the mind of the observer. . . . Every one of those impres-
> sions is the impression of the individual in his isolation, each mind
> keeping as a solitary prisoner its own dream of a world.[21]

The Romantics' "power" scarcely seems the appropriate term for the
activities of a subject of this description—a subject whose ideal condition Pater had described in "Diaphaneitè" (1864) as "a moral sex-
lessness, a kind of impotence, an ineffectual wholeness of nature."[22]

But in "Style" Pater needed to ascribe a virtue—and submission to
the shower of atoms would not do—to the exercise of literary style;
and, intending the essay to be the first in a volume dedicated in part
to writers of the Romantic period, he turned to the Romantic model
of an interactive mind and nature as something that might suggest
what was distinctive about the mental operations of the writers he
admired. The uncongeniality of the model—its metaphor is not sex-
lessness—is reflected in the revised description Pater offered of the
experience of experience:

> Into the mind sensitive to "form," a flood of random sounds, colours,
> incidents, is ever penetrating from the world without, to become, by
> sympathetic selection, a part of its very structure, and, in turn, the
> visible vesture and expression of that other world it sees so steadily
> within, nay, already with a partial conformity thereto, to be refined,
> enlarged, corrected, at a hundred points; and it is just there, just at
> those doubtful points that the function of style, as tact or taste, inter-
> venes.[23]

This is a sentence writ in water: everything it names it dissolves—putting "form" into quotation marks is the perfect Paterian touch—and
the unworkableness of the syntax around the word "nay" is a symptom
of the unworkableness of the model. What is refined, enlarged, and
corrected against the standard of what? And what is it that the mind
"sees" so steadily such that the sensible qualities of the outer world
are required to make it visible? In the "Conclusion," the character of
the inner life is continuous with the character of the outer—"that

strange, perpetual, weaving and unweaving of ourselves"[24]; in "Style," the physical world remains a stream of sensation, but Pater has tried to put some shape into his picture by granting the mind structure, steadiness, and the power to select.

Pater's difficulties here are in part a consequence of the paradox he was drawn into by attempting to derive ethical principles from a fairly uncompromising materialism, a paradox that afflicts the "Conclusion" as well—in the form of, "since we cannot 'do' anything, let us do this." His sentence becomes ambiguous at the moment it tries to account for the source of the mind's "other world" because about a subject whose contents are entirely the product of outer circumstance there is nothing ethical to be said. But some of the confusion is due to an inadequacy in the theory of the mind Pater's description relies on. For the problem with empiricist epistemology is not that it doubles the object, creating a mental one for every inaccessible "real" one— Berkeley had shown how that difficulty could be overcome—but that it doubles the mind. Every effort to make the best of the empiricist model is compelled at some point to invent an entity that performs with sense data inside the brain the very function it has already been asserted the brain cannot perform with the physical objects it contemplates. Even David Hume, who was determined to leave the mind nothing it could call its own, is caught in this redundancy when, undertaking to explode the fiction of personal identity, he calls the mind "a kind of theatre, where several perceptions successively make their appearance; pass, re-pass, glide away, and mingle in an infinite variety of postures and situations."[25] The metaphor betrays the argument, for in order to make sense of it, we need to imagine in attendance at this performance a tiny audience of one; and if we are to avoid giving this audience some sort of substance like "personal identity," we must further imagine it to have in attendance at *its* mental theater another tiny audience, and so forth.

Bergson's "intuition" is such a piece of internal machinery. It cannot go wrong; it is an infallible mind within the fallible one. And Pater becomes entangled in this famous Quaker-Oats-box-like regression when he posits an unnamed something that reads sensations in the same manner as common sense supposes the body's eye does objects in the world. Pater is not content to define "style" as that which a piece of writing presents, and a reader responds to, as the special flavor of the writer's way of experiencing, because style is not a game for two play-

ers; it is a discipline, and Pater wants the virtue he assigns to it—
"truth . . . to some personal sense of fact"—to be measurable:

> For just in proportion as the writer's aim, consciously or uncon-
> sciously, comes to be the transcribing, not of the world, not of mere
> fact, but of his sense of it, he becomes an artist, his work *fine* art; and
> good art . . . in proportion to the truth of his presentment.[26]

The empiricist's inner eye is not a disposable fiction; it is the gyroscope
in Pater's model. It stabilizes the picture so that expression can match
it.

"[H]is sincerity may be measured by a number of his images," Hulme
maintained of the poet in "A Lecture on Modern Poetry,"[27] and at
every point in Imagist theory where a practice requires legitimation,
this Paterian test is applied. It is Pound's argument for *vers libre*:

> I believe in an "absolute rhythm," a rhythm, that is, in poetry which
> corresponds exactly to the emotion or shade of emotion to be ex-
> pressed. A man's rhythm must be interpretative, it will be, therefore,
> in the end, his own, uncounterfeiting, uncounterfeitable.[28]

It is Ford's argument against literary allusion:

> Reading is an excellent thing; it is also experience. . . . But it is an
> experience that one should go through not in order to acquire imitative
> faculties but in order to find—oneself.[29]

And it is Aldington's defense of contemporary subject matter:

> . . . there is an escape from artificiality and sentimentality in poetry,
> and that is by rendering the moods, the emotions, the impressions of
> a single, sensitized personality confronted by the phenomena of mod-
> ern life, and by expressing these moods accurately, in concrete, pre-
> cise, racy language.[30]

The standard is the venerable one of sincerity, but its authority has
become drastically attenuated, for it is hard to feel that a self conceived of as merely attending, however earnestly, to the apparitions
that flash before it inside the metro station of the brain will have much
to be sincere about. Pound was, in fact, unhappy with the passive role
he felt some versions of Imagist theory—his friend Ford's Impressionism especially—assigned to the poet, and he tried with Vorticism to
license some *poiesis* for his poetic. But he did not want to give up any
of the epistemological ground Imagism had claimed; and so, though

the Vorticist poet may arrange his images in the manner most congenial to his design, the image is not simply the building block of his
poem; it is the only material permitted. "Every conception, every emotion presents itself to the vivid consciousness in some primary form,"
announces Pound's Vorticist manifesto in the 1914 *Blast,* and thus
"belongs to the art of this form." The "primary pigment" of poetry is
the image (the fundamental premise of the manifesto that each of the
arts has its own untranslatable mode is borrowed from the chapter on
"The School of Giorgione" in *The Renaissance;* the notion that experience naturally sorts itself into corresponding modes is Pound's contribution), and "The vorticist will use only the primary media of his
art."[31]

This was not, of course, the first time the visual connotation of
"image" proved a theoretical nuisance; but the implication that it is
the essence of poetry to produce pictures threatens the coherence of
the theory—"pigment" does not help matters either—and six months
after the *Blast* manifesto, Pound redefined, in the light of the new
doctrine, the term he had made the virtual dictator of his aesthetic
vocabulary:

> The Image can be of two sorts. It can arise within the mind. It is
> then "subjective." External causes play upon the mind, perhaps; if so,
> they are drawn into the mind, fused, transmitted, and emerge in an
> Image unlike themselves. Secondly, the Image can be objective. Emo-
> tion seizing up some external scene or action carries it intact into the
> mind; and that vortex purges it of all save the essential or dominant
> or dramatic qualities, and it emerges like the external original.[32]

Informing this definition is the strange alliance between empiricist
epistemology and a stripped-down Romantic theory of the imagination
that characterizes the Paterian tradition, and its difficulties could not
be more lucidly presented. In order to win for the poetic act the status
of objectivity, "subjective" is made to define a condition in which the
mind is acted upon by circumstance, "objective" to describe the result
of the mind's "seizing" upon an external "scene" and subjecting it to
mental operations. The minor mystery of why the object apparently
needs to be purged of its own extraneous qualities before it can be like
itself is explained by the doubled mind of the empiricist model: the
impression—the mental appearance of the object—is corrected against

the standard of what is real by an internal mechanism, here the vortex, whose performance is impeccable but unexplained.

Pound's distinction between two types of images corresponding to two types of mental behavior seems to depend for its persuasiveness not on an appeal to experience but on a resemblance to the Romantic distinction between "fancy" and "imagination"; and in the background of his description of image production can be detected the shadow of the familiar Wordsworthian formula for poetic composition—just as a late echo of Hazlitt's essay can be heard in Pater's "Style" and just as the authority called upon to clinch the argument in Hulme's "Romanticism and Classicism" turns out unexpectedly to be a sort of lowercase Coleridge. But though Wordsworth, leaning on a theory of associationism that might be taken for Vorticism's distant cousin, took the position that the imaginative response to things should be habitual, an impulse obeyed "blindly and mechanically," he argued that this impulse could be trusted only because the poet was someone who had first "thought long and deeply" and who hoped not to return the object to itself as it really is, but to direct the "understanding" and "affections" of the reader.[33] Pound was not so willing to assign a role to intellect. Eager to secure for his practice the sanction of a physiological process, he designed a model that would circumvent whatever smacked of intention, and he ended by making the stuff of poetry the product of a transaction between two machines:

> The best artist is the man whose machinery can stand the highest voltage. The better the machinery, the more precise, the stronger, the more exact will be the record of the voltage and of the various currents which have passed through it.[34]

Pound had intended to rescue the poet from the passivity of impressionism, but with Vorticism he seems to have driven the doctrine of the image as far back in the direction of its basis in sensation as it could be taken without leaving the artist with nothing to do.

2

T. S. Eliot arrived in London in the summer of 1914, a few weeks after the appearance of *Blast* and a few days after the start of the war that, as a by-blow of more significant disruptions, was to throw the alignments just beginning to sort themselves out in British cultural life into a prolonged state of confusion. The famous first meeting with Pound took place near the end of September, and shortly after it Eliot moved on to Oxford to pursue the studies his Harvard fellowship was providing for. They kept in touch. Pound began almost immediately his campaign to force "The Love Song of J. Alfred Prufrock" on a reluctant Harriet Monroe at *Poetry,* and in January he sent Eliot a long article on Vorticism he had written for the *Fortnightly Review.* Eliot wrote back thanking him politely for the article and adding that, since he distrusted theorizing about aesthetic matters, he had been glad to discover that Pound's ideas about art were not tied up to James or Bergson, and that Vorticism was not a philosophy.[35]

We do not know Pound's reaction to this remark, but it is hard to imagine that he took it as anything but a compliment. It had been, after all, one of the conclusions of Pater's theory about "the things we see and touch" that we do not have time to be making theories about those things, and Pound and Ford (unlike Hulme) liked to present their prescriptions for good art not as the fruits of a philosophical investigation but as the sort of sensible recommendations that might be expected to follow from a clear-eyed view of the case. But empiricism, too, styles itself a clear-eyed view of the case, and if we detect a trace of disingenuousness in Eliot's praise of Pound's article, it is perhaps because although Vorticism no doubt does not qualify as a philosophy, it certainly bears the characteristic stamp of a theory: it backs up its notion of what will work in art, as empiricism backs up its notion of what should count as knowledge, with a description of how the mind actually operates in experience. Eliot's distrust of theory was not, however, the antagonism of a man who thought that his assumptions about how we know were simple common sense; it was the premeditated position of someone who thought that about the question of how we know there is nothing theoretical to be said. For when he read Pound's article, Eliot was engaged in writing for the Harvard philosophy department a dissertation whose arguments amount to a demonstration of the pointlessness of doing, for any traditional philosophical reason, philosophy.

Different readers have discovered in Eliot's dissertation different Eliots. Hugh Kenner (1959) found "Experience and the Objects of Knowledge in the Philosophy of F. H. Bradley" to be a statement of

enlightened disillusionment with the intellect's pretension to competence as a mode of understanding and "evidence for [Eliot's] unqualified ingestion of certain perspectives of Bradley's which one does not
discover him ever to have repudiated." J. Hillis Miller (1965) read it
as an acknowledgment of "the inevitability of dualism," an expression
of the conviction that this state "is an alienation from reality," and an
announcement of the theme of Eliot's early poetry: "The pathos of the
human condition is man's inescapable exclusion from absolute experience." Lyndall Gordon (1977) took the dissertation to have been written by "a haunted young man, torn between the truth of his visions
and his rational distrust of them," "strain[ing] towards a final truth
contained in heightened moments of 'lived' experience." Walter Benn
Michaels (1981) found the same young man to be so far opposed to
notions such as that of "a final truth" as to be considered a pragmatist
and even something of a grammatologist.[36]

Every critic wants whatever is there to be a party to the case, and
the temptation when discussing Eliot's dissertation is to give it an explanatory power over his literary writings; the danger is that in order
to do so the dissertation will be endowed with a prescriptive character
which it seems determined not to possess. We shall not get very far
referring philosophical-sounding statements in Eliot's literary criticism
back to his dissertation for elucidation because the dissertation is not
a reservoir of explanations. It is an argument designed to expose the
factitiousness of certain philosophical givens and of the metaphysical
problems that have been invented to justify them; but it does not pretend that the problems do not arise as *practical* matters, and it does
not provide a more satisfactory set of terms for dealing with them. The
argument is aimed to destroy its targets, and the most that can be said
in favor of using it to explain Eliot's literary criticism is that some of
the things felt to be missing from the criticism can be found disman-
tled in the dissertation.

Eliot's title is not entirely helpful: "Experience and the Objects of
Knowledge in the Philosophy of F. H. Bradley" is not, as Kenner has
described it, an "account and defense of Bradley's position concerning
'immediate experience.' "[37] That concept is Eliot's single analytical
tool, but it is not itself immune from analysis. Eliot's critique of his
own key term is the opening dialectical move in the dissertation, and
if we have determined to find Eliot a faithful disciple of Bradley, it
marks the place we are likely to lose him.[38] "Immediate experience" is

the bottom layer of Bradley's three-tiered model of knowledge. "It means
for me," he says in *Appearance and Reality* (1893),

> first, the general condition before distinctions and relations have been
> developed, and where as yet neither any subject nor object exists. And
> it means, in the second place, anything which is present at any stage
> of mental life, in so far as that is only present and simply is.[39]

The emergence of relations, consequent upon the breakup of this felt
unity into things belonging to thought and things belonging to the objects of thought, initiates the second stage in Bradley's scheme and
gives us the world of appearance. And that is transcended in turn by
a third stage, in which, as had been prefigured at the level of immediate experience, subject is again fused with object and both are taken
up into the highest unity, Bradley's "Absolute." This way of slicing up
experience appears to hold out a promise very like the promise held
out by Bergsonism—that there is a something inaccessible to ordinary
habits of perception which if it can be known will enable us to know
truly. And Bradley's description of this something naturally provoked
the question, If immediate experience is a condition definitionally prior
to any distinction between a mind that experiences and a world that
is experienced, how can it be known, since knowing it would mean
making it an object of awareness? And if it cannot be known, can it
be said to exist? Bradley's response, set out in "On Our Knowledge of
Immediate Experience" (1909), was that while it would be illogical to
call immediate experience real, since "real" is a term of relation, it is
nonetheless undoubtedly *there:*

> There is an immediate feeling, a knowing and being in one, with which
> knowledge begins; and, though this in a manner is transcended, it
> nevertheless remains throughout as the present foundation of my known
> world. . . . It is not a stage which shows itself at the beginning and
> then disappears, but it remains at the bottom throughout as funda-
> mental.[40]

Though there can be no point of view outside of immediate experience
from which to know it, since "it contains within itself every development which in a sense transcends it," its existence is verified by experience: "At every moment my state, whatever else it is, is a whole
of which I am immediately aware." And Bradley ventured one step
further: immediate experience is not only an actual stage in life of the

species—it "comes first in fact," he says—but "it recurs even in the life of the developed individual."[41]

These claims lead in a direction Eliot was not willing to travel. Eliot thought "immediate experience" superior to the foundational concepts of other philosophies because it refuses to separate one element of experience out from the whole—as empiricism, for example, does with sense data—and confer on it the status of the irreducible atom of knowledge; and he therefore resisted Bradley's suggestion that his term names a distinctive condition we might find ourselves—as individuals or as a species—measurably closer to or farther from at any point. The notion of "immediate experience" has, in Eliot's view, no need for an ontological justification and no hope of finding one. Its philosophical soundness has nothing to do with such considerations as whether or not it describes accurately those moments in our experience we feel to be "most real." Bradley invented his concept for the simple reason that he could not have a theory without one—because, as Eliot explained it, "We are forced, in building up our theory of knowledge, to postulate something given upon which knowledge is founded"[42]—and it can therefore be justified only on grounds that it fulfills this essential requirement of theory-making with a satisfying adequacy. "Immediate experience" satisfies because it leaves nothing out; and every effort to establish the truth of the term by pointing to something in experience that it corresponds to only undermines its effectiveness. Its claim to validity is conditional on its willingness to remain hypothetical.

Theories of knowledge tend to become victims of their own strength, since the more explanatory authority they grant their givens the less they leave themselves to explain. Eliot felt this difficulty to be present in Bradley's philosophy in "an aggravated form," and having destabilized the concept at the base of that philosophy by showing that its value as a theoretical given depends on its being ungroundable, he was quick to give the screw yet another turn. For by virtue of the very inclusiveness that makes it admirable, the concept of "immediate experience" builds in to Bradley's philosophy a continuous running reminder of the metaphysical fraudulence of every distinction it will subsequently need—real, unreal; subject, object; act, content; percept, memory-image; and so on—to describe the way knowledge is structured in actual experience. "There is immediate experience, contrasted with ideal construction; which is prior, and in some sense, certainly, prior in time, to the ideal construction," Eliot conceded.

> But we go on to find that no actual experience could be merely im-
> mediate, for if it were we should certainly know nothing about it; and
> also that the line between the experienced, or the given, and the con-
> structed can nowhere be clearly drawn. Then we discover that the
> difference in no instance holds good outside of a relative and fluctuat-
> ing point of view. Experience alone is real, but everything can be
> experienced. . . . There is no absolute point of view from which real
> and ideal can be finally separated and labelled. All of our terms turn
> out to be unreal abstractions; but we can defend them, and give them
> a kind of reality and validity (the only validity which they can possess
> or can need) by showing that they express the theory of knowledge
> which is implicit in all our practical activity.[43]

The system Eliot adapted from Bradley is one that ironizes itself at
every point. Its terms of relation all show up as relative against the
background of "immediate experience," but when we try to grasp that
concept we find that it only points back to the terms it has discredited,
since it is founded on the paradox that whatever is "given" in our
experience cannot at the same time be present to us. Such a system is
a weapon, not a tool, and having equipped himself with it, Eliot proceeded to analyze away psychology's claim to have something scientific
to say about mental states and epistemology's claim to have something
theoretical to say about our knowledge of the world. There is, he concluded, "nothing mental, and there is certainly no such thing as consciousness if consciousness is to be an object or something independent
of the objects which it has"; and conversely, "there are no *objects* of
knowledge, when the object is treated as a hard and fast reality."[44]

The critiques of psychology and epistemology occupy Eliot for most
of the dissertation, but the assault is mounted on a somewhat grander
scale than the occasion would appear to require, and by the end it
begins to seem as though those subjects have simply strayed into the
line of fire, and that the real object of Eliot's attack is the claim of
metaphysics to have something true to say about experience. For although the terms of Eliot's analysis will allow us to say that as a practical matter each organism makes its own point of view hang together
with the help of notions such as "truth" and "error"—"and there must
certainly," Eliot suggests, "be analogies for truth and error in jellyfish
life"[45] (for even the jellyfish does not live in a world of immediate
experience)—it is the endeavor of metaphysics to make the points of

view of all organisms hang together, and Eliot's conception of experience has no provision for the success of such an undertaking:

> You start, or pretend to start, from experience—from any experience—and build your theory. You begin with truths which everyone will accept, perhaps, and you find connections which no one else has discovered. In the process, reality has changed . . . for the world of your theory is certainly a very different world from the world from which you began. . . . There occurs, in short, just what is sure to occur in a world in which subject and predicate are not one. Metaphysical systems are condemned to go up like a rocket and come down like a stick. The question can always be asked of the closest-woven theory: is this the reality of *my* world of appearance? and if I do not recognize the identity, then it is not.[46]

Readers whose primary concern is Eliot's poetry have naturally wanted to attach to judgments of this sort an emotional consequence, and the place they have usually found it convenient to start is the line in *The Waste Land*—"Thinking of the key, each confirms a prison"—that Eliot footnoted with the passage from Bradley beginning, "My external sensations are no less private to myself than are my thoughts or my feelings. . . ."[47] Miller chooses to start there, and sketches in the scenario that choice seems to require: attracted by the monistic vision held out at either end of the Bradleian scheme, Eliot is nevertheless driven by the argument of his dissertation to the conclusion that to be human is to be forever locked out of the unity of the Absolute, and he thus finds himself in solipsism's full embrace; his analysis of that condition provides his early poetry with its subject matter, and his sense of its unmitigability provides it with its pathos. With the prospect of his conversion and *Four Quartets* in the distance, this view of Eliot's career has a pleasing shapeliness; but the dissertation unfortunately comes first, and the reader who starts there in hopes of arriving at the thunder's statement about keys and prisons faces a trickier assignment. For, to begin with, the sentences that appear in Eliot's footnote are, as a number of commentators have pointed out,[48] not really representative of Bradley's position, and they are certainly not representative of the position Eliot takes in the dissertation. When Eliot quoted from the same section of *Appearance and Reality* in an article in *The Monist* in 1916, it was to make the point that the notion of completely private worlds amounted for Bradley to simply one of the ways in which experience might be regarded (though it represented a point of view Bradley was, in Eliot's opinion, somewhat overdisposed to emphasize); and Eliot went on to propose that experience might be described with equal fidelity to the doctrine of immediate experience as entirely *public,* on the grounds that other people can be said to understand my feelings better than I do—"as my oculist," says Eliot, "knows my eyes."[49] Extreme subjectivism gives us a picture of one aspect of a thing that can only be grasped dialectically, and if we feel the need to read *The Waste Land* as a poem with a claim to some sort of philosophical cogency, we might be warned against pointing to any single passage as the complete statement of the case by the circumstance that the thunder speaks, in proper dialectical spirit, with three voices.

It was precisely because it does not treat experience as merely an adjective of the subject that Bradley thought his philosophy to be in no danger of sliding into solipsism, and when Eliot takes up the matter in the dissertation, he considers it largely as a diversion for philosophical thrill-seekers. Though solipsism rests, he acknowledges, upon a truth, it is a truth only from one point of view—the point of view we get when we make the abstraction of a world appearing to one locus of experience, or, to use Bradley's term, one finite center. Reality is more, Eliot maintains, because each of us means it to be more, and it is from the intentions of many finite centers that the world is constructed.[50] Bradley's concept of an Absolute at the far side of the world of appearance offers a kind of metaphysical glue to hold those intentions together, but Eliot was not tempted to use it, and it was on this issue that he distinguished himself from Bradley most explicitly. His analysis in an article for the *Monist* on Bradley and Leibniz is firmly antitranscendentalist:

> The Absolute responds only to an imaginary demand of thought, and satisfies only an imaginary demand of feeling. Pretending to be something which makes finite centres cohere, it turns out to be merely the assertion that they do. And this assertion is only true so far as we here and now find it to be so.[51]

And he assigns it no role in the argument of the dissertation. His interest, he says there, is only with "some of the intermediate steps" in Bradley's model. For the fusion of subject and object can only mean, in fact, the disappearance of the relations that make possible not just our awareness of the world, but our awareness that we are aware; or as Eliot puts it, "immediate experience, at either the beginning or end of our journey, is annihilation and utter night."[52] From any conceivable human standpoint, nonrelational experience describes a condition indistinguishable from death, and it is difficult to see what sort of pathos could attach itself to the recognition of our exclusion from such a state.

Because to all appearances the dissertation is a purely intellectual exercise, and because Eliot does not describe anywhere in it his personal feelings about the conclusions his analysis has reached, Lyndall Gordon's claim, in her critical biography of Eliot, that the dissertation "resounds with confessions of suffering"[53] is not easily substantiated; but neither, for the same reasons, is it easily controverted. This is an interpretive impasse of a kind frequently run up against in discussions of modernism, and it arises out of the difficulty of translating what is written into what was experienced. Readers who set out to explain modernist literature as aesthetic compensation for the loss of epistemological or metaphysical certainty will want to locate the place in the life where belief had to be abandoned; and to those readers, the Eliot who remarked in his dissertation that "The virtue of metaphysical analysis is in showing the destructibility of everything"[54] will seem a young man who felt his world to be collapsing around him. But respect for the certainties they have inherited is not a thing young writers usually find, as a practical matter, they can afford much of, and the notion of "the destructibility of everything" offers promising material for poetry. So that we might feel equally justified in attributing to the Eliot of the dissertation not the despair of someone facing an unwished for crisis of belief, but the exhilaration of a young man who, bent on the cultivation of an unassailable ironism, suddenly finds in his hands an instrument whose touch turns every post-Cartesian philosophical brick into straw; and we might even assume further than the impression of having put himself at spiritual risk by using such an instrument was a desired feature of the attitude Eliot was seeking to perfect. Uncertainty is the modernist's literary capital; he cannot appear to have come by it cheaply, but he cannot do without it. This will seem a charge of dissimulation only if we assume adherence to the standard of sincerity to be unproblematic.

Whatever its usefulness to his poetry, Eliot's dissertation makes an unlikely preparation for someone about to begin, in 1916, a career as a literary critic. And the reason is easy to see: for the moment the

argument of the dissertation is trained on the aesthetic vocabulary of
the day, the authority for that vocabulary's key terms vanishes. Sensation, the home base of Imagist theory, becomes just another arbitrary starting place in the effort to put together an explanation of how
we know, since on the dissertation's strict constructionist reading of
the Bradleian doctrine of immediate experience, there *is* no stratum of
experience such that as we get closer to it we get better reports on
reality or feel more trustworthy emotions. "[T]he 'immediately given,' "
the dissertation warns the epistemological treasure hunter, "is the bag
of gold at the end of the rainbow."

> Knowledge is invariably a matter of degree: you cannot put your finger
> upon even the simplest datum and say "this we know." In the growth
> and construction of the world we live in, there is no one stage, and
> no one aspect, which you can take as the foundation. Radical empiri-
> cists assume that we have an "immediate" knowledge of a mysterious
> flux, and criticists assume that we know sense-data, or universals,
> immediately, as we do not know objects or other selves. But where we
> are first interested in knowing, there is the first thing known. . . .[55]

And sincerity, the virtue the writer's hard work is meant to secure,
turns out, in the light of the dissertation, to have been a shadow which
no visible object has cast; for

> the more accurately and scientifically one pursues the traces of men-
> tality in the "mind" of the individual, the less one finds; . . . [and]
> the more closely one scrutinizes the "external world," the more ea-
> gerly and positively one plucks at it, the less there is to see and touch.[56]

A theory of art designed to uphold the value of sincerity requires, as
we have seen, a distinction between what belongs to the world and
what belongs to the self to support it, and when the authority to enforce that distinction is withdrawn, the theory must collapse. For where
there is nothing that can be called mental, it makes no sense to talk
of an inner mechanism for sorting what truly matters out of the data
of the senses, and where there is nothing that can be called extramen-
tal, it makes no sense to talk of an inner vision to which the artist
might or might not be faithful.

Commentators eager to put so powerful a notion as immediate experience to work on behalf of some aesthetic good have offered to make
these difficulties disappear by suggesting that when Eliot moves from

the criticism of philosophy to the criticism of literature he takes his concept with him, translating it into an artistic ideal, the value of the work of art being measured by the extent to which it achieves a fusion of whatever dualism is understood to apply—object and subject, thought and feeling, individual talent and the tradition.[57] But whether Eliot's critical practice can be usefully explained in this way or not, as far as the dissertation is concerned, this suggestion is unsanctioned; the operation it describes is one that can only be performed in thin air. For things that cannot be convincingly separated cannot very well be convincingly rejoined. We cannot begin with "subject" on one side and "object" on the other, since by themselves those terms name nonentities; and we cannot end with a condition in which "subject" and "object" have disappeared into a greater unity, since such a condition would be unknowable—even by "intuition"—and therefore unrepresentable—even by "images." But beyond these inconveniences—and this is the triumphant point of the dissertation's ironism—given the entirely hypothetical character of those limits, we have no theoretically approved way of establishing the relative status of any stage "in between." It is possible that, wishing to cast some of his critical pronouncements in philosophical-sounding language, Eliot recalled terms and formulations from Bradley's writings; but it is not possible, by the lights of the dissertation, that Eliot's use of those terms could have been anything but ad hoc.

The perfect hopelessness of giving the dissertation's conception of immediate experience any practical critical work to do is nicely demonstrated by a recent dispute over a sentence in Eliot's 1920 essay on Swinburne: "Language in a healthy state presents the object, is so close to the object that the two are identified."[58] This seemed to Leslie Brisman, in an essay on "Swinburne's Semiotics" (1977), to be an assertion informed by a "rather powerful notion of the representational nature of words"—the notion that "Words substitute for presences"—and thus to partake of the dangerously metaphysical view that "it is [the] things behind the words that convey the meaning," a view apparently responsible for what Brisman calls "the tyrannizing presence of the Eliotic world of objects."[59] Walter Benn Michaels, in the single venture at tying Eliot's dissertation up to Eliot's criticism in an otherwise thorough and important discussion of the former, took issue with Brisman's assessment, and cited in Eliot's defense this passage in the dissertation:

No symbol, I maintain, is ever a mere symbol, but is continuous with that which it symbolizes. Without words, no objects. The object, purely experienced and not denominated, is not yet an object. . . . [W]e have no objects without language.[60]

Just as a subject divorced from all objects is an unreal abstraction, and just as objects disappear without subjects to intend them, words and things always appear together and always enter the room at the same time. "Eliot's denial that there can be an 'actual object of perception,' " Michaels concludes, "is a denial of the signified-in-itself, what Derrida calls the 'transcendental signified,' what Peirce called the 'transcendental object,'" and his refusal to separate word from thing or to give priority to either clears him of the charge of being a metaphysician of presence.[61] Michaels stops here, and his account is undeniably consistent with the position of the dissertation; but when we return, thus enlightened, to the sentence about Swinburne, we find that we can no longer make sense of it, for we are now faced with the question of what, if language and objects are by ontological necessity always identified, the phrase "in a healthy state" can possibly mean.

Literature is what the vocabulary being used to talk about it in any given historical moment makes it. (If this seems a definition superior to all other definitions by virtue of its apparent nonrestrictiveness, we might reflect that the historicist vocabulary of our time makes it seem so by making it impossible to define literature persuasively in any other way.) And Eliot wrote his critique of the assumptions of epistemology at a time when, as we have seen, the literary work had become conceived of as very nearly the paradigm of the traditional epistemological object—as the producer of an aesthetic sensation. Though the dissertation shears the philosophical ground away from every term needed to talk about literature in this way, it is, in accordance with its antitheoretical principles, not in the business of reconceiving experience for us, and it thus not only offers no alternative way of talking about such a thing as literature but also suggests that an "aesthetic experience" is one of those fictional constructs, like "the self," that can only be discussed in the vocabularies of the various makeshift theories on which their existences depend. "As it is metaphysics which has produced the self," the dissertation explains,

> so it is epistemology, we may say, which has produced knowledge. It is perhaps epistemology . . . that has given us the fine arts; for what was at first expression and behaviour may have developed under the

complications of self-consciousness, as we became aware of ourselves as reacting aesthetically to the object.[62]

The concept of immediate experience can give us, of course, no handle on our response to a work of art because it does not recognize a distinction between the work and our perception of it, and "when there are no bones," as Eliot says of immediate experience in general, "anybody can carve a goose." That the bones are needed is proved by the fact that we invent them:

> If we did not think that at some moments our consciousness is nearer to "pure" experience than at others, if we did not think of "sense-datum" as prior to "object," if we did not feel that "act" or "content," or "immanent" and "transcendent" object were not as independent of each other, as capable of entering into different contexts as a table and a chair, the fact of their difference would be a perfect example of useless knowledge.[63]

Distinctions are valid when they make a difference, and this pragmatic justification frees up the terms needed to talk about art in 1916: their use is permitted on the understanding that how aesthetic experience is carved up involves decisions on which no guidance can be expected from metaphysics. For it is the position of the dissertation that in every case where discriminations are wanted—when we undertake to criticize art, or to identify error, or to define the real—"the point at which a line may be drawn is always a question for partial and practical interests to decide."[64] Thus distinctions the dissertation has pronounced baseless—as when it warns, for instance, "There is no greater mistake than to think that feeling and thought are exclusive"—might be invoked to give meaning to critical statements that theory considers tautological (for instance, "A thought to Donne was an experience; it modified his sensibility" [1921]), and just as readily, when different needs arise, to underwrite claims that theory has declared impossible (for instance, "In Donne, there is a manifest fissure between thought and sensibility" [1931]).[65] For where judgment has been licensed to follow interest so brazenly, there is no reference point for choosing between contradictory conclusions; only the context can invalidate them. Eliot had great luck with contexts; and as the interests of its day required, his early criticism gave every earnest of Imagist loyalties, except for the difference an admission ultimately fatal to theories of the image makes—the admission that there is a politics of sensation.

3

Rescuing Literature from Itself

Descriptions of what the mind really does with experience and how language really works are features of every theory that calls upon the term "image" to legitimize a particular poetic practice; the point of using the term, after all, is to claim for literature an epistemological advantage over other kinds of writing. It is a discovery of every generation that makes this argument that one of the things jeopardizing its claims is the tendency of a poem to look, in fact, like a work of literature. Modernism, coming late in this tradition, confronted this difficulty in an especially exacerbated form; for to the extent that the efforts of earlier generations to strip literature of its conventional features seemed to have ended up by producing only a new style of conventionality, the modernists were naturally pressed to find more radical solutions. Which is why modernism sometimes seems to have been directed by an impulse to convert literature into a substance entirely without attributes, to create a literature that would have nothing literary about it. Imagism repeated, as we have seen, the epistemological arguments of the previous century, and it did so in drastically uncompromising terms; but it was not, finally, a response to a problem about ways of knowing. It was a response to a problem about the literariness of literature. Imagism was, to put it epigrammatically, about a problem with imagery.

T. S. Eliot began his career and established his reputation as a critic by attacking the claims of the literary avant-garde of his day.

Whether he did so from the position of a more uncompromising avant-gardism (for he did not appear to be defending the literary establishment) or from the position of an intelligent traditionalism (for his principles could not always be clearly identified with those of any announced avant-garde movement) was a matter he was careful to keep mysterious to his contemporaries. It was, in the circumstances, an ingenious strategy, and it enabled an extraordinary success. It also produced some notable inconsistencies. Those inconsistencies do not seem to have bothered Eliot, and they should not bother us, for they are among the things that give Eliot's early criticism its special interest to literary history. One way to put that interest is to say that if Imagism was a kind of literary minimalism, committed to the creation of a perfectly transparent art, Eliot was a postminimalist: he appreciated perfectly the point of Imagism's complaint about the mediated quality, the formal arbitrariness, the *literariness* of literature; but he thought that its solutions were simply opportunities for self-deception of a fairly spectacular sort, and he saw nothing to do about conditions that could not be evaded but to exploit them. More than that (and this is where the inconsistencies begin to surface), insofar as Imagist values were a part of the received conception of literature, Imagism itself was one of the conditions he was prepared to exploit.

"LITERARY! LITERARY!" complained Ford Madox Ford in a letter to an acquaintance who had sent him a volume of her poems. "Now that is the last thing that verse should ever be, for the moment a medium becomes literary it is remote from the life of the people, it is dulled, languishing, moribund and at last dead."[1] "Every literaryism, every book word," Ezra Pound informed Harriet Monroe a few years later, "fritters away a scrap of the reader's patience, a scrap of his sense of your sincerity."[2] These sentiments are likely to strike us as unexceptionable, for the cultural dispensation under which "literature" operates as an honorific term and "literary" as a vaguely pejorative one is well established; but the negative connotation of "literary" and the coinage of "literaryism" belong to the late nineteenth century,[3] and by calling upon literature to avoid not the characteristics associated with other types of writing but precisely the things that give a text the appearance of being literature, those terms state the conditions of what would become a familiar avant-garde problem. For a thing that is suspect for looking like itself is an onion that can be peeled indefinitely.

Ford, for instance, objected not only to poetry's tendency to draw on a specialized vocabulary—a complaint as ancient as the institution of literary criticism—but to its "detestable assonances and inexactitudes," its similes, its rhyme, its rhythm, and its "egoism."[4] "Is there something," he asked,

> about the mere framing of verse, the mere sound of it in the ear, that it must at once throw its practitioner or its devotee into an artificial frame of mind? . . . [M]ust it necessarily quicken them to the perception only of the sentimental, the false, the hackneyed aspects of life?[5]

And Pound concluded, in an essay on French poetry, that "all attempts to be poetic in some manner or other defeat their own end,"[6] a statement which, though it seems perfectly sensible, leaves dangling the question of how else the impulse to make a poem might be described.

Vorticism, in keeping with Pound's penchant for solving problems of this sort by manifesto, tried to make the difficulties disappear by declaring the poetry invisible, thereby creating difficulties of a different kind. These difficulties were not peculiar to Pound, but they had in his case peculiar consequences, consequences that point to one limitation of the Imagist project. The limitation arises, somewhat paradoxically, from the inclusiveness of the Vorticist poetic. For everything that is fed into the vortex—memories, facts, beliefs, sententiae, quotations from other poems—emerges as an image; and thus everything in a poem can be justified by Vorticist standards once it is treated not as a means of expression but as an object. Pound needed a theoretical blanket of this type of the *Cantos,* a poem he called in its early stages "Phanopoeia"—"image-making"—and which he told Joyce would be "all about everything."[7] One of the consequences of the license Pound granted himself was the creation of what has been described (and criticized) as the *Cantos'* "poetry of surface":[8] it is useless to try to distinguish figure from ground, grammar from expression in that poem because everything has been weighted equally. The diligent reader will be able to find, as Hugh Kenner has, the significant pattern of a given passage in its scansion alone;[9] and the critic skeptical of the claim that though ideology is in the poem the poem is not ideological will not find it easy to explain what is unacceptable about suggestions like the one Delmore Schwartz once offered about "Canto XLV": "in this particu-

lar Canto," Schwartz proposed, "the attack on usury as a poetic statement can be separated from its connection with a particular economic
theory by the mere device of substituting another three-syllable word
with the same accents, for example, 'capital.' "[10]

Changing the focus of critical attention so that what had been taken
for form suddenly appears as content, or what had been read as content takes on the properties of form, is a strategy adaptable to any text;
that its results are often convincing is one of the reasons poems have
interpretive histories. Pound's case is unusual only because his theory
seems explicitly to authorize this sort of critical play with his poem.
But his permissiveness had a hidden cost. The Imagists' prescriptions
for good writing bank for their persuasiveness in part on the habit of
thinking of language as, in ordinary use, a means a little too weak for
its ends, perpetually falling short of the matter to be expressed by
spending its force inefficiently on the production of verbiage. A poetic
that, relying on Pater's faith that "there is . . . for every lineament
of the vision within, the one word, the one acceptable word,"[11] calls
for each word to perform at its full capacity, seems a promise to get
language up to the level of experience. We may choose to doubt this
promise simply by noting that it is a rare occasion when one word will
do, and by suggesting that in many cases this is not because one word
says too little, but because it says too much. Our ordinary speech is
marked up with a cross-hatching of redundancies, retractions, and
contradictions partly because unobstructed words are too powerful; they
carry too much significance into the sentence, and wordiness is a way
of muting the force of individual words in the hope that the whole will
be more compatible with the modesty of our intentions. Every kind of
writing—even literary writing, in which the connotative power of words
is expected to be most dramatically displayed—has a stock of conventions, "arbitrary" to the matter, that drag on the signifying tendencies
of words to the degree necessary to subdue them to the capacities of
the understanding. "If he is not careful he will take to meaning what
he says instead of saying what he means," warned Edward Thomas
about Pound's preoccupation, in a volume of the pre-Imagist period,
with the manner of expression.[12] In freeing all the language of the
Cantos to participate equally in the patterning of the poem, and in
endowing everything with the rights and privileges of the image, Pound
must have eventually felt himself, as Thomas had foretold, the prisoner of his own technique, and he may have found his poem unfinish-

able in part because by always saying so much with every fresh image he added to it, he could never manage to say finally only as much as he meant.

As with most modernist dissatisfactions, the worry that a poem's effectiveness is interfered with by the requirement that it look like a poem—the worry Pound chose to settle in this uncompromising way—was shared by contemporaries less committed to iconoclasm. Even Harold Monro, the publisher of the Georgian anthologies, could suggest, in a review of the literary events of the 1910s, that "The mere act of versification is often responsible for insincerities, conscious or unconscious."[13] But Monro thought Imagism a strange solution to the problem, and, asked to contribute to a special Imagist number of *The Egoist* in 1915, he made a poem of John Gould Fletcher's called "London Excursion" the example of its troubles:

> Mr. Fletcher makes an excursion to London, let us suppose with the object of writing a poem. . . . He finds things distinctly unlike their representation in old-fashioned poetry, yet, at the same time, tantalizingly like. However like they be, he *must* write something different. He is resolved, too, on accuracy of observation, of rhythm, and of expression. But each hampers the others. His observations land him in a series of crude statements. These should be modified by their rhythm. Rhythm is found to embarrass their accuracy. His expression, again, must precisely reproduce his observation. It cannot, however, because what he has observed cannot be reproduced in poetry. . . . The reader is so held by the contortions of Mr. Fletcher battling with his difficult art that the emotional values of the poem almost escape him.

And in a critique in the same essay of H.D.'s 'Oread" ("Whirl up, sea . . .")—already an Imagist touchstone—he registered a further complaint: "It can be said in the one minute before lunch. . . . Such images should appear by the dozen in poetry."[14] In the next month's issue, May Sinclair came to the movement's defense—"Imagery is one of the old worn-out decorations the Imagists have scrapped. . . . What the Imagists are 'out for' is direct naked contact with reality"[15]—but by pretending to miss the point completely, Monro had scored a hit. For nothing looks more deliberately crafted, more decorative—more literary—than an Imagist poem.

Given the origins of the doctrine, though, this is not a surprising judgment of the practice. The "literaryisms" the Imagists undertook

to eliminate Pater called "surplusage"—"the ornamental word, the figure, the accessory form or colour or reference"; and he enjoined their
use on the grounds that they created (the term points up nicely the
sensationalist basis of Pater's aesthetic) disruptive "brainwaves."[16] But
without the temptations of excess, stylistic excellence would not be
possible; for like most literary guides who begin by advising the writer
to resolve all matters of style by being true to himself, Pater provided
specific directions for how the impression of sincerity might most convincingly be managed: "the true artist," he suggested, "may be best
recognised by his tact of omission."[17] The mot juste is made much of
in "Style," as it is in the critical writings of the Imagists, but the right
word in Pater's essay stands not so much for its object as for all the
words that have been considered and rejected as not being right enough;
and Pater's real argument seems to be that the inner being—the true
object of literary representation—is most clearly apprehended not
through what is written but through our sense of what might have
been written and was not—just as the saint has nothing to show in
this world for all the sins he has refrained from committing but his
lack. This difficult virtue of "restraint"[18] Pater thought exemplified
by Flaubert, whom he made not the hero (for style has no heroes) but
the martyr of style.

Edward Thomas, in his critical study of Pater (1913), took excep-
tion to this manner of praising Flaubert, and used his disagreement as
an occasion for pointing out the defect in Pater's own literary style.
Flaubert, he explained,

> was only less quickly satisfied than most men by words that rose to
> his call when writing, only more conscious of the approach of that
> satisfaction. It was his misfortune. In Pater's case, it sometimes ap-
> pears to be his fault. He gave cause for being supposed to think labo-
> riousness in itself a virtue, and he has left some writing which has no
> other virtue.[19]

But the impression of extraordinary pains taken, the sensation Monro
objected to in Fletcher's poem of having had to overcome what other
writers would not even have recognized as difficulties, was just the
effect Pater had in mind. For though language, being a public thing,
will do for "facts," which are objects of public knowledge, the writer's
particular "sense of fact," a thing whose essence in Pater's view is
always private, can be expressed only by the shape his resistance to

the departicularizing tendencies of his medium takes. The fineness of
the resistance (including, of course, the willingness in the end to grant
the conventional its triumph) is the measure of the exquisiteness of
the artist's inner vision and therefore—the standard is applied everywhere in Pater's criticism—of the value of the work of art. By remov-
ing the traditional object of mimesis from the outer world to the inner,
Pater must have thought he had found a way to make it representable,
since it no longer depended on a correspondence relation to language;
and he did not intend to appear hyperbolic when he asserted that "in
truth all art does but consist in the removal of surplusage."[20]

Thomas complained that "Pater has no sense but vision, and he can
adapt to it all things presented to him," suggesting, as Wilde had suggested before him, that Pater seems to be interested not so much in
what a sentence says or how it sounds as in the way it looks.[21] And
Pater's vocabulary always does seem to be slipping into spatial metaphors, treating a page of writing as though it were a piece of sculpture.
But this is the consequence of Pater's critical obsession: he wants the
literary work to have the virtue of a thing looked at—a thing which,
like a table or a lamp or a jewel, can be admired *only* for its style. Like
any nineteenth-century economist, Pater calculates the worth of a
commodity by the labor required to produce it, and he therefore—it is
the taste of a society that subscribes to a labor theory of value—prizes
detail and finish. He needs the labor to be visible. The interest of a
sculpture does not consist in anything the stone expresses, but in what
the hand of the sculptor has cut away, and if we think of language as
a block of crude material, we will be interested, Pater thinks, only in
how the individual mind has cut a sentence out of it. The rarer the
cutting ("Literature is not for connoisseurs," Thomas protested,[22] but
Pater was for connoisseurship in all things), the more exquisite the
sensibility that produced it:

> Self-restraint, a skilful economy of means, *ascêsis,* that too has a
> beauty of its own; and for the reader supposed there will be an aes-
> thetic satisfaction in that frugal closeness of style which makes the
> most of a word, in the exaction from every sentence of a precise relief,
> in the just spacing out of word to thought, in the logically filled space
> connected always with the delightful sense of difficulty overcome.[23]

Pound called the image a "statement that has not yet SPENT itself in
expression,"[24] and we can see why he wanted to reify poetic language
to this extent if we think of the Imagist poem as a work built to the

specifications of Pater's critical doctrine. The poem is an object to be
looked at, and the response it produces is therefore owed to the hard
work of the person who made it. Pound in fact liked to emphasize the
time it took him to produce a short poem: "I waited three years to find
the words for 'Piccadilly,' " he explains in "How I Began" (1913), "it
is eight lines long, and they tell me now it is 'sentiment.' " The two
lines of "In a Station of the Metro," he says in the same article, required "well over a year";[25] it was cut down, we learn in "Vorticism"
(1914), from a poem of thirty lines.[26] At other times, of course, he
preferred to stress virtuosity. There is a story sometimes told of his
comment to a young literary aspirant who had handed him a new poem:
"It took you 97 words to do it," he remarked after reading it through;
"I find it could have been managed in 56."[27] But there is no inconsistency in this: a virtuoso is not a person in a rush; he is someone who
can produce quickly a thing that has the same value as another thing
that would ordinarily take twice as long to make.

The size of an Imagist poem is therefore in a sense the emblem of
its value—such an enormous quantity of superfluity has been cut away—
and its austerity is offered as the guarantee of the authenticity of the
emotion. The reader is not being tricked because the writer has done
his homework. We may be suspicious of the guarantee, but the re-
quest the aesthetic makes of us is not an unfamiliar one. We know
exactly what it means to read a piece of writing for its style: it means
that we are to read it as "literature." In its enthusiasm for ridding
itself of the literary, Imagism ended by getting rid of everything *but*
the literary; it moved the quality of literariness to the center of the
poem, and then began to trim away what was left around the edges.
The consequence, as with any minimalist enterprise, was the production of a kind of work that could be dealt with only as an example of
the very thing whose conventional features it had so programmatically
effaced: only as literature—"pure literature," if one thought of literature as writing in which the ordinary difficulties of representation can
be transcended; "mere literature," if one thought of it as simply a
particular mode of expression, or as a toy for the emotions, or as the
ornament of discourse.

Eliot's earliest literary essays were written for *The New Statesman,*
a journal that had been founded by two Fabians, the Webbs, and whose
literary editor, J. C. Squire, was a champion of the Georgian anthologies and an antagonist of Imagism. The essays that appeared in this

unlikely forum are mounted as little skirmishes with faddishness—
with the vogue for *vers libre* and the artistic pretensions of the prose
poem—and they are therefore, as exercises in that critical genre, committed to as thorough a routing of the enemy as might be compatible
with a manner of perfect nonchalance. But the spirit of wholesale
dismissiveness gives them the value of exhibiting in fairly unmodulated
form a kind of skepticism which, as his critical career progressed, Eliot
seems to have found either better and better ways of disguising (if we
assume that it is the ultimate ambition of every ironist to produce
statements indistinguishable from conventional opinion) or more and
more successful means of curing (if we assume that a too outer-directed
irony was one of the hubristic traits the later Eliot wished to efface).
And their critiques are run on the paradox that supplies many of Eliot's
early essays with their critical edge (and many of his later essays with
their polemical content)—the paradox that a work of literature derives
its authority from the very thing that makes it seem synthetic.

The argument of "Reflections on *vers libre*" (March 1917) is cut
with a hatchet, and it is a thorough job. Its strategy is to define the
term *"vers libre"* entirely in negatives—"(1) absence of pattern, (2)
absence of rhyme, (3) absence of metre"[28]—and then to attack it for
failing to refer to anything. Various passages in what looks like *vers
libre* are shown to depend for their effectiveness on pattern, rhyme,
and meter, and various passages of apparently conventional verse are
shown to succeed by avoiding those things to one degree or another,
with the conclusion that "the division between Conservative Verse and
Vers Libre does not exist, for there is only good verse, bad verse, and
chaos."[29] As an argument about poetics, this is perfectly cogent: it is
hard to imagine a poem to which no form can be attributed, and a
poem with a completely unvaried metrical pattern, if there is such a
thing, is not likely to hold much aesthetic interest. But it is also entirely beside the point. For the verslibrist does not claim that his poem
makes no pattern, or that effects by rhyme are illegitimate, or that his
line cannot be scanned. He only claims to have subjected his use of
those devices to what Richard Aldington, in his unsigned preface to
Amy Lowell's edition of *Some Imagist Poets, 1916,* called "the laws of
cadenced verse":

> The definition of *vers libre* is—a verse-form based upon cadence. . . .
> It is the sense of perfect balance of flow and rhythm. Not only must

> the syllables so fall as to increase and continue the movement, but the
> whole poem must be as rounded and recurring as the circular swing
> of a balanced pendulum.[30]

This might, to a skeptical view, sound less like a law than a license
for compositional whim, but it describes a type of poetry that by 1917
was well established and easily recognizable, and for which a technical
vocabulary existed. Although it is surely possible to do so, discussing
Leaves of Grass as a series of departures from metrical norms, as "Reflections on *vers libre*" appears to require, would not have seemed to
Eliot's contemporaries a particularly efficient way of proceeding. But
the student of Laforgue and author of "Prufrock" knew these things
as well as anyone, of course, and though it presents itself as a dispute
about poetics, Eliot's essay is at bottom a dispute about poetic ideology.
It is a quarrel not with the letter of "the laws of cadenced verse" but
with their spirit.

The spirit of a statutory law is the cushion that keeps its letter from
being broken by every anomaly; ethics consists not in remarking on the
fragility of the letter but in measuring the resiliency of the spirit. The
verslibrist of 1917 made two appeals to the ethical sense of those readers who felt themselves to be unprepared for a metrically informal
poem—one in the name of individuality, the second in the name of
art. Eliot was the sort of strict constructionist who cannot see the
point of trying to claim the sanction of the very rules one is transgress-
ing—not because he wants the rules to be inviolable, but because he
wants the transgression to be worth something. And he therefore not
only had answers to both those appeals; he eventually found a way to
make them seem contradictory.

The first line of the verslibrist's defense was backed by a familiar
principle. "We do not insist upon 'free-verse' as the only method of
writing poetry," explains the preface to the first volume of the Lowell
anthologies (1915):

> We fight for it as a principle of liberty. We believe that the individu-
> ality of a poet may often be better expressed in free-verse than in con-
> ventional forms. In poetry, a new cadence means a new idea.[31]

There was nothing exceptional in this manner of self-presentation. It
is an appeal to the standard of sincerity—what is within needs to create its own shape when it becomes something without; to require it to
conform to a conventional pattern is to make it betray its originality—

and the general sentiment might be found in the writings of the Georgians (though they took an officially dim view of *vers libre*) and the Vorticists (though they took a dim view, officially and unofficially, of Amy Lowell). It is a sort of muscular Paterianism, and it derives its authority from a Paterian definition: "Poetry," in the words of Aldington's 1916 preface, "is the vision in a man's soul which he translates as best he can with the means at his disposal."[32] One soul is different from the next, so poems must be different; modern souls are different from Victorian ones, and so poetry must be different too.

Eliot's response was deflating: "*Vers libre . . .* is a battle-cry of freedom," his essay announces, "and there is no freedom in art."[33] But this is not quite the totalitarian position it seems—and for a reason that belongs to the characteristic logic of Eliot's early criticism. For Eliot did not want to get rid of the value of sincerity; he only wanted to get rid of its metaphysics. And he therefore makes his argument turn on considerations of a strictly practical nature: the writer who seeks to escape from convention in order to be truer to himself, Eliot suggests, is giving up a useful restriction for a worthless liberty. The suggestion seems to be based on a calculation as simple as this: insofar as poems are prized for their sincerity, the impression of being sincere is what the poet will need to create; and if the threat of conventionality does not loom somewhere in the poem, the impression will not appear genuine. For if the forms of expression were understood to be perfectly adaptable to whatever it is that the individual soul wishes to express, if saying what one feels were thought to be simply a matter of writing as one likes, what grounds would we have for calling sincerity a literary virtue? It is not enough that the writer tell the truth; the requirement is that he tell the truth and make a poem at the same time. And his success will depend in part on impressing the reader with the difficulty of his task. "We may therefore," Eliot proposes,

> formulate as follows: the ghost of some simple metre should lurk behind the arras in even the "freest" verse; to advance menacingly as we doze, and withdraw as we rouse. Or, freedom is only truly freedom when it appears against the background of an artificial limitation.[34]

The last sentence of this paragraph manages to be both perfectly coherent and philosophically useless, since it is impossible to determine from its language just what is real and what is appearance. But the metaphysics does not matter. It is what is perceived that makes the difference. "Reflections on *vers libre*" is one of Eliot's livelier essays, and it has much to say about how verse forms develop and decay and why theories are put forward to give new ones legitimacy; but there is nothing in it to suggest that a particular poetic form works because it has a correspondence relation to something else—to the subject of the poem, or to the condition of the world in which the poem was written, or to the soul of the person who wrote it.

The verslibrist's second appeal was to the literary tradition. The principles shared by the writers collected in *Some Imagist Poets* "are not new," announces the 1915 preface; "they have fallen into desuetude. They are the essentials of all great poetry, indeed of all great literature."[35] We are so accustomed to this manner of self-justification in the arts that it is likely to seem merely obligatory; but it carries a particular message, and it was especially prevalent in the modernist period for reasons that require separate discussion.[36] Eliot, of course, was a master of the technique, and he did not object to its propriety; he only objected to the particular lessons the verslibrist claimed the study of the literary past had taught.

The preface to the second Lowell anthology provided a brief sketch of a genealogy: Arnold, Milton, Dryden, and Chaucer, it suggested, all approved of free verse before *vers libre*. But in her introduction to *The New Poetry,* an anthology assembled by the editors of *Poetry* and published in February 1917, Harriet Monroe made the question of the verslibrist's relation to tradition the chief issue in the case for modern poetry, and she undertook to litigate it. In "trying to make the modern manifestations of poetry less a matter of rules and formulae, and more a thing of the spirit," she contended, the "new poets" were not performing an act of aesthetic isolationism:

> In this enthusiastic labor they are following not only a strong inward impulse, not only the love of freedom which Chaucer followed—and Spenser and Shakespeare, Shelley and Coleridge and all the masters— but they are moved also by influences from afar. They have studied the French *symbolistes* of the 'nineties, and the more recent Parisian *vers-libristes*. Moreover, some of them have listened to the pure lyricism of the Provençal troubadours, have studied the more elaborate mechanism of early Italian sonneteers and canzonists, have read Greek poetry from a new angle of vision; and last, but perhaps most important of all, have bowed to winds from the East.

And thus it could even be said that:

> There is more of the great authentic classic tradition . . . in the *Spoon River Anthology* than in the *Idylls of the King, Balaustian's Adventure,* and *Sohrab and Rustum* combined. And the free rhythms of Whitman, Mallarmé, Pound, Sandburg and others, in their inspired passages, are more truly in line with the biblical, the Greek, the Anglo-Saxon, and even the Shakespearean tradition, than all the exact iambics of Dryden and Pope, the patterned alexandrines of Racine, or the closely woven metrics of Tennyson and Swinburne.[37]

The purpose of all this study, in short, had been "to find out what poetry really is";[38] and what was discovered was that the essence of all genuine literature is the effort to escape from literariness.

Eliot certainly knew Monroe's introduction—he was represented in *The New Poetry* himself by "Portrait of a Lady"—and although he does not refer to it in the second of his *New Statesman* pieces, "The Borderline of Prose" (May 1917), that essay is in effect a response to its claims. The explicit occasion Eliot chose for his critique was the recent prose poetry of Richard Aldington, and the strategy he adopted was the same he had used to unravel the concept of *vers libre:* he defined prose poetry so that it does not refer to anything that cannot be called simply poetry or prose. The genre of the prose poem, Eliot pointed out, depends on the notion that "prose" and "poetry" are the names not for tangible forms but for intangible qualities—that there is, as Monroe had argued the verslibrist's historical studies had proved, something independent of the particular form a poem takes that might be thought of as the essence of poetry. This seemed to Eliot the sponsoring of a snark hunt:

> I know that the difference between poetry and prose is a topic for school debating societies, but I am not aware that the debating societies have arrived at a solution. . . . There are doubtless many empirical generalisations which one may draw from a study of existing poetry and prose, but after much reflection I conclude that the only absolute distinction to be drawn is that poetry is written in verse, and prose is written in prose; or, in other words, that there is prose rhythm and verse rhythm. And any other essential difference is still to seek.[39]

Of course, when we use a term like "poetic," we must mean something by it; but if we look at the prose that seems to exhibit this quality, says Eliot, we find that it does so by obeying the laws of its own form. Thus the excellence of Rimbaud's *Illuminations* is owed not to any formal innovation but to its prose being "good French prose";

and thus the bird's-eye view of Europe in Ruskin's "The Nature of Gothic" and the snapdragon passage in Newman's *Apologia Pro Vita Sua* and even Bradley's answer to the materialist's picture of the universe in his *Principles of Logic* (all quoted by Eliot) are justifiably called "poetic," because they are technically "pure prose." No experiment in form can transcend the fact of a piece of writing's being either prose or poetry, and why would the writer wish it to? For as in the case of *vers libre,* the writer who aspires to escape the bounds of form is giving up an opportunity for a muddle. "We admire Pope," Eliot maintains, "because he has sometimes given impeccable and inevitable verse form to the 'prosaic,' and so has made (whatever the nineteenth century may have said) permanent poetry. We admire several prose writers because they have given impeccable and inevitable prose form to what we had supposed limited to verse." And to the claim of the "new poet" that literature succeeds when it seems to have nothing conventional about it, Eliot answers that this is an effect which only a mastery of convention can make possible:

> There is a prose arbitrariness and a verse arbitrariness; whichever we are writing, there are moments when we simply have to conform to the limitations of the medium we have chosen; there is a verse monotone and a prose monotone, and success in either verse or prose consists in the most skilful variations of music, all the while we never allow this ground-monotone to become entirely inaudible.[40]

What literary history teaches is that literature is a kind of writing defined—and identified—by laws whose letter is without spirit; successful literary expression consists in making obedience to those laws seem the act of a free will.

In June 1917, a month after "The Borderline of Prose" appeared, Eliot became an assistant editor of *The Egoist.* The association was significant for Eliot—it was in the offices of *The Egoist* that he became, when the manuscript chapters began to arrive in late 1918, one of the first readers of *Ulysses*—and it was significant for the fortunes of the literary avant-garde. For *The Egoist* had been, from its days as *The New Freewoman* (June to December 1913), the magazine of Imagism—until 1915 under the auspices of Ezra Pound and since then, as part of a kind of anti-Pound backlash, under the sign of Amy Lowell. And the editor Eliot replaced was Richard Aldington. But if Eliot's skepticism was a challenge to the avant-garde, it seem that the avant-garde was a challenge to Eliot's skepticism too. Mocking the aspirations of the verslibrists for the delectation of J. C. Squire at *The New Statesman* was a different matter from provoking those writers on their own ground and as one of their number. The job of critiquing the avant-garde in the leading avant-garde forum of the day led Eliot to try to contrive an aesthetic vocabulary that would sustain a program of experimentalism in literature without the metaphysics of *vers libre;* the result was an essay, appropriately appearing in the last issue of the magazine, that manages to turn the doctrine of the image on its head. The essay is "Tradition and the Individual Talent" (1919), and among its other finalities, it closes the argument about "pure poetry" that the Imagists had begun.

In September 1917, Eliot began in *The Egoist* a series of "Reflections on Contemporary Poetry." The general subject of those essays— there are four—is the manner in which contemporary poetry tries to be contemporary; and though their tone is more sympathetic and their strategy subtler, they effectively continue the business of exposing the limitations of "new poetry" poetics started by the essays for *The New Statesman.* The tone is sympathetic because the essays adopt an aggressively condescending attitude, congenial to the modern poet's self-conception, toward the poetry of the nineteenth century. The strategy is subtle because it is the point of the essays to suggest that the farther contemporary poetry pursues the policies which it imagines distinguish it from the poetry of the previous century, the more like the poetry it will become.

Thus the first of the "Reflections" opens by observing that:

> One of the ways by which contemporary verse has tried to escape the rhetorical, the abstract, the moralizing, to recover (for that is its purpose) the accents of direct speech, is to concentrate its attention upon trivial or accidental or commonplace objects.[41]

And the example of Wordsworth is adduced as a caution: the emotions in Wordsworth's poetry are generally "of the object and not of human life" (it is not worth pausing to try to make sense of this as a judgment of Wordsworth; the attitude is the important thing), and since he therefore has to supply with reflective power the significance his emotional or imaginative power is not strong enough to provide, his poems tend toward "a moral or philosophical conclusion." The modern poet will want to avoid this fate by letting his objects carry with them a human emotion that makes his poem meaningful without moralizing. But it is at just this point that the project begins to turn against itself. For an object's significance must come from someplace; it does not come from the object. Worsdworth at least had a philosophy ("though ill apprehended from foreign teachers"); the modern poet, distrusting intellectual systems for fear of abstraction, has no source for the moral point of his poem, and thus, "when he diverts his attention from birds, fields, and villages, is subject to lapses of rhetoric from which Words-worth, with his complete innocence of other emotions than those in which he specialized, is comparatively free."[42] The punch line of the argument is left unstated, but it is clear enough: having no other source for the significance he attaches to his objects, the modern poet will borrow the significance he finds attached to them in the poetry of the past—from sentiments, in other words, that, having lost the context that once gave them life, now belong to rhetoric. Wordsworth, in the Arnoldian phrase Eliot later endorsed,[43] may not have known enough; the modern poet, aspiring to know nothing in order simply to feel, will end by knowing only Wordsworth.

Subsequent entries propose similar complications. The second essay in the series (October 1917) makes a problem of the notion that mod-ern poetry ought to concern itself with the "things that are real to modern man." Eliot's suggestion is that it is precisely the spirit of the up-to-date that makes Victorian poetry seem so old-fashioned: "A care-ful study of the nineteenth-century poetry based on 'things real to modern man' would be interesting, beginning with Princess Ida and her fluid haze of light."[44] To substitute the electron for Laplace's ne-bular hypothesis, he warns, is to invite the same obsolescence. The third of the "Reflections" (November 1917) is a review of *The New Poetry,* and it takes issue with the title—it "lead[s] me to wonder whether a whole generation can arise together and insurrect"—and with the suggestion of the introduction that an escape from rhetoric is possible on such a scale:

> [T]here is a great push at the door, and some cases of suffocation. But what is rhetoric? . . . There is rhetoric even among the new poets. Furthermore, I am inclined to believe that Tennyson's verse is a "cry from the heart"—only it is the heart of Tennyson, Latitudinarian, Whig, Laureate. The style of William Morris is a "style like speech," only it is the speech of Morris, and therefore rather poor stuff. The

"Idylls of the King" sound often like Tennyson talking to Queen Victoria in heaven; and the "Earthly Paradise" like an idealized Morris talking to an idealized Burne-Jones.[45]

Insofar as the nonrhetorical is conceived of similarly by an entire generation of poets, that is, it becomes the rhetoric of that generation. Or as Eliot put it somewhat later, "the avoidance of the rhetorical expression of older writers has become a form."[46]

The last of the "Reflections on Contemporary Poetry" did not appear until July 1919. It is perhaps the most remarkable of Eliot's uncollected essays, and it leaves us on the doorstep of "Tradition and the Individual Talent." The essay is important because it is the first to make good on the critique of modern poetics Eliot had been prosecuting for more than two years: it offers an explanation for art's effectiveness that does not depend on a theoretical account of how we know, or of how language works, or of how the individual soul impresses itself on tangible things. But to say that the explanation is without metaphysics is not to say that it is inhospitable to metaphysical suggestion, and the fourth of the "Reflections" is remarkable because it packages its answer to the Imagist's problem in a theory of inspiration that is so essentially Romantic that it seems to have been lifted straight out of *On the Sublime*.

Eliot begins with the proposition that literary maturity requires literary experience, by which he means more than an acquaintance with the great writers ("Admiration for the great," he says, "is only a sort of discipline to keep us in order, a necessary snobbism to make us mind our places") and more than a self-appointed discipleship under an admired predecessor ("Admiration leads most often to imitation; we can seldom remain long unconscious of our imitating another, and the awareness of our debt naturally leads us to hatred of the object imitated"). He means something he can describe only on the analogy of personal experience:

Th[e] relation is a feeling of profound kinship, or rather of a peculiar personal intimacy, with another, probably a dead author. It may overcome us suddenly, on first or after long acquaintance; it is certainly a crisis; and when a young writer is seized with his first passion of this sort he may be changed, metamorphosed almost, within a few weeks even, from a bundle of second-hand sentiments into a person. The imperative intimacy arouses for the first time a real, an unshakeable confidence. That you possess this secret knowledge, this intimacy, with the dead man, that after a few or many years or centuries you should have appeared, with this indubitable claim to distinction; who can penetrate at once the thick and dusty circumlocutions about his reputation, can call yourself alone his friend: it is something more than *encouragement* to you. It is a cause of development, like personal relations in life. Like personal intimacies in life, it may and probably will pass, but it will be ineffaceable.[47]

This might be called a theory of creativity, or even of originality, but it is not yet a theory of art. The accomplishment it describes is personal to the poet; to make an aesthetic, a consequence for the reader needs to be proved. For surely few things are more common in art than an afflatus that dies in the work. Longinus called the writer's inability to induce the reader to share his passion *parenthyrsus,* and he made it one of the tropes of failed sublimity. Eliot's response is that the writer's private affair has plugged him, whether he consents or not, into a public thing; the analogy might be that love seems private to each, but marriage, even in secret, is an institution. "[W]e have not borrowed," Eliot says of the writer who has discovered an "imperative intimacy," "we have been awakened, and we become bearers of a tradition."

But—and this is the crucial moment in the argument—this connection between the writer and the literary past is not simply metaphorical; the connection is real precisely when it is visible. For where the past shows through for the reader, the poem draws on a power greater than any the poet alone could command:

> fly where men feel
> The cunning axletree: and those that suffer
> Beneath the chariot of the snowy Bear

is beautiful; and the beauty only appears more substantial if we conjecture that Chapman may have absorbed the recurring phrase of Seneca in

> signum celsi glaciale poli
> septem stellis Arcados ursae
> lucem verso termone vocat. . . .
>
>> sub cardine
> glacialis ursae . . .

a union, at a point at least, of the Tudor and the Greek through the Senecan phrase.

The example is important, for it indicates how concretely influence, as Eliot understood it, translates into an aesthetic effect. "Reflections on Contemporary Poetry" has the value of showing that whatever it may eventually have come to mean, Eliot's concept of tradition did not start out as an Arnoldian generality about the continuity of high-culture values. It was in the first instance a practical observation about how literature works.

The complaint against contemporary poetry, then, is that it is "deficient in tradition":

> We can raise no objection to "experiments" if the experimenters are qualified; but we can object that almost none of the experimenters hold fast to anything permanent under the varied phenomena of experiment. . . . No dead voices speak through the living voice; no reincarnation, no re-creation. Not even the *saturation* which sometimes combusts spontaneously into originality.[48]

For with all its poetic committed to the service of newness, modern poetry has denied itself the use of the one thing needed for newness to matter aesthetically. Asked to invent a story, all tellers will tend, however different their tales, to sound the same; but when each is asked to recount the same familiar story, it will be what is different that is noticed, and the differences will belong to the tellers. Two months after the last of the "Reflections on Contemporary Poetry," "Tradition and the Individual Talent" reminds the proponent of artistic individuality of this fact of perception: "We say: it appears to conform, and is perhaps individual, or it appears individual, and may conform; but we are hardly likely to find that it is one and not the other."[49]

In the remark about saturation in tradition spontaneously combusting into originality we can see the ground being laid for the prescriptive psychology of "Tradition and the Individual Talent," with its advice about what the poet must do with the impediment of his own personality, its warnings about the hard work necessary to acquire tradition, its enforcement of a distinction between the suffering man and the creating mind—"my programme," as Eliot called it, "for the *métier* of poetry."[50] This preoccupation with the artist's creative hygiene belongs to another side of Eliot's critique of modern literary values. No doubt he did not consider it detachable from his argument about the uses of tradition, and it is in any case a kind of warranty of that argument's respectability; it is easy to see, for instance, how it meets the contemporary requirement that good writing have a high labor cost. But if we cut around it, we are left with an observation about the source of literature's effectiveness that can stand on its own, and that can be verified by our experience with new works of art: a poem's greatest strength derives from the fact that it looks like a poem. For what a poet can provide is nearly negligible compared with what the reader can bring with him, and if the reader is prepared to meet a poem, he will bring everything that "poetry" means—including the authority of all the literature whose value is already established. Absent this borrowed legitimacy, everything contributed by the poet from his own experience, no matter how genuine—the sound of his voice, the impressions of his mind, the objects of the contemporary world— will seem fake.

But the problem has one more twist. In 1915, Marcel Duchamp hung a snow shovel in a gallery in New York. It was a gesture comprehending many ironies, and some are directed at the sort of position Eliot would shortly begin working toward in his *Egoist* essays. "As an artist," Duchamp told an interviewer in 1916, "I consider that shovel the most beautiful object I have ever seen."[51] And, as Eliot suggests in his critique of the modern poem, insofar as the shovel is indeed an object of aesthetic interest, it is most completely so in a context that identifies it as art. In a hardware store or a garage, it might be admired in a casual way by a self-conscious observer as "beautiful"; but mounted in an art gallery, it partakes automatically of all the achievements of the history of art. As we have seen, Eliot did his best to make the new artist earn his piece of the reputation every artist before him had labored to establish. But this professional ethic is one of the things Duchamp's ready-mades mock. For part of the shovel's effect on us has to do with our sense of how little time and tribulation were needed for it to be transformed from raw material into an art object; and it is often just this sense of a fortuitousness having been at work, of a kind of aesthetic luck having nothing to do with Flaubertian ordeal, that makes the experience of successful new art so exhilarating.

This is not a view of aesthetic value we find Eliot showing much interest in at any stage of his career; but Duchamp's snow shovel was also the messenger of a darker irony, and one that Eliot was more disposed to appreciate. In a society in which "art" has become a term of disputed authority, its use for aesthetic effect will have consequences riddled with ambiguity beyond the artist's control, and this is just the society that ready-mades and, to the extent that they are the expression of a programmatic hostility to the poetical, even Imagist poems are harbingers of. For just as the snow shovel takes on the reputation of art when it appears in a gallery, so art begins to take on the reputation of the shovel—and what exactly is the status of a tradition to which a snow shovel now belongs? In December 1919, in the same month that the concluding sections of "Tradition and the Individual Talent" were appearing in the final number of *The Egoist,* Eliot wrote to his mother of his determination to begin the "long poem I have had on my mind for a long time." [52] It is characteristic of his temperament that having just completed the construction of a theory of art based on the value of the cultural tradition, Eliot should at the same moment have seen the opportunity for exploiting it, and should turn to the composition of a poem in which culture figures as an agent of the most doubtful reliability.

4

Problems About Texts

The composition of *The Waste Land* was a famously difficult business. The story of Eliot's troubles is now well enough known to have become, for many readers, part of the experience of the poem.[1] Having been shoring fragments for a long work since his first year in England, Eliot announced his intention to begin putting his poem together in the fall of 1919, but apparently found it almost impossible to proceed. "[E]very evening, he went home to his flat hoping that he could start writing again, and with every confidence that the material was *there* and waiting," he told Conrad Aiken, but "night after night the hope proved illusory: the sharpened pencil lay unused by the untouched sheet of paper. What could be the matter? He didn't know."[2] His writer's block was aggravated by circumstances: the demands of his job at Lloyds Bank, and of the various freelance lecturing assignments he took on to supplement his salary, left him with little energy for poetry; his wife's father became ill, then his wife, then Eliot himself; and a visit from his mother and sister in the summer of 1921 seems to have precipitated a crisis. He took three months' leave from the bank in October 1921, and went first to Margate for a month, then to Lausanne to undergo therapy; and there, working in solitude, he was able to complete a draft of the poem. Pound performed his editorial role in January, and *The Waste Land* seems finally to have been finished in the late spring or early summer of 1922.

Eliot alludes often in his letters during this period to personal troubles—to concern about the state of his marriage, anxiety about his career, recurrent nervous exhaustion, even the fear of mental illness—and it may be, as Ronald Bush has suggested, that the combined traumatic weight of these worries made writing poetry under ordinary conditions impossible by compelling Eliot to confront emotional material that a commitment to literary honesty made nearly intractable.[3] And there seems to have been a purely professional pressure on Eliot as well, the pressure caused by the regular appearance on his desk at *The Egoist* of the chapters of *Ulysses* in manuscript from, which made him feel about his own work, as he explained it to an interviewer many years later, that "[w]hat he was tentatively attempting to do, with the usual false starts and despairs, had already been done, done superbly and, it seemed to him finally, in prose which without being poetic in the older sense, had the intensity and texture of poetry."[4]

But *The Waste Land* must have been difficult to write for another, simpler reason. It was the promised major work of a writer who, in his criticism, had exposed the delusiveness of virtually every conventional prescription for poetical newness. In a period when avant-garde literature seemed a function of theories and manifestos, Eliot was an avant-gardist without a program. Having demonstrated the factitiousness of the traditional building blocks of poetic theory—the definition of what literature is, the epistemological explanation of how literature works, the notion that sincerity is a matter of being true to oneself—Eliot must have found himself with nothing to construct a poem on. Whatever their insight into the way literature is perceived, his prescriptive essays are, from a writer's point of view, entirely impractical: the fourth of the "Reflections on Contemporary Poetry" describes genuine creativity as a business as unpremeditated as falling in love, and "Tradition and the Individual Talent" assigns the poet the whole of the Western tradition as homework but says nothing about how that learning might, in the actual process of composition, be put to use.

"[I]f we are to express ourselves, our variety of thoughts and feelings, on a variety of subjects with inevitable rightness," one of the early essays counsels the modern poet, "we must adapt our manner to the moment with infinite variations."[5] The sentence might have been the model for many of Eliot's early critical prescriptions. It is a formula whose lack of metaphysical content may be satisfying to the skeptic, but whose lack of almost every other sort of content leaves the practitioner somewhat worse off than he was without the advice, for it provokes the question, What *is* one's manner if it is a thing infinitely adaptable? But let us suppose that this was a question that Eliot, as he sat, a poem in his mind but a blank sheet before him, asked himself at some point. It would not have seemed unfamiliar to him, for it is a particular instance of the general question posed by the extreme ontological relativism of his dissertation: if each thing is entirely a function of its perceived relation to every other thing, what sense does it make for us to speak—as we do speak—of an object's distinctive character? Individuality—the set of qualities that "belong" to the object—is, by the lights of the dissertation, a phantom; it is an accident of the shape ordinary knowledge happens to take, the inexplicable residue that remains after everything else about a thing has been explained, or the unlikeness that is left after all likenesses have been used up. The notion that there are qualities original to the object persists because we have made the decision to treat certain aspects of our experience as discrete. But philosophically these discriminations have no standing; they cannot survive analysis, whose virtue, the dissertation reminds us, "is in showing the destructibility of everything."[6]

This might seem a problem whose working out will be of interest only to metaphysicians and their antagonists; but it is one of those apparently empty philosophical topics that take on life in controversies in which the issues seem quite tangible and the consequences are real enough. The question that Eliot might, in some form or other, have asked himself—What is "mine" about my poem?—is a version of this problem, and it belongs to an important line of nineteenth-century thought. The line is important because it was one of the ways the nineteenth century undertook to defend the status of human endeavor against the implications of scientific determinism, and its consequences mattered because the way the question is answered has an effect on the value that is attributed to art. There is much in Eliot's early writing that can be explained by this nineteenth-century intellectual background; but it is, characteristically, hard to know which side of the issue Eliot wanted to come down on. For if "Tradition and the Individual Talent" seems to lean toward one sort of answer to the question, *The Waste Land* seems to lean in a rather different direction. As is the case with many of the issues that figure in modernist writing, the alternative ways of thinking about the problem can be found articulated in particularly vivid forms in the literature of the 1890s.

Oscar Wilde thought the essay on "Style" the least successful in Pater's *Appreciations*. He considered the subject too theoretical, and felt that Pater did better things when he was engaged with particular works of art. But still, he added, there was something so Paterian about Pater's treatment of his abstract theme that perhaps the essay could be regarded as a success after all: "I think I have been wrong in saying that the subject is too abstract. In Mr. Pater's hands it becomes very real to us indeed."[7]

The ambivalence is typical of Wilde—he always seems willing to be seduced by a pleasing surface—and like so much else in his thought, it was learned from Pater himself. For when it is the writer's unique set of fingerprints we are interested in, it will not matter what he picks up. Pater had made the fingerprints interesting by assigning everything else to determinism, leaving us to choose only the manner in which we submit ourselves to its authority. "Natural laws we shall never modify, embarrass us as they may," advises Pater's essay on Winckelmann; "but there is still something in the nobler or less noble attitude with which we watch their fatal combinations."[8] It is a familiar alliance: aestheticism underwritten by a radical materialism; and "embarrass" is the word that gives the sentence its nineteenth-century flavor. The eighteenth-century empiricist did not consider himself embarrassed by the recognition that he was dependent on imperfect sense data for his knowledge of the world; but Darwin had shamed humankind by showing it to be descended from the apes.

For a nineteenth-century cultural historian like Pater, Darwinism had a double aspect: it made the job of understanding the past problematic in a new way, but it seemed at the same time to hold out the promise of an extraordinary solution. Evolutionary theory exacerbated the skepticism inherent in the empiricist tradition by suggesting that the men and women of the past were different from ourselves not just in the way the contents of one center of consciousness are different from and ultimately inaccessible to the contents of another, but because those men and women had different physiologies. And the historian who undertook to reconstruct that world of slightly alien creatures was therefore the prisoner not merely of his subjectivity, but of the configuration of his own particular moment in the evolutionary process as well. "Human nature" was no longer a stable paradigm. But in closing off the last window to an objective view of the past—the window afforded by the notion that although its contents may differ, the structure of human consciousness is always the same—Darwinism seemed to make the problem of objectivity disappear. For it suggested that the relation between the historian and the object of his study might now be conceived in a new way: the historian was himself—as a *subject*—the product of the past he was seeking to understand. And his best way of knowing the past was therefore not to try to get outside himself, to aspire to some extrapersonal or ahistorical vantage point, but to remain true to his subjectivity, since that subjectivity was in the end not his own at all, but the property of history itself. "The fancy of a perpetual life, sweeping together ten thousand experiences, is an old one," Pater concludes his famous description of the face of the Mona Lisa; "and modern thought has conceived the idea of humanity as wrought upon by, and summing up in itself, all modes of thought and life. Certainly Lady Lisa might stand as the embodiment of the old fancy, the symbol of the modern idea."[9]

For Pater, the awareness of the determining hand of the past gave the coloring of tragedy to the contemplation of life. In the greatest art, he says, "this entanglement, this network of law, becomes the tragic situation, in which certain groups of noble men and women work out for themselves a supreme *dénouement*."[10] But like any good disciple, Wilde had the courage of his teacher's convictions, and he stripped Darwinism of this Paterian pathos and put it to the essentially comedic service of turning received values upside down, making style (as in his change of mind about Pater's essay) take precedence over substance, artificiality over sincerity, criticism over creation.

Wilde's most ambitious performances in this mode are those imaginary dialogues in *Intentions* (1891), "The Decay of Lying" and "The Critic as Artist," which strike us today as thoroughly Victorian in taste and nearly postmodern in conviction. Gilbert, the protagonist of "The Critic as Artist," has studied Pater's passage on the Mona Lisa carefully. He seems, in fact, to know it by heart: "By revealing to us the absolute mechanism of all action, and so freeing us from the self-imposed and trammelling burden of moral responsibility," he explains to Ernest,

> the scientific principle of Heredity has become, as it were, the warrant for the contemplative life. It has shown us that we are never less free than when we try to act. . . . It is the only one of the Gods whose real name we know. . . . And so, it is not our own life that we live, but the lives of the dead, and the soul that dwells within us is no single spiritual entity, making us personal and individual, created for our service, and entering into us for our joy. It is something that has

dwelt in fearful places, and in ancient sepulchres has made its abode. It is sick with many maladies, and has memories of curious sins. It is wiser than we are, and its wisdom is bitter. It fills us with impossible desires, and makes us follow what we know we cannot gain. . . . [T]he imagination is the result of heredity. It is simply concentrated race-experience.[11]

For Wilde, as for Pater, Darwinism made the history of culture hang together in a new way—as a string of subjective moments, each giving meaning to the others by reinterpreting them. It was a conception that turned history into a kind of autobiography. History, like the autobiographical subject, reveals itself only in the process of contemplating itself (so that a Paterian novel like Joyce's A *Portrait of the Artist as a Young Man* [1916] has in this sense, to borrow Gillian Beer's useful phrase, a Darwinian plot). And like the autobiographical subject, history is a whole whose surface is constantly being reinscribed but whose integrity can be empirically tested: we know it to be there because we feel ourselves to be here. Thus the thought of Pater and Wilde exhibits the common characteristic of late-nineteenth-century historicist philosophies: the belief, as Peter Allan Dale has described it, that "the human mind finds its highest expression in the weaving of a vast and continuous system of human culture through time and that the meaning of man in the present can be no more or less than as a participant in that historical culture."[12]

This is a line of thought to which "Tradition and the Individual Talent"—not in spite of, but because of the severity of its strictures on the hypostasization of personality—quite clearly belongs. "No poet, no artist of any art, has his complete meaning alone," runs the familiar passage in Eliot's essay:

. . . The necessity that he shall conform, that he shall cohere, is not one-sided; what happens when a new work of art is created is something that happens simultaneously to all the works of art which preceded it. The existing monuments form an ideal order among themselves, which is modified by the introduction of the new (the really new) work of art among them. The existing order is complete before the new work arrives; for order to persist after the supervention of novelty, the *whole* existing order must be, if ever so slightly, altered; and so the relations, proportions, values of each work of art toward the whole are readjusted; and this is conformity between the old and the new.[13]

It is the modernist edition of the nineteenth-century historicist argument: if we abandon the atomistic conception of subjectivity—the fiction that "personality" is a thing autonomous and coherent enough to express itself—the subject will be revealed to be a nondetachable part of a greater whole, with the capacity to express, and by expressing to remake, something "more valuable"[14] than itself. For by giving up the search for what is original with the poet, Eliot's essay explains, "we shall often find that not only the best, but the most individual parts of his work may be those in which the dead poets, his ancestors, assert their immortality most vigorously."[15]

Sitting at his desk with a blank sheet before him, Eliot must thus have felt that in order to write a poem about the experience of contemporary life, he would have to write a poem that took in everything. And *The Waste Land* is indeed a literary work that seems to regard the present moment—as it is experienced by the individual subject—as a reinscription of the whole of the cultural past, and the cultural past as though it were the autobiography of a single consciousness. Or so, at least, the notes to the poem suggest. "Tiresias," explains the note to line 218,

> although a mere spectator and not indeed a "character," is yet the most important personage in the poem, uniting all the rest. Just as the one-eyed merchant, seller of currants, melts into the Phoenecian Sailor, and the latter is not wholly distinct from Ferdinand Prince of Naples, so all the women are one woman, and the two sexes meet in Tiresias. What Tiresias *sees,* in fact, is the substance of the poem.[16]

And the "one woman" of which all the women in the poem are said to be types seems very like a version of Pater's emblem for the evolutionary history of consciousness summed up in the expression of a single face, La Gioconda. Eliot's symbol of perpetual life appears first in the epigraph as the ancient Sybil who cannot die, and again, perhaps, in "The Burial of the Dead" as "Belladonna, the Lady of the Rocks" ("She is older than the rocks among which she sits . . ." runs Pater's description).[17] She is the woman in "The Game of Chess," surrounded by "her strange synthetic perfumes" and on whose dressing-room walls hang the "withered stumps of time"—the artistic record of the mythical past (". . . and all this has been to her but as the sound of lyres and flutes, and lives only in the delicacy with which it has moulded the changing lineaments, and tinged the eyelids and the hands"). And she appears, finally, in "The Fire Sermon," where she draws "her long black hair out tight," while

> bats with baby faces in the violet light
> Whistled, and beat their wings
> And crawled head downward down a blackened wall

(". . . like the vampire, she has been dead many times, and learned the secrets of the grave").[18]

But *The Waste Land* makes a strange gloss on "Tradition and the Individual Talent," for it seems infected with a doubt not addressed by the essay, but implicit in the intellectual tradition to which the essay belongs. The doubt stems from the assault the historicist thesis, in the name of subjectivity, makes on the integrity of the individual subject: for after everything in the poem that belongs to the tradition has been subtracted, what sort of value can be claimed for what is left? Pater called the remainder "style," and he made it the signal—in fact, the single—virtue of the literary object; but in Eliot's essay, all the emphasis is directed the other way. The writer who, in obedience to "Tradition and the Individual Talent" 's "programme for the *métier* of poetry,"[19] undertakes to produce the "really new" work of art, is given no place to look for its origins; the program is distinctly inhospitable to such notions as the Paterian "inner vision." And the suspicion thus arises that newness is nothing more than a kind of accident, a mistake that could not, in the end, be avoided. The manner in which *The Waste Land* dramatizes this doubt derives from the critique of the historicist defense of culture, a critique to which Eliot himself, in his brief career as a philosopher, made a relevant contribution.

Wilde's thought, unlike Pater's, leaned in the direction of Utopianism, and he saw in the acceptance of an extreme materialism the chance to make a number of false issues about literary values go away. To begin with, materialism seemed to him to solve the problem of artistic content. For if ethical standards, on a deterministic view like Gilbert's, are simply things thrown out and then swallowed up again by the evolutionary flux, we no longer need to trouble ourselves about making our response to a work of art answerable to the moral fashions of our time, since the content of one statement is as good as the content of another. There are only differences in the forms the statements take, and those differences must be what matters. "From time to time the world cries out against some charming artistic poet, because, to use its hackneyed and silly phrase, he has 'nothing to say,' " Gilbert declares. "But if he had something to say, he would probably say it, and the result would be tedious. It is just because he has no new message, that he can do beautiful work."[20] All the poet's material is given culturally (as all the components of personality are given genetically), but the shape into which that received information is molded will always be unique (just as each person carries off his assigned role in the evolutionary program differently). The form of an artistic statement can therefore be treated as a behavioral gesture: an attitude, a style, a pose—something that does not require us to engage in pointless debate over its meaning or moral intentions, as my way of walking is expressive but has no message to deliver.

Emptying out the content seems to liberate the notion of interpretation as well, since if it makes no sense to speak of originality of conception, it is pointless to draw a distinction between creation and criticism. Not only does objectivity become a problem to be solved by being ignored, but it is in fact, says Gilbert, the critic's "duty" to misinterpret: "To give an accurate description of what has never occurred is not merely the proper occupation of the historian, but the inalienable privilege of any man of parts and culture."[21] For it is of a series of misinterpretations that history is made. When we look for a reality in the past that we might describe, we find only the descriptions others have made; and our understanding of those prior descriptions will scarcely be objective, since the organ of our understanding is itself one of the things they have created ("the imagination is . . . simply concentrated race-experience"). Because it never affirmeth, art is the best record of our misreadings: "The fact is," explains Vivian in "The Decay of Lying," "that we look back on the ages entirely through the medium of Art, and Art, very fortunately, has never once told us the truth."[22] And the critic will therefore want the same freedom to make a new thing out of his failure to achieve an accurate representation of the object of his attention as the artist has traditionally been granted.

In extending the implications of Pater's thought, Wilde was, of course, continuing the work that has been taken up anew by each generation of aesthetic theorists in modern times—the task of adapting the values of art to a new phase of the progressive disenchantment of the world. The strategy Wilde had learned from Pater was a radical one. He did not try to oppose aesthetic values to scientific ones, to force his contemporaries to choose among competing *Weltanschuuangen;* he made his

argument for the superiority of the language of art turn precisely on
an acceptance of the most advanced scientific view of things. He made
science underwrite an argument for its own inadequacy. But it was a
risky business, and it required, as we have seen, extreme measures.
For like any formalist ideology, aestheticism invites the complaint that
in order to preserve art's special status, it effectively gets rid of everything that makes art matter to most people. In rescuing art from the
threat of determinism, Wilde not only felt himself obliged to jettison
the notion of valid interpretation, the notion that we can have an understanding of a work of art that corresponds to the artist's intention
and to the understandings of other people; he had to subvert or abandon the values of content, representation, and originality as well. It
was Wilde's contention that art was well rid of these things, that it
only made itself richer by handing them over to the enemy, but he had
embarked on a line of reasoning that has no natural stopping place.
For if the matter of our expressions is not ours, why is the manner?

It was in fact the belief of some of Wilde's contemporaries that *every*
aesthetic value, even the value of style, is reducible, without remainder, to a scientific explanation. "The mysterious gift of inspiration,
essential to all literary and artistic genius," explained J. F. Nisbet in
The Insanity of Genius (1891), "is evidently nothing but the automatic
activity of the nerve-cells of the brain—a phase of that morbid condition which finds its highest expression in insanity."[23] Nisbet described
the method of his book as the assertion of "the principle of a fatalism
in the lives of great men," and he proposed, by replacing the mystical
notion of the brain as spirit with the scientific notion of the brain as
matter, to account for every attribute of extraordinary behavior physiologically. It is in the structure of the brain, he announced, that "the
solution of such problems as reason, judgment, imagination, and inspiration is to be sought," and he proceeded to give a material explanation not only of inspiration, but of such elements of style as rhyme
and meter (a "special susceptibility of the motor as well as of the au-
ditory centres and their connections"), assonance, imagery, puns, wit,
clarity, and the mot juste.[24]

Nisbet's book belongs to the phenomenon Allon White has described
as the rise of symptomatic reading, the method of treating literature
as the record of a state of affairs which, by definition, the writer cannot manipulate—as the symptom of the writer's historical situation, or
of his unconscious impulses, or of his neurological health.[25] Because

everything has been given over to determining forces, what the writer intended to say—even what he intended to say about his unconscious impulses or the conditions of his time—cannot count; it is what he could not help saying, what he has said in spite of himself, that is his meaning. Symptomatic reading is the practical critical response to the notion of art as behavior: my way of walking will tell you something about me only as long as it remains unpremeditated; if I deliberately change its style, what will be revealing will be not the new manner of walking itself, but the fact of my having chosen to adopt it.

Symptomatic reading is a way of setting up the game so that the critic will always be one move ahead of the writer (though White has shown how the modern writer, by adopting the literary strategy of obscurity, took revenge on his interpreters). Its most celebrated practitioner in Wilde's day was Max Nordau, whose *Degeneration* (1892) is still in some ways the summa of all the attacks that have ever been made on modernism in art. "[T]he application of the term 'degenerates' to the originators of all the *fin-de-siècle* movements in art and literature," Nordau maintained, "is . . . no baseless conceit, but a fact." And he offered what amounted to an improvement on Nisbet's method: he did not need, he argued, "to measure the cranium of an author" to prove his assertion, for he had available the literary work itself, whose attributes could be analyzed as one would analyze the symptoms—Nordau called them the stigmata—of the diseased person.[26]

Nisbet had classed the artist with the lunatic; Nordau, taking his cue from Cesare Lombroso's physiological studies of the "born criminal," classed him with the sociopath. And, ascribing to the popular speeded-up Darwinism of the time,[27] he explained genetically inscribed sociopathic tendencies by environmental change. Modern life— bigger cities, faster railways, a greater rate and volume of economic activity—added up to a "vastly increased number of sense impressions and organic reactions, and therefore of perceptions, judgments, and motor impulses." But civilized humanity, Nordau argued, "had no time to adapt itself to its changed conditions of life. . . . It grew fatigued and exhausted, and this fatigue and exhaustion showed themselves in the first generation, under the form of acquired hysteria; in the second, as hereditary hysteria." Nordau meant his diagnosis literally: "railway-spine" and "railway-brain" (the consequences of "the constant vibrations undergone in railway travelling") had brought about

an actual physiological alteration—first directly, and then through ge-
netic transmission—in the organ of perception.[28] Thus an Impression-
ist painting, for example, was not the product of a conscious effort to
adapt artistic form to the subject matter of modern life; it was an
accurate representation of the optical image produced by a nervous
system in the process of devolution:

> The degenerate artist who suffers from *nystagmus,* or trembling of the
> eyeball, will, in fact, perceive the phenomena of nature trembling,
> restless, devoid of firm outline, and, it he is a conscientious painter,
> will give us pictures reminding us of the mode practised by the
> draughtsmen of the *Fliegende Blätter* when they represent a wet dog
> shaking himself vigorously.[29]

And by the same token, the poses of the aesthete, precisely because
they differ from the behavior of the normal person, are the symptoms
of a deviation that calls for a psychological diagnosis:

> The predilection for strange costume is a pathological aberration of
> a racial instinct. . . . When . . . an Oscar Wilde goes about in "aes-
> thetic costume" among gazing Philistines, exciting either their ridicule
> or their wrath, it is no indication of independence of character, but
> rather from a purely anti-socialistic, ego-maniacal recklessness and
> hysterical longing to make a sensation. . . .[30]

The artist who subscribes to Wilde's position has no good way of
defending himself against this sort of critical treatment, since although
he can, according to the Wildean view of artistic content, say what he
likes, he has effectively relinquished control over what he means. *Degeneration* is the nightmare version of late-nineteenth-century aestheticism; it is the danger Wilde was flirting with when he enlisted scientific determinism in his defense of art. Pater and Wilde had
undertaken to preserve the status of art under a materialist dispensation by assigning value to whatever it is that gives a thing its distinctive form, that makes it what it is and not another thing. The work of
art is the type of the distinctive object; its style is the sign of its
uniqueness, and the evidence of the artist's triumph—in the aggre-
gate, of humanity's triumph—over impersonal process. Nordau responded, in effect, by pointing out that materialism leaves no room for
an independent intention, so that whatever distinguishes a thing from
the norm is analyzable as the symptom of an evolutionary aberration.
To claim that the history of culture, taken as a series of misinterpre-

tations, is coherent on grounds that it is the evolutionary record of the subject is to claim that a list of errors adds up to the truth. Participation in culture cannot be the meaning of human life, because culture is purely reflexive; it adds nothing to what is there: "every work of art," says Nordau, "always comprises in itself truth and reality in so far as, if it does not reflect the external world, it surely reflects the mental life of the artist."[31] In Nordau's version of Darwinian historicism, wholeness becomes totality: the evolutionary law covers every case, and reduces everything to its terms. Nordau, like Nisbet, explained the distinctive act physiologically for the simple reason that on his view it could not be accounted for in any other way. He thus made the artist the victim of his own individuality, of the very quality the aesthete had hoped would save him.

The 1890s is the missing chapter in many versions of the history of literary modernism, in part because all the issues in its cultural controversies appear to be overdrawn, so that it is not easy to know just how seriously to take them. If Nordau's position seems absurd, Wilde's seems deliberately calculated to provoke absurdity. But however self-consciously extravagant it may have been, the aestheticist valorization of style had a significant role in the formation of the ideology of modern art, and the problem Nordau's argument makes for it is a real one.

Nor is it the only difficulty that can be pointed to. In December 1913, T. S. Eliot read a paper on a problem in comparative anthropology to Josiah Royce's graduate seminar at Harvard. Eliot's particular examples were Jane Harrison's *Themis: A Study of the Social Origins of Greek Religion* (1912) and Frazer's *Golden Bough,* and his argument was that the efforts of those writers to describe religious ritual scientifically were misconceived, and could lead to no conclusive results.[32] The problem, Eliot maintained, was not merely the traditional epistemlogical problem of uncertainty, the problem of having no way of knowing when our knowing is objectively true. We assume, of course, that the scientist's interpretations will interfere with the facts of the phenomenon he is trying to provide an account of, that those interpretations will disappear into the data and emerge in the analysis as "descriptions." But this difficulty is exacerbated in the case of a social phenomenon such as a religious ritual by the circumstance that the person who performs the ritual will have his own interpretation of its meaning, and this interpretation will be an additional fact to be described. For unless the description of an action takes account of the meaning it has for the actor, Eliot argued, it treats behavior as "mere mechanism."[33]

But when we look to the internal meaning of an action, we find ourselves confronting a further problem, the problem that the individual participant's interpretation of a ritual cannot be taken as definitive, that it will be an interpretation "probably not in accordance with the facts of [the ritual's] origin."[34] Because a religious ritual is a social activity, its meaning cannot be the meaning given to it by one of the participants (an "[i]nterpretation which the individual makes is not made by the group," as Eliot put it, "and hence [is] not the cause"[35]). And since a ritual is, furthermore, an activity that has a history, it cannot even be, at any given moment, the sum of all the meanings given to it by all the participants; for each time the ritual is performed, it will mean something different, the interpretations of each new generation constituting a reinterpretation of a phenomenon which is already defined in part by the interpretations of the previous group, and so forth backward in time. "Interpretation is thus ever a new problem added to increase the difficulty of the old," Eliot concluded; and the comparative study of religions, he noted, was a subject "especially good to bring this out, for here interpretation has succeeded interpretation, not because the older opinions were refuted, but because the point of view has changed."[36]

Royce commented on Eliot's paper by suggesting that in everyday life we might solve problems of interpretation by asking questions until a mutual understanding was reached. But Eliot did not see how this proposal met the case, and he replied by asking Royce: "Is there no essential distinction between a social statement in language which asks for interpretation and a something not intended as a sign?"[37] It is a nice question, for the answer would seem to be that there is a distinction, since we make it all the time, but that there is nothing essential about it, since a thing is a sign when it is treated as one and not a sign when it is not, as when you suddenly interpret my habit of raising my eyebrows as skepticism. But even on these relative terms, the distinction has a consequence for our understanding. The point of Eliot's response to Royce is that once something is regarded as behavior, interpretation becomes not merely a problem (as Royce had hope to leave the matter) but problematic. The meaning of a statement that was intended to have a meaning can be ascertained, if only in a rough and ready way, as when I ask if this is what you meant by something you said, and you say yes. But the meaning of behavior is indeterminate: my interpretation of my way of walking is not definitive; it is just one more piece of the puzzle, and one that cannot now be left out. But it was precisely by thinking of art as like a way of walking that Wilde had hoped to avoid the goose chase after meanings.

All the difficulties with the late-nineteenth-century idea of style seem to be summed up in *The Waste Land*. It is, to begin with, a poem that includes an interpretation—and one "probably not in accordance with the facts of its origin"—*as part of the poem,* and it is therefore a poem that makes a problem of its meaning precisely by virtue of its apparent (and apparently inadequate) effort to explain itself. We cannot understand the poem without knowing what it meant to its author, but we must also assume that what the poem meant to its author will not be its meaning. The notes to *The Waste Land* are, by the logic of Eliot's philosophical critique of interpretation, simply another riddle—and not a separate one—to be solved. They are, we might say, the poem's way of treating itself as a reflex, a "something not intended as a sign," a gesture whose full significance it is impossible, by virtue of the nature of gestures, for the gesturer to explain.[38]

And the structure of the poem—a text followed by an explanation—is a reproduction of a pattern that, as the notes themselves emphasize, is repeated in miniature many times inside the poem itself, where cultural expressions are transformed, by the mechanics of allusion, into cultural gestures. For each time a literary phrase or a cultural motif is transposed into a new context—and the borrowed motifs in *The Waste Land* are shown to have themselves been borrowed by a succession of cultures[39]—it is reinterpreted, its previous meaning becoming incorporated by distortion into a new meaning suitable to a new use. So that the work of Frazer and Weston is relevant both because it presents the history of religion as a series of appropriations and reinscriptions of cultural motifs, and because it is itself an unreliable reinterpretation of the phenomena it attempts to describe. The poem (as A. Walton Litz argued some time ago) is, in other words, not *about* spiritual dryness so much as it is about the ways in which spiritual dryness has been *perceived.*[40] And the relation of the notes to the poem proper seems further emblematic of the relation of the work as a whole to the cultural tradition it is a commentary on. *The Waste Land* is presented as a contemporary reading of the Western tradition, which (unlike the "ideal order" of "Tradition and the Individual Talent") is treated as a sequence of gestures whose original meaning is unknown, but which every new text that is added to it makes a bad guess at.

The author of the notes seems to class himself with the cultural anthropologists whose work he cites. He reads the poem as a coherent expression of the spiritual condition of the social group in which it was produced. But the author of the *poem,* we might say, does not enjoy this luxury of detachment. He seems, in fact, determined to confound, even at the cost of his own sense of coherence, the kind of interpretive knowingness displayed by the author of the notes. The author of the poem classes himself with the diseased characters of his own work—the clairvoyante with a cold, the woman whose nerves are bad, the king whose insanity may or may not be feigned. He cannot distinguish what he intends to reveal about himself from what he cannot help revealing: he would like to believe that his poem is expressive of some general reality, but he fears that it is only the symptom of a private disorder. For when he looks to the culture around him, everything appears only as a reflection of his own breakdown: characters and objects metamorphose up and down the evolutionary scale; races and religions lose their purity ("Bin gar keine Russin, stamm' aus Litauen, echt deutsch"); an adulterated "To His Coy Mistress" describes the tryst between Sweeney and Mrs. Porter, and a fragmented *Tempest* frames the liaison of the typist and the young man carbuncular; "London bridge is falling down." The poem itself, as a literary object, seems an imitation of this vision of degeneration: nothing in it can be said to point to the poet, since none of its stylistic features is continuous, and it has no phrases or images that cannot be suspected of—where they are not in fact identified as—belonging to someone else. *The Waste Land* appears to be a poem designed to make trouble for the conceptual mechanics not just of ordinary reading (for what poem does not try to disrupt those mechanics?) but of *literary* reading. For insofar as reading a piece of writing as literature is understood to mean reading it for its style, Eliot's poem eludes a literary grasp.

But the composition of *The Waste Land* was not a reflex, of course, and Eliot was not trying to produce a text determined entirely by submission to outer circumstance and inner compulsion; he was trying, I think, to write a poem that would be "his own." And for such an intention, "style," as the late nineteenth century conceived it, would have restricted what was his in his poem precisely by drawing a line between what could and could not be helped. For, as we have seen, in preserving something in the work of art the artist can truly call his own, Wilde and Pater handed over nearly everything to external forces— to the given. But by renouncing as an illusion the very value aestheti- cism had rescued from the flux, Eliot's poem seems to have won an even greater authority. For it was the common argument of *The Waste Land's* early champions—Wilson (1922), Richards (1925), Leavis (1932)—that the poem was held together not by its meaning, or by its author's beliefs, or by metaphysics, but by the unity of a single, co- herent authorial presence.[41] If we want to account for this perception of a work that appears so radically decentered—and to do so by saying something more specific to the case than that *The Waste Land* is a poem that takes advantage of the universal habit of reading by which we infer an author for every text—we might suggest that insofar as style had become a problematic literary value, *The Waste Land* was a poem that succeeded by presenting itself as a symptom. For the result of this strategy is that since nothing in *The Waste Land* (except the notes, of course, whose self-consciously "authorial" manner only makes the symptomatic character of the rest appear more striking) is more "Eliot's" than anything else, everything in *The Waste Land* is Eliot's. Eliot appears nowhere, but his fingerprints are on everything. And this gives him a victory over hermeneutics as well, for there is no level of reading of Eliot's poem at which it is possible to say that we have reached a meaning that might not have been put there by Eliot him- self.

This view of *The Waste Land* belongs to the school that takes the poem to be a work of "decreation," as Frank Kermode has called it, or a "roadway to nowhere," in Eloise Knapp Hay's more recent phrase;[42] it differs from the school that takes the poem to be a signpost pointing toward "a further stage in [Eliot's] development," or an account of "the trials of a life in the process of becoming exemplary."[43] If the poem was indeed intended as a kind of deliberate dead end, an explo- sion of the nineteenth-century metaphysics of style leaving nothing in its place, this ambition was perhaps one of the things Eliot learned from Joyce. *Ulysses,* Eliot told Virginia Woolf in a famous conversa- tion, "destroyed the whole of the 19th century. It left Joyce with noth- ing to write another book on. It showed up the futility of all the En- glish styles. . . . [T]here was no 'great conception': that was not Joyce's

intention. . . . Joyce did completely what he meant to do."[44] An essay
Eliot published in the *Nouvelle Revue Française* a few months after
this conversation gives us a better idea of the nature of the accomplishment he had in mind: "The influence of [the style of] Walter Pater,"
he says there,

> . . . culminates and disappears, I believe, in the work of James Joyce.
> . . . In *Ulysses* this influence, like the influence of Ibsen and every
> other influence to which Mr. Joyce has submitted, is reduced to zero.
> It is my opinion that *Ulysses* is not so distinctly a precursor of a new
> epoch as it is a gigantic culmination of an old. In this book Joyce has
> arrived at a very singular and perhaps unique literary distinction: the
> distinction of having, not in a negative but a very positive sense, no
> style at all. I mean that every sentence Mr. Joyce writes is peculiarly
> and absolutely his own; that his work is not a pastiche; but that never-
> theless, it has none of the marks by which a "style" may be distin-
> guished.
>
> Mr. Joyce's work puts an end to the tradition of Walter Pater, as it
> puts an end to a great many other things. . . .[45]

We are likely to feel that traditions are not so easily killed off as the
modernists supposed, that they live on long after their metaphysics
have been demolished. But this strange life of the buried past is one
of the things *The Waste Land*—and its tradition—are all about.

The notion that cultural history is the product of a series of errors,
that the new appears as the result of a misinterpretation of what is
received, is articulated in Eliot's paper on ritual and seems to inform
the structure of *The Waste Land;* but it is left dangling, as we have
noted, in "Tradition and the Individual Talent." Eliot appears to have
been concerned almost immediately after the publication of *The Waste
Land* to withdraw "Tradition and the Individual Talent" 's apparent
invitation to subjectivism. An interpretation, he announced in "The
Function of Criticism" (October 1923), "is only legitimate when it is
not an interpretation at all, but merely putting the reader in possession
of facts which he would otherwise have missed." And its goal, thus
conceived, lies entirely outside the historicist hermeneutical system: it
is the "possibility of arriving at something outside of ourselves, which
may provisionally be called truth."[46]

But this "official" view of the editor of *The Criterion* is sometimes
subverted, in unobtrusive places, in Eliot's later writings. His intro-

duction to his mother's dramatic poem *Savonarola* (1926), for instance, is rather weak on the importance of the positivistic "sense of fact" endorsed by "The Function of Criticism":

> [A] work of historical fiction is much more a document on its own time than on the time portrayed. Equally relative, because equally passed through the sieve of our interpretation, but enabling us to extend and solidify this interpretation of the past which is its meaning, its sense, for us. By comparing the period described in *Romola* as we know that period, with George Eliot's interpretation of it, we can supplement our knowledge (which is itself an interpretation and relative) of the mind and of the epoch of George Eliot. But unless George Eliot's novel gave a faithful presentation of Romola's time to George Eliot's contemporaries, it would have little to say to us about George Eliot's time.[47]

And in his introduction to G. Wilson Knight's *Wheel of Fire* (1930), Eliot seems to have been seduced even farther away from an objectivist position by the allurements of a theory of explicitly *bad* interpretation:

> [O]ur impulse to interpret a work of art . . . is exactly as imperative and fundamental as our impulse to interpret the universe by metaphysics. . . . And Bradley's apothegm that "metaphysics is the finding of bad reasons for what we believe upon instinct; but to find these reasons is no less an instinct," applies as precisely to the interpretation of poetry.
>
> . . . [I]t occurs to me as possible that there may be an essential part of error in all interpretation, without which it would not be interpretation at all. . . . The work of Shakespeare is like life itself something to be lived through. If we lived it completely we should need no interpretation; but on our plane of appearances our interpretations themselves are a part of our living.[48]

We have Eliot's final thoughts on this problem only at third hand, from Joseph Summers's report of a conversation with F. O. Matthiessen in 1950. Eliot, according to Matthiessen, had

> thought of writing a book to be entitled "The Fruitfulness of Misunderstanding." The central idea was that many of the significant changes in poetry have occurred when a writer who is attempting to imitate another or others, through misunderstanding of his model or models creates inadvertently something new. The specific cases Eliot intended to develop . . . were Coleridge's misunderstanding of German philosophers, Poe's misunderstanding of Coleridge, Baudelaire's and the

French *symbolistes'* misunderstanding of Poe, and Eliot's own misunderstanding of the French writers.[49]

This is a lovely piece of self-directed irony, and it exhibits a fatalism even a determinist might admire, since it manages to tie Eliot, by an incredible run of bad luck, to the very tradition he had devoted most of his career to distinguishing himself from.

II
The Literary Vocation

5

Literature and Professionalism

T. S. Eliot was married to Vivien Haigh-Wood on June 26, 1915. It was the end of his first year at Oxford on a fellowship from the Harvard philosophy department, but Eliot did not plan to return to Cambridge, and two days after the wedding Ezra Pound sat down and drafted a letter to the father of the groom. "[Y]our son asks me to write this letter," Pound explained; "I think he expects me to send you some sort of apologia for the literary life." But the apologia was not Pound's preferred mode of persuasion:

> . . . Of the conceit of artists there is no end, but this letter is between ourselves and I see no reason to beat about the bush.
> . . . Apart from all questions of "inspiration" and "star born genius" I should say that the arts, as the sciences, progress by infinitesimal stages, that each inventor does little more than make some slight, but revolutionizing change, alteration in the work of his predecessors. Browning in his *Dramatis Personae* and in his *Men and Women* developed a new form of poem which had lain dormant since Ovid's *Heroides* or since Theocritus. Ovid's poems are, to be sure, written as if they were letters, from Helen to Paris, from Paris to Oenone, etc. In Theocritus (IV.2 I think) we have a monologue comparable to those of Browning (much more passionate, to be sure, but still comparable as a form.)
> The Anglo Saxon *Seafarer* and Rihaku's *Exile's Letter* are also poems of this sort. Nevertheless, Browning's poems came as a new thing in their day. In my own first book I tried to rid this sort of poem of all

irrelevant discussion, of Browning's talk *about* this, that and the other, to confine my words strictly to what might have been the emotional speech of the character under such or such crisis. Browning had cast his poems mostly in Renaissance Italy, I cast mine in medieval Provence, which was a change without any essential difference. T.S.E. has gone farther and begun with the much more difficult job of setting his "personae" in modern life, with the discouragingly "unpoetic" modern surroundings.

. . . As to his coming to London, anything else is a waste of time and energy. No one in London cares a hang what is written in America. After getting an American audience a man has to begin all over again here if he plans for an international hearing. He even begins at a disadvantage. London likes discovering her own gods. . . . The situation has been very well summed up in the sentence: "Henry James stayed in Paris and read Turgenev and Flaubert, Mr. Howells returned to America and read Henry James."

. . . Again if a man is doing the fine thing and the rare thing, London is the only possible place for him to exist. Only here is there a disciplinary body of fine taste, of powerful writers who "keep the editors under," who make it imperative that a publisher act in accordance, occasionally, with some dictates other than those of sheer commercialism.

And the letter concludes with a postscript indicating that "a man" might need $500 the first year and $250 the second to get a literary career underway.[1]

Pound was one of the most political and least politic of men, and as he would do more spectacularly on more famous occasions, he seems here to have contrived a piece of complete miscalculation. Henry Ware Eliot, Sr., was a manufacturer of bricks; what he would have made of the collegial reference to Theocritus IV.2—"much more passionate, to be sure, but still comparable as a form"—or the helpful examples of *The Seafarer* and Rihaku can scarcely be imagined. In the event, much of the literary talk was apparently deleted—perhaps at Eliot's suggestion—before the letter was sent. But even the edited version has something slightly comic about it. Pound's little winks of familiarity ("but this letter is between ourselves . . .") seem to fall into the gap across which, as we tend to imagine it, the artist and the industrialist, each in the separate stronghold of his own view of what matters, contemplate each other with mutual distrust.

But society is not so atomistic. Those occupational antagonisms are local things; and though Pound's letter was unsuccessful—Eliot's father was still unreconciled to his son's career when he died in 1919—its confidence that its recipient will appreciate the general thrust of its argument was not entirely misplaced. This is so not simply because of Pound's pragmatic attitude toward literary fortune, his insistence that the producer of cultural goods needs to seek out the most profitable markets. That part of the letter was no doubt calculated by its author to have a particularly telling effect by virtue of its appeal to the commercial instincts of his correspondent (though Henry Eliot might have replied in the same vein that he had not invested so heavily in a philosopher in order to end up with a poet). But practical arguments in favor of impractical careers are part of the history of parents and children, and Pound's worldliness is the traditional tone for the intermediary in such a quarrel to take. What gives the letter its strange suitability is in fact that part of the argument that seems so misconceived—the sketch of a literary tradition.

Though it is obviously in some respects a slightly eccentric case, Pound's letter conforms to a practice that seems standard enough. It passes up an individualistic style of justification for the artistic career (here the argument that Eliot is a born writer, a young man whose sense of fulfillment can only come from the exercise of his talents) in favor of an institutional one (the claim that Eliot's work is important because it carries on in a useful and time-honored way the traditions of an ancient vocation). We are so accustomed to this manner of explaining the value of the artistic enterprise that we are apt to regard it as perfectly noncontroversial; but its use in the modernist period was a response to a specific process of social change, and it therefore had a specific ideological content. The process it reflected was the rise of professionalism—the evolution in the second half of the nineteenth century of the conception of the high-status occupation, in the course of which professional standards of conduct gradually came to overlay, and in some cases to displace, the vocational values of independence, ingenuity, and entrepreneurship. This process exerted pressure on a way of conceiving literature that had become customary since Romanticism; so that (to summarize in simplified terms an extremely complicated phenomenon) insofar as literature was understood generally to be an activity pursued by individual artists answering solely to the dictates of their own genius and producing objects whose value was to a significant degree a function of their originality—insofar as this view was part of the reputation of literature—it became necessary to find new ways of describing the proper practice of literature and the definitive characteristics of the worthy literary object if the social status of the literary vocation, and thus to some extent the perceived value of literature itself, were to be preserved.

The argument of this chapter depends on two hypotheses: first, that the ideology of professionalism during the late nineteenth and early twentieth centuries developed in discriminable stages, stages that responded both to instabilities in previous editions of the construct "professional" and to concrete social developments; and, secondly, that the emergence of the values associated with professionalism influenced to some degree the way literature was perceived by its audience. The consequence of these developments (assuming the rough validity of the hypotheses) was not that literature became a different thing, or that writers began to think of themselves differently—claims that would in any case be impossible to substantiate—but that the critical vocabulary used to distinguish good literature from other kinds of writing, and to justify the social importance of the literary vocation, adapted itself to meet the standards of a set of altered occupational values.

Ideological change of the nondisruptive sort involved here tends to take the line of least resistance, and this is especially true of changes in the ideology of an activity as dependent on a sense of continuity and history as literature. So that it was not necessary—it was not even desirable—to discard the existing formulas for literary excellence; it was only necessary to rewrite them. And this helps to explain one of the peculiarities of the modernist enterprise—the fact that, as many commentators have discovered, its activities can be explained with almost equal cogency in the critical vocabularies of Romanticism and of anti-Romantic or "classical" modernism.[2] Two features of modernist criticism—features that Eliot in particular is strongly associated with— seem to stand in an especially significant relation to the developing ideology of professionalism: one is the notion of tradition, and the other is the programmatic disparagement of the literature of the nineteenth century.

Pound's letter to Henry Eliot suggests an obvious irony in the situation this chapter describes—the irony that the manner in which the modern artist tried to keep his ideological distance from the business-man, to guard the autonomy of his work, was also one of the ways in which the artist and the businessman were both, in spite of their self-conceptions, bound together. But the irony is easily cheapened if too much store is set by it. For even an activity that undertakes to stand in an independent and critical relation to the life of the group as a whole, as modern high-culture art once proposed to stand, requires for its effectiveness a legitimacy that can only come from an appeal to the standards of the group itself. "Autonomy" would mean nothing if it were not a relative term.

1

Looking to a literary work for an analysis of the condition of literature seems a risky business, for how can a literary writer be disinterested enough to qualify as the sociologist of his own vocation? But the practice is a common one, and it might be justified by answering that a literary text tends to be more overdetermined, to screen out less, than other kinds of writing, and that it therefore takes on significances beyond the scope of its author's conscious intentions—even to the point of standing as a record of its own circumstances. Whether this is so or not, it is certainly the case that few literary works have seemed as overdetermined, and as accommodating to multiple readings, as Joseph Conrad's *Heart of Darkness,* and I propose to take advantage of that work's reputation by showing it to tell, in addition to its other stories, a story about itself. That story has a double plot—one about the changing character of the nineteenth-century capitalist, and the other about the predicament of modern art—and, because these plots are made to overlap each other, it states, in a particularly concise and forceful way, the terms of a problem with the reputation of literature.

The first plot takes us along the surface of the narrative (to use a dubious but Marlovian metaphor). Five men, on the deck of a yacht in the Thames estuary, are waiting for the tide to turn so that they can begin what is presumably to be a recreational cruise. The host is a businessman, "The Director of Companies,"[3] and his guests are a lawyer, an accountant, the narrator (his occupation is not identified, but we will have a guess at it later on, when we reach the second plot), and Marlow. The setting makes a convenient stage for the introduction of the triple parallel of imperialisms that becomes the explicit context for Marlow's story—the Roman invasion of Britain, the English conquest of the New World, and the nineteenth-century European colonization of Africa. But it is also, halfway between the city and the sea, useful as a reminder of an occupational difference between Marlow and the others: the five are friends, explains the narrator, because of "the bond of the sea,"[4] but only Marlow has remained a seaman, and this fact gives his story a significant tilt. For it is clear that Marlow's listeners regard him as a man who, having taken an independent and solitary path, can afford the luxury of high-mindedness, and are therefore prepared to discount his moral pronouncements according to the standards of a more worldly economy; and it is equally clear that Marlow knows this. The consequence is a certain amount of deliberate vagueness in the telling of the story and a certain degree of willful impercipience in the immediate audience's understanding of it (the Anglophilia sometimes attributed to the book, for instance, is the narrator's, not Marlow's[5]). And the narrator's famous remark about the fuzziness of Marlow's stories—"to him the meaning of an episode was not inside like a kernel but outside, enveloping the tale which brought it out only as a glow brings out a haze"[6]—might be taken to mean simply that in the interests of companionship Marlow has agreed to make the point of his story obscure, and the others have agreed to miss it.

Marlow's narrative is in a sense an explanation for his decision to remain, as the narrator calls him, "a wanderer."[7] The Wordsworthian association is suggestive: to his listeners Marlow is a late incarnation of a familiar Romantic type—a sort of scholar-gypsy, though with a touch of the Victorian moralist about him, too, since he evidently conceives it a duty to report back occasionally to his brothers in the prison of convention. And since it is a defense of his own choice of career, Marlow's story can be expected to contain an implicit judgment on his friends'—the choices, which have placed them at the financial and administrative heart of the world's greatest empire. But the judgment Marlow passes is not a condemnation for complicity in the crimes of imperialism. For capitalism is a world economy—no one would have known this better than a late-nineteenth-century seaman, especially a freelancer like Marlow—and, as he does in all his books, Conrad takes a totalizing view of the situation: one is either exploiting or exploited. Conrad was not a reformer, and it is one of the lessons of Marlow's experience that there are no scholar-gypsies. Marlow's story is not a political tract; it is a tract about character. And this is why he is so certain that his listeners will not understand the part of the tale that is the most important for him—the mystery of his admiration for Kurtz.

Kurtz's character is established almost entirely by rumor. This is appropriate because genius is a rumor to the rest of us, and Kurtz is a genius. The term is Marlow's; he is not quite sure what he means by it, but it is somehow connected in his mind with being an amateur. "I am unable to say what was Kurtz's profession," he confesses near the end of his story,

> whether he ever had any—which was the greatest of his talents. I had taken him for a painter who wrote for the papers, or else for a journalist who could paint—but even [Kurtz's] cousin . . . could not tell me what he had been—exactly. He was a universal genius—on that point I agreed. . . .[8]

And everything we hear about Kurtz has the same air of vagueness: " 'He is a very remarkable person,' " the chief accountant tells Marlow at the coastal station; " 'He is a prodigy. . . . He is an emissary of pity, and science, and progress, and devil knows what else,' " explains the "brickmaker" at the Central Station; and the manager refers to him as "an exceptional man, of the greatest importance to the company."[9] The men who furnish Marlow with these descriptions are not geniuses, and the nature of their talents is not in doubt. They are company men, and their ordinariness is made a point of, particularly the ordinariness of the station manager, which is so complete that it provokes from Marlow a kind of praise:

> He was commonplace in complexion, in feature, in manners, and in voice. He was of middle size and of ordinary build. . . . He was a common trader, from his youth up employed in these parts—nothing more. He was obeyed, yet he inspired neither love nor fear, nor even respect. . . . He originated nothing, he could keep the routine going—that's all. But he was great. He was great by this little thing that it was impossible to tell what could control such a man. He never gave that secret away. Perhaps there was nothing within him.[10]

The passage is famous, because it is the sketch of a figure that has haunted much of twentieth-century thought: the man (and it invariably is a man) whose success follows from his ability to conform everything about himself to the requirements of the institution he serves, to guide his work by its needs and with indifference to his own interests or scruples. It is, in its most primitive form, the figure of the professional: he is able, as we say, to keep his personal feelings out of it; and his identification with his institution is what gives him his absolute superiority over the most gifted amateur.[11] For he *is* a success: the station manager after all emerges victorious from his contest with the exceptional man. He has a rather easy time of it, in fact; for once the instinct for economic domination has organized itself with such bureaucratic thoroughness, it conquers by sheer momentum. Personality has nothing to do with its progress and is powerless to impede it. Confronted by this choice of types, Marlow, of course, gives his loyalty to Kurtz. To say this much is simply a way of restating a familiar reading of Conrad's novel. But the story of Marlow's choice makes a kind of parable of nineteenth-century economic history, and of British economic history in particular, a parable that is summarized in the fact that although the station manager has no use for Kurtz, he is glad to get the ivory.

Kurtz is identified by the "brickmaker" at the Central Station as one of "the new gang—the gang of virtue," by which he means that Kurtz is one of the Belgian imperialists who have allied themselves with humanitarian causes to gain political leverage at home against competing colonial traders.[12] He belongs, that is (or at first appears to belong), to a higher stage in the evolution of the professional: he can articulate an ethic to justify his right to practice. And he is therefore regarded by the "brickmaker" and his patron the station manager with the jealousy and fear of men seeing themselves being replaced by an outsider who has been brought in because he has the talents needed to play the game by rules that are new to them and whose purpose they do not understand. But Kurtz does not remain one of the new type for long, for although he has a talent for expression, he has none for hypocrisy (there is no suggestion that Kurtz did not believe his humanitarian cover story when he embarked for Africa); and at some point during his enormously successful tenure as chief of the Inner Station he becomes a throwback, the incarnation of an earlier era in the history of capitalist expansion.

Kurtz figures in most readings of Conrad's story as the hypocrisy of liberal imperialism personified, a sort of picture of Dorian Gray of the late-nineteenth-century colonial trader. But it makes no sense to think of Kurtz as, for instance, what the station manager would look like if his surface of ordinariness were peeled away; it is precisely the point about the station manager that there is no inner man. The later Kurtz is not the station manager's hidden side because he is not, figuratively speaking the station manager's contemporary. The indictment Conrad clearly intended to make of the modern imperialist has a historical dimension (otherwise Marlow's admiration is, I think, simply a perversity). Kurtz becomes, in the course of his regression, his own economic grandfather—which is why, for instance, Marlow's journey up the river is repeatedly figured as a journey back in time. And it is because Kurtz is no longer the latest edition of the professional type that the grudging awe the station manager had felt toward the man who arrived from Brussels speaking the powerful language of the new imperialism is so easily supplanted by the contempt he feels for the man he has to drag out of the jungle. " 'Mr. Kurtz is a remarkable man.' " ventures Marlow after the picture of Kurtz's degeneration has become clear; " 'he *was*,' " replies the station manager.[13] It is the reply of a man who suddenly appreciates his own position in a new light.

It is the station master's triumphant point that in spite of the remarkable amount of ivory he has collected, Kurtz has ruined the district, and his explanation is the verdict of the organization man: " 'the method,' " he tells Marlow, " 'is unsound.' " " 'No method at all,' " is Marlow's response.[14] The station manager is right because the method is one he recognizes. It is the method associated with the early industrial capitalist: purely empirical, ruthlessly utilitarian but with never more than the short run in view, controlling by treating everything as the extension of his own personality. And Marlow is right, too, because those men seemed to have had no models to practice on. They did not simply administer an economic machine already in place and collect its receipts, and they did not merely squeeze profits from markets waiting to be exploited. They made something where there had never been anything like it before. The conditions, perhaps, were given to them—the means for transporting raw materials and finished goods, the mass of unskilled labor, the elementary technology of the first machine age—but the extraordinary effort by which those resources were transformed into the modern worldwide market economy was largely an effort of primitive will. So at least—whatever the historical truth may have been—the nineteenth century perceived it; and Kurtz's final cry at the jungle, as it is given in the manuscript version of the novel, is the echo of that spirit: " 'Oh! but I will make you serve my ends.' "[15]

Marlow, of course, does not admire Kurtz for what he has done, only for the strength of character that has let him do it without self-deception—and because Kurtz has exposed the utter venality of the whole colonial enterprise. For if Kurtz's brief career is a reenactment of the first industrial revolution, it is a reenactment in the style of the-second-time-as-farce. The drama is played out this time in an environment whose only challenge is to the animal health of the principals, and in which glass beads and bits of cotton suffice for a wage fund and "production" consists of digging buried ivory out of the ground. The exercise of entrepreneurial willpower in such a setting produces results that are absurdly over the mark, since there is no need to disguise its motives with the slogans of respectability and no countervailing economic or political force to resist it. Kurtz's way seems dangerous and its results spectacular, but the station manager is right in holding such things in contempt. *His* way is merely efficient, but it ensures survival and is the strategy appropriate to the business at hand. For far from marking a resurgence of the entrepreneurial spirit, the imperialist project of the late nineteenth century was one of the symptoms of that spirit's degeneration.[16]

Victorian Britain owed its position in the world economy to the head start its early industrialization had given it, and its dominance allowed it in the middle years of the century to maintain by informal means a de facto commercial empire that was virtually worldwide. The sudden efflorescence of formal empire building by the industrial powers in the last decades of the century thus represented for Britain something of a setback. Informal empires are cheaper than formal ones, and selling to the developing nations, as Britain had amassed its wealth by doing, presents a different challenge to the economy from selling to captive markets in the underdeveloped world. But the program of colonization pursued by the industrial nations provided the British economy with a second and deceptively brilliant opportunity. For Britain's earlier domination of international trade had left it in possession of an enormous commercial system: a huge merchant fleet, extensive diplomatic connections, unsurpassed financial machinery—the superstructure needed to conduct the business of empire. These were things countries with less international experience were willing to pay for, and as it had once been the world's greatest producer of coal and steel, Britain became in the second half of the nineteenth century the leading supplier of commercial services—shipping, banking, insurance, finance, and so on. The result was an economy that still enjoyed a preeminent position in international trade, but whose manufacturing base, on which its competitiveness ultimately depended, was gradually and invisibly eroding as the capital that might have underwritten the remodernization of Britain's own industrial plant flowed into investments abroad. Though it was the financial center of world trade, Britain had become by the end of the century, as E. J. Hobsbawm has put it, "a parasitic rather than a competitive economy, living off the remains of world monopoly, the underdeveloped world, her past accumulations of wealth and the advance of her rivals."[17]

A director on the boards of trading companies, a lawyer, and an accountant are therefore the appropriate representatives of the British empire in 1899—specialists, administrators, professionals. And Marlow's interest is thus in making them "see"[18] not only the present fact of what goes on at the other end of the vast machine they superintend (that story would not require a Kurtz to make its point) but what was done in the past to make the professional life possible—how the ivory was got in the first place. For professionalism is a way of not having to look those things in the face. The early industrialist (the picture is drawn in every nineteenth-century condition-of-England novel) lived in the daily and immediate knowledge—buffered only by the most transparently self-serving of economic theories as his excuse—of the price others had to pay for his comforts; the imperial administrator of 1899 was distanced by half the world from the human consequences of his decisions and by nearly a century from the violent transformations required to create the machinery he used to operate a world economy. But Marlow is sure that his pedagogic project will meet with no success, and for a particular reason. For with the change in the basic activity of the British economy had come a change in the ethos of the workplace. The late-nineteenth-century British man of business, like any third-generation figure, viewed the entrepreneurial aggressiveness of his grandfather with distaste. His standards and practices were those of the public school and the country estate. He preferred acquiring property (land, or perhaps yachts) to pursuing profits; he prized manners over matter ("Try to be civil," one of Marlow's listeners finds it necessary to remonstrate with him partway through the story); he held to a sporting ethic that was essentially noncompetitive.[19] The heroism of Kurtz's assault on the wilderness and the honesty of his self-confrontation are therefore, as Marlow understands it, things the lawyer and the accountant and the company director will fail to appreciate—not because they can be expected to disapprove of the results of those struggles, but because they will not see the point of anyone's choosing to engage in them in the first place. When the rules of the contest are no longer recognizable, even defeat is not likely to have much meaning.

But *Heart of Darkness* has other aspirations than to serve as a guide to conduct. It wants to be a work of art. And these two projects—we might call the first project Marlow's plot and the second Conrad's— cut against each other in a way that, in the end, proves advantageous to both. Marlow's certainty that his story will not be completely clear to his audience is nicely complemented by Conrad's anxiety that his will: the obscurity Marlow drapes over his tale in deference to his listeners' sensibilities is, from another point of view, the suggestiveness Conrad uses to invest his novel with the indeterminacy that is, by the lights of late-nineteenth-century aesthetic theory, one of the features of the autotelic art object. And the complementarity goes a little further: just as Marlow fears that his vagueness will be perceived simply as indeterminacy, a lesson to which contradictory morals can be attached, so Conrad despairs that his indeterminacy is in the end simply obscurity, that the truly original work of art is beyond his capacity to create or his audience's to comprehend. This second occupational crisis makes the other plot of the story *Heart of Darkness* tells about itself.

When Marlow finally arrives at Kurtz's Inner Station, he is met by that strange character, the young Russian deserter and adventurer, whose only function at first seems to be to distance the account of Kurtz's activities by the thickness of yet another narrating presence. He is first and most consistently identified for Marlow by his costume:

> His clothes had been made of some stuff that was brown holland probably, but it was covered with patches all over, with bright patches, blue, red, and yellow,—patches on the back, patches on the front, patches on elbows, on knees; coloured binding around his jacket, scarlet edging at the bottom of his trousers. . . .

The outfit seems to Marlow to have a significance he cannot quite place:

> His aspect reminded me of something I had seen—something funny I had seen somewhere. As I maneuvered to get alongside, I was asking myself, "What does this fellow look like?"[20]

Marlow's answer to himself is that the fellow looks like a harlequin, which is an answer that will do, but which is not the only one indicated by the text. For the Russian also looks like something *we* have seen somewhere before: he looks like a map. When Marlow visits the company's offices in Brussels to receive his commission, he stands in the waiting room while his name is taken in to "the great man," and he looks around:

> Deal table in the middle, plain chairs all round the walls, on one end a large shining map, marked with all the colours of a rainbow. There was a vast amount of red—good to see at any time, because one knows that some real work is done in there, a deuce of a lot of blue, a little green, smears of orange, and, on the East Coast, a purple patch, to show where the jolly pioneers of progress drink the jolly lager-beer. However, I wasn't going into any of these. I was going into the yellow.[21]

When this map reappears hundreds of miles up the Congo River in the person of Kurtz's disciple, it is as a parody of its former self: colors that once were signs for meanings easily grasped now seem to make a mockery of signification. But the note of ambiguity is struck at every crossing in this text, and there is also a sense in which the Russian's outfit may be more than parodic, though it will be hard for us to see it, just as there is a sense in which Kurtz may be more than the parody of an entrepreneur, though Marlow's listeners will not see why. And this is because the world of the Inner Station, as Marlow experiences it, is a world in which it is no longer possible to tell what is simply nonsensical from what is inscrutable.

Marlow's epistemological difficulties are insisted on at many points in the story of his journey up the river: when he comes upon villagers dancing by the shore, he cannot tell from their cries whether they are cursing or welcoming him; when he arrives at the hut below the station, he finds a flag flying whose colors are no longer recognizable and a book—Towson's *Inquiry into Some Points of Seamanship*—filled with marginalia apparently written in cipher. His ability to estimate time and distance deserts him, he tells us, since each day comes to seem so much like the others; and when the mists settle in, as he nears the camp, he cannot judge his position relative to the shore. But Marlow's most striking failure of perception, of course, is the one involving the posts that stand outside the house in Kurtz's compound. This is his first view:

> There was no enclosure or fence of any kind; but there had been one
> apparently, for near the house half-a-dozen slim posts remained in a
> row, roughly trimmed, and with their upper ends ornamented with
> round curved balls.

But a little later, with an armed vision:

> . . . I went carefully from post to post with my glass, and I saw my
> mistake. These round knobs were not ornamental but symbolic; they
> were expressive and puzzling, striking and disturbing—food for thought
> and also for the vultures if there had been any looking down from the
> sky; but at all events for such ants as were industrious enough to
> ascend the pole. They would have been even more impressive, those
> heads on the stakes, if their faces had not been turned to the house.[22]

The sequence of perceptions is the reverse of normal—we ordinarily
think of a created object as beginning as a symbol, food for many
thoughts, and becoming through repetition an ornament, food for none—
because Marlow's journey is a backward one. There is much play in
Heart of Darkness with the notion of the taken-for-granted changing
places with the exotic, and some of it, such as the Montaignesque
ironies involving the cannibals and "pilgrims" on the steamer, sponsors
a moralism generalized enough to appeal even to Marlow's listeners,
since by implicating everyone it blames no one—and who would be a
cannibal just to possess a cannibal's virtues? But the knobs on a garden
gate becoming the shrunken heads on the posts in Kurtz's yard and
the fixed tokens of a businessman's map exploding into the anarchy of
the Russian's patchwork costume are ironies directed at a different
target. For a place where the decorative and conventional is transformed back into the totemic and iconoclastic is a place where art has
become new again; and if that kind of art now seems grotesque and
even a little ridiculous—as Marlow cannot help making Kurtz, in spite
of everything else about him, seem a little ridiculous—where does that
leave Conrad's novel?

The two plots meet in the character of Kurtz. And again it is better
to decline the text's apparent invitation to universalize: just as Marlow's plot, to make its point, requires that Kurtz be recognized as
something more historically specific than a type of the charismatic man,
it is important to Conrad's plot that Kurtz not simply be taken allegor-
ically for the ahistorical figure of "the artist." It is one of the attributes
of Kurtz's character, after all, that he cannot be identified with any

occupation. It is enough to say that the qualities that made Kurtz the representative for Malrow's plot of a certain phase in the ideology of capitalist enterprise can be taken for qualities that made him belong for Conrad's to a certain phase in the ideology of art as well—that the world of the first-generation industrial capitalist was also the world of the first-generation Romantic artist. It does not matter, so far as Conrad's novel is concerned, what the early capitalist and the Romantic artist actually *were,* since it is precisely for their mythic qualities that they are wanted: what matters is how they looked from the other end of the century. And what they shared from that perspective was the mystique of originality. The impulse that created, as though *ex nihilo,* the physical plant of the modern world and the impulse that gave birth to the symbols of its imaginative life seemed indistinguishable. That they were also understood, in most particular cases, to have been antagonistic only made the resemblance closer, for true originality is naturally a competition with what exists.

Nothing in professional life is *ex nihilo;* professionalism is the art of precedent. And the fin-de-siècle artist, *Heart of Darkness* seems to suggest by this strange juxtaposition, is living, like the fin-de-siècle man of business, on precedent, on the last energies of the exertion of willpower that first thrust the imaginative structures of Romanticism onto a hostile world. The world of 1899 is hostile no longer, and the symbols of Romanticism have become domesticated into the stock devices and decorative embellishments of aestheticism. "[A]n animated image of death carved out of old ivory"[23] is Marlow's description of his first sight of Kurtz. It might be a description of the spirit of Romanticism— the culture's buried ivory—come back to mock the efforts of its epigones. But ghosts are absurd things—Kurtz is absurd—and it is in the nature of epigones to find it impossible to take them completely seriously.

We might join the two plots more intimately by suggesting a third reading of *Heart of Darkness,* one that has the attraction of being wholly speculative: It is the story of Conrad's journey to visit the spirit of his father, the poet and Polish freedom fighter who dressed his young son in red, white, and blue, because they were colors once given the power of symbols by the collective burst of imagination of the French Revolution. Conrad makes the journey in the company of his uncle, a man who seems to have been able to express his affection for his nephew only in accounting terms, and who marked the occasion of Conrad's thirtieth birthday by noting: "Thus the making of a man out of Mr. Konrad has cost—apart from the 3,600 given as capital—17,454."[24] And the unnamed narrator who listens so attentively and with such doubtful success for the meaning of Marlow's tale is a figure well known to Conrad himself—the figure of the former seaman turned professional writer.

Heart of Darkness has usually been read as a story about hypocrisy, about the instinct for domination and the mask of civility. The reading I have given it only assigns to this familiar interpretation a historical specificity. It makes Conrad's story a story not about the universal price of civilization, but about the moral transaction costs of a particular social change. And to the extent that this change involved the depreciation of values that had been traditionally associated with literature, my reading suggests, *Heart of Darkness* marks a point of crisis in the reputation of the literary vocation.[25] The crisis manifests itself in Conrad's writing as a certain melodramatic quality, a hint of sensationalism which readers sometimes tend to discount as an unintended idiosyncrasy of tone. But it does not need to be discounted; it can be understood as the signal the story gives that the high style has become, like many other virtuous things, debilitated. Suggesting the persistence in his stories of a stratum of romantic cliché that a self-conscious, slightly overwrought style labors to but cannot quite transcend is one of the ways Conrad discovered for holding up his own writing as a symptom of the meanness of contemporary life. It is a constant theme, expressed as an agonized skepticism about the value of his work, in his letters to Cunninghame Graham; and it becomes in one form or another a feature of the novels from *Heart of Darkness* on. (In *The Secret Agent* [1907], for example, the imputation of a slightly sordid sensationalism to the novel itself is suggested by the opening description of Verloc's pornographic bookshop.)

Making capital out of the worn-out quality of received literary form is, of course, one of the techniques of modernism generally. It seems to be the fundamental strategy of Eliot's "Preludes";[26] and we find it deployed on a much grander scale in *Ulysses* and *The Waste Land,* works that create some of their effects by ridiculing their own artistic pretensions. This is the side of modernism that points to the end of the high-culture line, that presents itself as the cautionary object of history's lesson. But there is another, prescriptive side to modernism as well, the side that seemed to many of its admirers to constitute a reinvention, or a rediscovery, of formal possibilities for serious art. The incompatibility of these two aspects of the modernist enterprise generates a distinctive ambivalence: when we examine a modernist literary work as an instance of modernist theory in practice, we can never quite be certain whether we are looking at an example of the critical prescription being applied successfully or an example of the disease the prescription is supposed to cure. Conrad's injunction in the preface to *The Nigger of the "Narcissus"* (1897) to make the reader "see" seems to be subverted by the lesson of Marlow's narrative in *Heart of Darkness* that it is impossible to make anyone see anything other than what he wants to see; the formula of the "objective correlative" loses some of its cogency coming from the author of poems of such apparently free-floating anxiety as the "Preludes" and "Sweeney among the Nightingales"; and the "mythic method" Eliot identified in 1923 as the technique by which *Ulysses* and, by implication, *The Waste Land* give "a shape and a significance to the immense panorama of futility and anarchy which is contemporary history"[27] seems to be parodied by the footnotes to his own poem. It is therefore useful to keep in mind, in the discussion that follows of the vocabulary modernist criticism proposed as a corrective to what it regarded as the obsolete vocabulary of popularized Romanticism, that modernist literature holds many funds of irony to mock its own prescriptions.

2

Professionalism is a phenomenon born of contradictory impulses—which is part of the explanation for its ambiguous reputation. It clearly belongs to the movement toward a democratic social system and a free-market economy: it promises to open careers to talents; it extends the characteristic capitalist system of the division of labor to all areas of work; it provides the specialists necessary to serve the legal, financial, and technological needs of a competitive and highly interdependent economy. But some of its attributes seem neither democratic nor laissez-faire: it threatens to replace class elitism with elitism of another kind; it seeks to monopolize not only the production of certain highly rewarded social services but even, by dictating the requirements for the vocational training of the professional class, the production of those

services' producers; its ideology emphasizes self-consciously precapital-
ist "quality of life" values over the competition for profits—so that, as
Magali Sarfatti Larson has argued in *The Rise of Professionalism* (1977),
professionalism can be regarded both as an extension of laissez-faire
capitalism and, from another perspective, as part of a countermove-
ment against it.[28] Thus, every profession has a side that is turned
away from the anarchy of open competition, a side that shelters its
members from the day-to-day vicissitudes of the market and fosters the
values of continuity, autonomy, and disinterestedness in a system in
which most economic activity seems to be given over to uncertainty,
government by externalities, and the pursuit of self-interest. And thus,
at the same time, every profession does these things precisely in order
to win a competitive advantage—if possible a monopoly—in the marketplace: it aggrandizes itself most effectively by identifying with a
higher standard than self-interest. This double motive is reflected in
the argument all professions offer as their justification, the argument
that in order to serve the needs of others properly, professions must
be accountable only to themselves.

The second half of the nineteenth century was the era of the professionalization of occupation. So that when G. H. Lewes announced
in 1865 that "Literature . . . has become a profession,"[29] he was not
objecting to the demystification of the literary vocation; he was claiming for it its proper place in the occupational structure of his time.
Lewes thought that what he saw as the professionalization of literature
was an excellent thing, for a reason that reads a little like a conflation
of Arnold and Darwin:

> [I]n the development of the social organism, as the life of nations be-
> comes more complex, Thought assumes a more imperial character; and
> Literature, in its widest sense, becomes a delicate index of social evo-
> lution. . . . Literature is at once the cause and the effect of social
> progress. . . . As its importance emerges into more general recogni-
> tion, it necessarily draws after it a larger crowd of servitors, filling
> noble minds with a noble ambition.

Any activity, once it is perceived to make a social difference, invites
guidance; and Lewes therefore saw no reason to consider the career of
the imaginative writer any differently from the career of the physician
or the politician. If it was an agent of "social progress," it was worth

pursuing with the same purposiveness; he therefore proposed "to define, if possible, the Principles of Success" in literature.[30]

It is easy to understand why Lewes saw in the emergence of professional standards of vocational conduct an opportunity to put literature on a footing with other high-status occupations of his day, for the professionalist argument in favor of self-regulation seems perfectly suited to the activity of art. But in spelling out the principles of literary success in a professionalist vocabulary, Lewes ran unavoidably into the contradiction every profession must find a solution for: the contradiction between its business ethic—how it looks to its practitioners—and its service ethic—how it looks to its customers. This is a contradiction that cuts especially sharply against efforts to revise the formulas for success in a field of endeavor as dependent on a sense of history and continuity as literature is; its consequences for Lewes's argument are a good illustration of the problem.

Lewes's first concern was to disencumber the literary vocation of its amateur reputation. Properly considered, he maintained, literature was neither an amusement for the idle nor a showplace for the clever:

> To write for a livelihood, even on a complete misapprehension of our powers, is at least a respectable impulse. To play at Literature is altogether inexcusable: the motive is vanity, the object notoriety, the end contempt.

And in clearing out the dilettanti, he needed to clear out the gifted as well—"Talent," he explained, ". . . holds a very subordinate position in Literature to that usually assigned to it"—for, as we have seen, genius, that which is given and cannot be earned, is not the basis for the professional's claim to superiority. Having thus put genuine literary achievement within the reach of the honest worker, Lewes proceeded to relocate the standard of success to a place inside the bounds of ordinary understanding. Public success, he declared, could be considered "an absolute test" of literary merit:

> We may lay it down as a rule that no work ever succeeded, even for a day, but it deserved that success. . . . Success, temporary or enduring, is the measure of the relation, temporary or enduring, which exists between a work and the public mind.[31]

But when we ask by what means public success is to be had, we find that we have reached the limit of Lewes's Horatian pragmatism, the point at which a language of professionalism no longer meets the case. For it turns out that literary success cannot be won by calculation. The writer will need, for instance, to be sincere (here as elsewhere in Lewes's criticism the main literary virtue); but he will find that the impression of sincerity is not something that can be contrived, for the familiar reason that if it could be it would have no value. "He must believe what he says," Lewes explained, "or we shall not believe it." Adherence to the principle of sincerity, along with the principle of vision and the principle of beauty, is said to lead, "with the inexorable sequence of a physical law," to success in literature.[32] But at this point, the reader is likely to feel that the Darwinism has got the upper hand in Lewes's argument, and that the chance for literary achievement, having been held out so invitingly, has been snatched back and turned over to a greater power. It is now clear that if a writer cannot already hit the target on his own (or if the target refuses to be pierced by his arrows), no amount of coaching can make a difference. Lewes's problem, in short, was the consequence of trying to treat professionally an activity whose value depended on its amateur reputation; it was that literature in 1865 was a kind of writing most likely to produce successful effects precisely when it seemed most innocent of the intention to produce an effect.

Late-nineteenth-century aestheticism, more daring with literature's reputation, seems in some respects more compatible with the values of professionalism. Wilde's "The Soul of Man under Socialism" (1891), with its argument that the radical autonomy of the artist is a precondition for, and a prefigurement of, the ideal community, is in many ways a classic statement of the professional project. But there were still certain items in the package that art could not afford, and the suitability of some aspects of the professionalist ethos to the artistic vocation made the impropriety of others especially conspicuous. In his paradoxical moods, Wilde himself was a master of the ironies involved: "I have no knowledge of the views of ordinary individuals," he replied during one of his trials to a question about the effect *Dorian Gray* might be expected to have on the views of the ordinary reader. "You did not prevent the ordinary individual from buying your book?" returned his cross-examiner. "I have never discouraged him," was Wilde's response.[33] Wilde's replies cover both ends of the professionalist contradiction: as a practitioner, Wilde was naturally indifferent to the interests of his readers, but as a businessman, so to speak, he saw that indifference was a pose that would sell books. The exchange shows the aestheticist attitude at its most clairvoyant. It seems to see right through to the time when an apparent contempt for the views of the audience would be a chief ingredient of artistic success, the sign that the artist really cares. But it was not an attitude the nineteenth century was, on the whole, accommodating to, and Wilde, of course, was not able to sustain it much longer, for its dangers in his time were real enough.

By the end of the century, then, as *Heart of Darkness* suggests, the terms of the problem had become clear: putting the literary vocation on a respectable standing among occupations, in order to prevent it from seeming, like Kurtz, outmoded and slightly absurd, risked sacrificing all the advantages derived from the general perception of its essential *difference* from respectable kinds of work. Spontaneity, originality, inspiration—qualities viewed with increasing suspicion in the world of practical affairs—were among the very things that seemed to define the artistic, and, as Lewes discovered in spite of his intentions, they are things that defy prescription. Thus Conrad's own habit, often remarked by his biographers,[34] of presenting his career as a seaman as the result of a series of carefully deliberated decisions (though much of it seems to have been fortuitous) and his career as a novelist as the result of a series of accidents (though he appears to have prepared himself for it quite conscientiously) might be understood as an effort to preserve something like an amateur status, to give the impression that his writing was something he could not help in order to claim for it an origin in the unpremeditated impulses responsible for true art. And at about the time that Conrad was beginning his literary career, we find "professional" first being applied satirically to other areas of life commonly thought of as best left undisturbed by occupational considerations, as in "professional beauty" (1887) and the phrase that makes prostitution "the most ancient profession" (1888).[35]

But a facetious usage suggests that the thing a term ordinarily describes has become, for the moment at least, one of the facts of life; and by the early twentieth century, the ideology of professionalism had established itself to the extent of making anything that smacked of amateurism look second-rate. Insofar as art still banked on the unprofessional side of its reputation, the artist was therefore beginning to lose vocational ground; for to the professional view, "inspiration" will seem like self-indulgence, and innocence of design will imply ineffectuality. If aestheticism might be said to belong to the phase of professionalism's first serious challenge to occupational values, modernism belongs to the phase of its successful hegemony over them.

The product of the struggle for ideological control of an occupation that is becoming professionalized is the association, and the emergence of the professional association marks the middle stage in the evolution of the mature profession. The proliferation of associations—particularly of so-called qualifying associations, whose function is to certify competence for professional practice—is a phenomenon, in both England and America, of the late nineteenth century.[36] The chief economic benefit of an established association is, of course, the increase in market power enjoyed by each member. The weakest professional, because he is backed by the collective authority of his group, has an almost unassailable advantage in the market for his services over the strongest nonprofessional operating on his own, since the nonprofessional must build a reputation by his own toil, while the professional's credibility is given to him. He does not need to win it by his own exertions; he can only be judged, at some future point, to be no longer worthy of the endowment. And the proponents of professionalism were able to identify advantages to association-making of a less obviously practical kind as well. Emile Durkheim, for instance, suggested in the preface to the second edition (1902) of *De la division du travail social* that the incorporation of occupational groups worked a psychological benefit: it provided the sense of continuity once preserved in a more stable class system by institutions like the family, and it thus protected against the danger of *anomie*.[37] The Fabians, in a report on "Professional Associations" (1917), concluded that the self-sufficiency of the association, its relative invulnerability to the political pressures of the moment, made it the only "effective organ of criticism" of public policy in the modern state.[38] And R. H. Tawney, in 1921, urged industry to rid itself of whatever still persisted of the entrepreneurial ethos and to reorganize itself along corporate lines and by "professional standards" in the name of a greater efficiency: "the time has come when absolutism in industry may still win its battles, but loses the campaign, and loses it on the very ground of economic efficiency which was of its own selection."[39]

Whatever their merits as social policy, these arguments point to a redistribution of certain social values: the autonomous individual is now figured as less free than the person who operates as the extension of an organization—less free because less secure in his sense of identity, less likely to get done what he wants done, less able to hold his course in the winds of competing interests. And these are not simply effects of size; every organization will want to be self-limiting, since it is clear that the tighter the identification of the individual with his group, the more sharply defined and effective will be the authority he derives from it. The evolution of professional associations therefore tends to follow a pattern of a large organization with a general rubric and an informally regulated membership breaking up into independent and restricted associations of specialists, until the parent association eventually falls away. Thus, to take one example from many in the same period, the American Social Science Association, founded in 1865 as a group for amateur students of a broadly defined range of social science subjects, split up rather rapidly in the 1880s into separate associations of modern language teachers and scholars (1883), historians (1884), economists (1885), church historians (1888), folklorists (1888), and political scientists (1889)—all university-based communities of academic professionals, jealous of the autonomy of their disciplines and (as is still the case, of course) with no umbrella organization coordinating their researches.[40]

Poetry around the time of the First World War was to a significant extent a group activity: the characteristic mode of publication was the anthology, and the characteristic manner of self-presentation was the -*ism*. In, say, 1916, we find actively operating in London: the Georgians, with two anthologies in the bookshops and three more to come; the Imagists, some of them formerly the Imagistes in Pound's *Des Imagistes* anthology (1915) but now represented by Amy Lowell's *Some Imagist Poets* (1915, 1916, 1917); the Vorticists, under whose standard Pound was by then enrolled, and whose work—a good deal of it in the genre of the manifesto—had appeared in Wyndham Lewis's magazine *Blast* (1914–1915); and the Cyclists, contributors to Edith Sitwell's annual anthology *Wheels* (1916–1921). We might count as well the numerous coterie magazines, which came and went like mayflies on the literary landscape; the various collections advertised on more comprehensive terms, such as Pound's *Catholic Anthology* (1915) and Monroe and Henderson's *The New Poetry* (1917); and the inexorable procession, beginning almost with the first fatality, of war poetry anthologies. This was not the first time, of course, that artists had presented themselves as members of a group sharing a common purpose. And it could hardly be maintained that the proliferation of anthologies in the London literary world in the 1910s was a phenomenon explained by the emergence in the recent past of professional associations in most other high-status occupations. But the tendency toward group publication in the early modernist period does seem in certain significant respects to reflect the general practice of associationism, to stand as an example of its advantages and, at the same time, of its limitations. For although these various literary alliances were formed with different ends in view—some had polemical intentions, others simply commercial ones—they all had an associational function: they lent the little-known writer the identity of a movement and the prestige of a group (most were careful to include an established name or two in the table of contents), and they all tended to follow the characteristic associational practice of presenting their ranks as open to anyone with talent and their specialties as simply the revival of the tradition of good writing—even though each had obvious ideological requirements for admission and represented a readily distinguishable stylistic school.

The story of the first—and in many respects the model—of the literary groups that announced themselves by the publication of an anthology is a nice case in point. The *Georgian Poetry* anthologies (1912–1922) began as an effort to promote the work of one poet, Rupert Brooke. It was the bright idea of Brooke and his friend and admirer Edward Marsh that a young poet just entering the literary marketplace would have a better chance at making himself known if he could manage to tie his name to a provocative concept than if he had nothing but the quality of his poems to distinguish him from every other unknown. The concept they settled on was the notion of a new literary generation—the Georgians—and the manner of introduction they conceived was the anthology. Newness needs sanction, and it was Marsh's idea to include several figures from an older generation among the less recognizable names. He asked Housman, Chesterton, and Sturge Moore for contributions, and Chesterton and Moore obliged. The plan was dreamed up in September 1912, and its realization took only a matter of weeks, for Marsh saw the importance of having the volume in the bookstores for Christmas shoppers. It was, and its success was something of a surprise even to its producers. It was certainly a surprise to most of the poets involved, who were astonished by the occasional royalty checks Marsh sent them as sales mounted. The reception of the first volume led to a series. Each time a new *Georgian Poetry* was proposed, it was objected—even by many of the poets who were asked to contribute—that the public had had enough, that contemporary poetry was not meant to be packaged in such a form; but each time the edition was filled and thousands of copies were sold. For *Georgian Poetry 1911–1912* had, by its success, contributed to the creation of a set of conditions in which it had become increasingly difficult for a writer to attract a piece of the literary audience's attention unless he appeared under the banner of a group.

But the tendency toward group publication involved public relations problems each literary faction responded to in its own way; for the notion of literature as a group activity made trouble for certain traditional literary values. Among other things, it subverted the standard of sincerity by subordinating the uniqueness of a poem to its conformity to the group ideal. The poets in the Georgian anthologies, on the whole, resisted identifying themselves, outside the covers of the anthology, with a group; their work, as Marsh advertised it, was for "the lovers of poetry,"[41] and they therefore wished to preserve something of the individualistic character such an audience could be expected to demand. But more avant-garde writers made a special point of the advantages of the corporate approach. The Imagistes, for instance, were presented by Rebecca West in 1913 as writers who conceived of their vocation in a new and modern manner (though she could not seem to decide at which end of the occupational scale it would be most advantageous to place them):

> [T]here has arisen a little band who desire the poet to be as disciplined and efficient at this job as the stevedore. Just as Taylor and Gilbreth want to introduce scientific management into industry so the *imagistes* want to discover the most puisant way of whirling the scattered star dust of words into a new star of passion.[42]

The Imagistes could be considered collectively, that is, because they were engaged on a problem that was not personal—how the writer might best express himself—but institutional—how literature might be made more effective. The analogues West cited were the American efficiency engineers Frederick Taylor and Frank Gilbreth, whose work on "scientific management"[43] belongs to the history of the professionalization of industry; it is a risky comparison, but its riskiness is an index of how drastic the avant-gardist, in one of her poses at least, meant the overhaul of the conventional notion of the literary vocation to be. And we might recall that it was in the same terms that, two years later, Pound put the case to Eliot's father: there was a job of work to be done, and a respectable living to be made by doing it properly.

But the period of association-building was only a phase in the evolution of the modern profession, and the period of the literary group, as prepotent as the arrangement seemed for a time, was only a phase in the development of the modern writer—and for reasons that are parallel. The limitation of the professional association is that it is, in the end, too visible. It makes too easy a target, and the individual practitioner who borrows its credibility also takes on the problem of how to distance himself from those of its "official" positions he finds inconvenient or unacceptable without losing his piece of its authority. The consummation of the professional project therefore occurs not (as Larson, for instance, suggests[44]) when the association has achieved independence from outside control, but when the association is no longer perceived as the true source of the professional's authority. Though we expect the lawyer, for instance, to have been certified by all the appropriate institutions, his social status derives from the sense of his belonging not to the Bar Association (a nineteenth-century requirement) but to the ancient profession of the law. Like any social perception, this is a sense that must be created before it can be taken for granted, and it is against the background of this final phase in the evolution of professionalism that some of the reasons for the effectiveness of T. S. Eliot's early criticism become apparent.

By the time Eliot began making his name known as a critic, a reaction against the tendencies of literary collectivism had set in. Though they continued to find a market, the Georgian anthologies were attacked, along with their more avant-garde imitators, for the "corporate flavour"[45] of their contents; and various alliances, notably the Imagists and the Vorticists, were beginning—with the help, of course, of the war—to unravel. And we can find, outside literary circles, parallel indications of a general skepticism about the beneficence of the organizational spirit, signs of a renewed effort to assess the social cost of efficiency. Max Weber's famous expressions of divided sentiments about the nature of work in the modern world, "Politics as a Vocation" and "Science as a Vocation," were delivered as lectures in Germany in

1918. Among less tempered considerations of the matter we find, in the *American Journal of Sociology* (1915–16), an article claiming a pathological consequence for the worker whose identification with his profession is too close to absolute;[46] a book on *Professionalism and Originality* (1917) by Frank Hayward, a British writer on the philosophy of education, condemning professionalism for, among other vices, its self-concern, its cultivation of jargon and complexity, its passionlessness, its uncreativeness, and its ordinariness;[47] and an attack in the *Times Literary Supplement* (1918) on "Professionalism in Art," which maintained that

> Decadence in art is always caused by professionalism, which makes the technique of art too difficult, and so destroys the artist's energy and joy in his practice of it. . . . The value of the Romantic movement lay, not in its escape to the wonders of the past, but in its escape from professionalism and all its self-imposed and easy difficulties. For it is much easier to write professional verses in any style than to write songs of innocence.[48]

"An attitude which might find voice in words like these," replied T. S. Eliot, "is behind all of British slackness for a hundred years and more: the dislike of the specialist."[49] This was the judgment of a man who had lived in England for a little more than three years—for two of those years as a student—and it was therefore a judgment of peculiarly imposing authority. For Eliot possessed what no Georgian could possess, but what was, in the literary situation of 1918, precisely the thing needed: the voice of the outsider. This was a circumstance whose opportunities Eliot seems to have understood almost immediately: "There are advantages, indeed, in coming from a large flat country which no one wants to visit," he wrote in an essay on Henry James.[50] They are the same advantages as those enjoyed by the man from Mars; the trick, as Eliot might have learned from Pound's mistake, was to appear not as an American, but as a man without a country. A passage in one of Eliot's early pieces, a review of Edward Garnett's study of Turgenev (1917), might have been a recipe for his own career:

> Turgenev was, in fact, a perfect example of the benefits of transplantation; there was nothing lost by it; he understood at once how to take Paris, how to make use of it. A position which for a smaller man may be merely a compromise, or a means of disappearance, was for Turgenev (who knew how to maintain the rôle of foreigner with integrity)

a source of authority, in addressing either Russian or European; authority but also isolation. He has a position which he literally made
for himself, and indeed almost may be said to have invented.[51]

It might be objected that a position made for oneself can only be a
position made with mirrors, that Eliot's argument (which he repeated
elsewhere in his early writings[52]) requires both that nationality be a
highly determining circumstance and that possibilities exist for step-
ping outside it. But in his own case, the perception was the thing that
mattered. Eliot had no stake in the received reputation of the imaginative writer; he had never drawn on it before a public to his own
advantage. And he was therefore ideally suited to play a significant
part in the transformation of that reputation—the transformation needed
to protect the status of the literature and the literary vocation in the
changing value structure of his time. His role has an analogy in the
development of the modern professions: every successful effort to pro-
fessionalize an occupation, as Larson points out,[53] comes from outside.
The traditional practitioner has no incentive to renounce the reputation he has inherited, but those who have nothing will be eager to
renounce it for him. When the American Social Science Association
broke up into its separate disciplines, its members were not profession-
alizing themselves; they were being displaced by a new type—the academic specialist—and, in the end, their displacement meant their
exclusion from the "official" discourse that would subsequently define
their subjects. The task of the usurping practitioner is to make his
discourse seem not a new, but in fact the traditional discourse, and to
make the language of the amateur he is supplanting appear to be an
aberration. And this was exactly the procedure modernism followed in
distinguishing itself from and claiming superiority to the established
literary culture of its time. In the case of Eliot's criticism, the mode
to be exposed as specious was the mode identified with the Georgian
anthologies; the mode to be revealed as traditional was, of course, his
own.

Eliot discredited the Georgians by attacking the authority of their
tradition, and he discredited the authority of their tradition by attacking them. If one wanted to know what Georgian poetry was worth,
one needed only to look at the literary traditions of the nineteenth
century, and if one wanted to know what those traditions were worth,
one had only to look through the Georgian anthologies. It was a nearly
foolproof strategy, and its effectiveness was enhanced by Marsh's re-

fusal to permit American poets to be represented in *Georgian Poetry*[54]— a bit of chauvinism which for Eliot's purposes focused the issue nicely. For the problem with Georgian poetry, Eliot charged, was that it was "inbred":[55] one poem tended to borrow its features from another, and all together tried to sound like a respectful imitation of the literature of the previous century. If there was anything to be learned from that century, he maintained, it would require an energetic *dis*respect the English poet was too gentlemanly to exert:

> The Englishman, completely untrained in critical judgment, looks complacently back over the nineteenth century as an accumulation of Great Writers. England puts her Great Writers away securely in a Safe Deposit Vault, and curls to sleep like Fafner. There they go rotten; for if our predecessors cannot teach us to write better than themselves, they will surely teach us to write worse; because we have never learned to criticize Keats, Shelley, and Wordsworth (poets of assured though modest merit), Keats, Shelley, and Wordsworth punish us from their graves with the annual scourge of the Georgian anthology.[56]

Examined with a critical eye, Eliot proposed, the literature of the nineteenth century teaches by negative example the value of what he did not scruple to call literary professionalism:

> The opposite of the professional is not the dilettante, the elegant amateur, the dabbler who in fact only attests the existence of the specialist. The opposite of the professional, the enemy, is the man of mixed motives. Conspicuously the Victorian epoch is anti-professional; Carlyle as an historian, Ruskin as an economist; Thackeray who could write such good prose as the Steyne episode, and considered himself a kindly but penetrating satirist; George Eliot who could write *Amos Barton* and steadily degenerate. Decadence in art is caused by mixed motives. The art of the Victorians is spoiled by mixed motives, and Oscar Wilde finally added ingredients to the mixture which made it a ludicrous emetic.
> . . . Surely professionalism in art is hard work on style with singleness of purpose.[57]

This is a judgment of the Victorians that we find everywhere in Eliot's remarks at this period: Matthew Arnold, he said, was "a popularizer";[58] John Stuart Mill was "an amateur";[59] Browning, he told Virginia Woolf, "was lazy: they are all [the poets since Johnson] lazy. . . . And Macaulay spoilt English prose."[60] The Victorian error, like the Georgian error, had been to mistake Romanticism for a tradition—

a misperception Eliot addressed in a review with the polemical title,
"The Romantic Generation, If It Existed." The period 1788–1832, he
maintained,

> was not a period; or two periods. . . . [W]e cannot overlook the fact
> that four of the greatest minds—great in different degrees and kinds—
> remained apart from the general ideas of the time, and shared little or
> not at all in the time's approval. Crabbe, Blake, Landor and Jane Aus-
> ten are precisely the spirits who should have guided and informed the
> period of transition from the eighteenth century; they all preserved
> the best formal or intellectual tradition of that century, and they are
> all not only original but unique. But the generation after 1830 pre-
> ferred to form itself upon a decadence, though a decadence of genius:
> Wordsworth; and upon an immaturity, though an immaturity of ge-
> nius: Keats and Shelley; and the development of English literature was
> retarded.

The "intellectual chaos" of the Romantic period (if it can be called a
period) "leads us," Eliot suggested, "to speculate whether the age, as
an age, can ever exert much influence upon any age to come; and it
provokes the suspicion that our own age may be similarly chaotic and
ineffectual."[61]

Eliot's "London Letters" to the American *Dial* (1921–22) indulge
this suspicion generously: they are filled with comments on English
culture's "lack of ambition, laziness, and refusal to recognize foreign
competition."[62] An essay on Baudelaire (1921) complains that "If French
culture is too uniform, monotonous, English culture, when it is found,
is too freakish and odd."[63] And in Wyndham Lewis's *Tyro* in 1922
Eliot described the situation in English literature as one might describe a corporation ripe for takeover:

> The advance of "American literature" has been accelerated by the
> complete collapse of literary effort in England. One may even say that
> the present situation here has now become a scandal impossible to
> conceal from foreign nations; that literature is chiefly in the hands of
> persons who may be interested in almost anything else; that literature
> presents the appearance of a garden unmulched, untrimmed, un-
> weeded, and choked by vegetation sprung only from the chance ger-
> mination of the seed of last year's plants.[64]

This all seems now like calculated overkill, but it appears to have
been just what the postwar literary audience was ready to hear. For
although there were many who resisted Eliot's brand of criticism and

his style of poetry, it is hard to find anywhere a complaint about his treatment of the nineteenth century. Eliot did not, though he has sometimes received credit for it, create the reaction against that century. British writers had been trying to find a way to make a break with Victorianism on and off for twenty-five years before Eliot's arrival on the cultural scene. A. C. Bradley, in 1914, thought that the reputation of Tennyson, for instance, could hardly sink much lower;[65] and who was there, by the end of the war, to offer a serious defense of Tennyson, or Matthew Arnold, or Shelley? Eliot only put the reaction to its appropriate ideological use: he wrote it into literary history as part of the definition of the twentieth-century writer. The modernist writer, of course, could hardly have conceived of his vocation or written his poems in indifference to the nineteenth-century traditions he and his audience were saturated in—as revisionist commentators on modernist literature have repeatedly pointed out. But this made no difference to the effectiveness of Eliot's polemic. What mattered was that the modernist writer was able to present himself and his work as belonging to a tradition older than Romanticism. The apparent contradiction in Eliot's notion of tradition—that in spite of its valorization of continuity, ideal order, and so on, it proposed a line of development that leapfrogged over most of the previous century—was really its great strength. For that contradiction shares the irony that characterizes the final phase of every professionalist project: having been thrown up in the first place by the emerging capitalist system, the modern professions finally established themselves by persuading their practitioners and their public of their essential difference from that system, by declaring their independence, so to speak, of their own origins.

Thus, when Herbert Spencer surveyed "Professional Institutions" in *The Principles of Sociology* (1896)—a heading under which he included not only law and medicine, but painting, music, dance, philosophy, history, education, and belles lettres—he began his history of each activity in antiquity and illustrated his account with anthropological parallels.[66] The modern lawyer or man of letters, Spencer's way of treating the subject suggested, is only the latest in a line that begins with society itself and has representatives in all cultures and every social formation. This sense of its traditional character belongs, of course, to the side of professionalism that keeps its face turned away from the market in order to preserve market power, and it is the source of the mature professional's legitimacy: his way of doing things, and the need for it, are ratified not by organizational muscle but by history. Durkheim, as we have seen, called upon this organicist argument in suggesting that professions provide continuity in a system otherwise given over to flux; and we find even in Hayward's *Professionalism and Originality* the concession that professionalism "is one of the half-dozen indispensable things of civilization," because "it is an important link with the past."[67]

By appearing to conceive of their task as a group activity, the Georgians, like their modernist rivals, laid themselves open, as we have seen, to the charge of corporatism. Eliot joined in the complaint. Groups, he suggested in 1919, "are easier to find, easier to talk about, and their multiplied activity is more inspiriting to watch than the silent struggles of a single man." But it is in the silent struggles that literature is preserved:

> Every one of the writers of "Wheels" [an anthology of poets—the Cyclists—associated with the Sitwells] must make a choice. They can either hang together, and make a small place for themselves in the history of literature by being the interesting fashion of a day, or they can choose to run the risk of being individuals. . . . If they will make the choice of standing each for himself, some of them will instantly disappear in oblivion; the rest will have an opportunity of being lonely and unappreciated and above the possible mutations of public taste.[68]

But when the association has fallen away, where is the artist to plant his feet? Three months after Eliot's advice to the Cyclists, we find him disparaging Yeats precisely for choosing to run the risk of being an individual:

> Mr. Yeats's dream is identical with Mr. Yeats's reality. *His* dream is a qualification or continuation of himself. . . . His remoteness is not an escape from the world, for he is innocent of any world to escape from; his procedure is blameless, but he does not start where we do. His mind is, in fact, extreme in egoism. . . .[69]

Eliot's answer to this dilemma, of course, was "Tradition and the Individual Talent": the writer stands on the heritage of that part of his work that does not change, ground more secure for having no visible aspect. He derives his authority not from an inner vision to which his work is true, not from the validity of the principles of the literary movement with which he is allied, but from the "tradition." We do not need, in fact, to wait until "Tradition and the Individual Talent"

(September 1919) to find this argument articulated. In April 1919, Clive Bell provided a version of it in *The Athenaeum;* it is far less powerful than Eliot's, but its values are distributed in the same places:

> An artist, seen as the protagonist of a movement, the exponent of a theory and the clue to an age, has a certain interest for all active-minded people; whereas, seen merely as an artist, which is how he must be seen if he is to be seen in the tradition, he is of interest only to those who really care for art. . . . [S]et him in the tradition, and his one important characteristic is the one he shares with all the rest— his being an artist. In the tradition a work of art loses its value as a means. We must contemplate it as an end—as a direct means to an aesthetic emotion—or let it be. Tradition, in fact, has to do with art alone. . . . The tradition of art begins with the first artist that ever lived, and will end with the last.[70]

How is the professional to establish his claim to a place in the tradition (be it genuine or factitious) of his vocation? The strategy is a simple one: it is to isolate the one feature of an activity that is most likely to require full-time attention, to make that feature the chief criterion of whether the activity is done well or not, and then to argue that every previous worker has historically taken the isolated characteristic to be the most important one as well. For the artist, this is the argument of formalism, and it is why formalism can be understood as a reflection of worldly values precisely by virtue of its effort to establish art as an autonomous sphere of activity. Again, we can find the argument being advanced outside modernist circles. John Drinkwater, one of the original Georgians, in an essay on "Tradition and Technique" (1912):

> We [poets] inherit the thought, the impulse, the spirit of our forerunners only as a part of the cumulative experience which goes to make up the world that we contemplate. But the technique, the expression, the body of poetry, in so far as it is fashioned by example and not as the result of unaided discovery, comes from the poets alone. . . . [T]here are . . . a certain familiarity with metrical construction, a sense of word values and a power to distinguish between music and mere formal regularity, that can be acquired, and, indeed, cannot be mastered without more or less mature consideration of the practice of a poet's predecessors.

This concern with technique persists in indifference to historical circumstance, and it is the true work of the poet to preserve its purity:

The spirit of poetry is immutable and immortal, untouched by the siege of years. But it may well come to be the chief distinction of this age that it preserved a worthy and beautiful expression for the service of this spirit in the midst of a danger rarely equalled in the history of our literature.[71]

"Surely professionalism in art," Eliot wrote six years later, "is hard work on style with singleness of purpose."

The general principles of The Sacred Wood, and the argument of "Tradition and the Individual Talent" in particular, therefore appear to have answered a need for a redefinition of the artistic enterprise— and to have done so by providing a vocabulary that managed to be compatible with a professionalist-sounding conception of the literary vocation, and at the same time (and this seems crucial to an explanation of the book's success) to have consisted in some respects of little more than restatements of generally accepted aesthetic values.[72] The appearance of iconoclasm was important because it suggested a fresh start under a new ideological dispensation. The ersatz products of unqualified practitioners could now be written out of the field on the authority of standards freshly articulated and generated from within the discipline—from the consideration of poetry as poetry, and not another thing (a standard so severe that Eliot sometimes gives the impression that ordinary life has no language to meet it, as in this sentence on Coleridge's inadequacy as a critic: "a literary critic should have no emotions except those immediately provoked by a work of art— and these (as I have already hinted) are, when valid, perhaps not to be called emotions at all"[73]). The sense, on the other hand, that nothing essential was being discarded, that the "new" standards were discovered merely by reviving the traditional discourse (a sense the preponderance of essays on Renaissance writers helped sustain) was important because it was in the name of a transhistorical continuity that the social value of the literary enterprise was being claimed. Thus, in "Tradition and the Individual Talent," the criterion of "impersonality" frees the writer from the vaguely disreputable aspects of individualism, but the notion of "tradition" gives him an even greater abstraction than his personality to be true to—just as the professional is a worker whose identification with his job is most complete because there is, ideally, so little that is personal about it. Because in the performance of his work he submits his own interests to the interests of "the law," the lawyer is always—even at the beach, or sitting on his yacht—a lawyer. It is the same for Eliot's artist: being an artist is part of his personality, but it is not personal.

The argument of "Tradition and the Individual Talent" takes on greater force by virtue of the general depreciation of the nineteenth century in the essays that surround it. One reason for the effectiveness of Eliot's attack on nineteenth-century cultural values was simply that the more ancient the line of precedent, the greater the authority for the present practice. That the historically specific characteristics of the work of earlier practitioners will have to be discounted for the line of precedent to appear relevant—that the tradition will, in most essential respects, have to be invented—matters less than that continuity is proved. "History" can, in fact (as it does in the critical doctrine of some of Eliot's followers), drop out of the equation altogether, since, like the changing tastes of the audience of outsiders, it is one of the contingencies serious art transcends. "Culture is traditional, and loves novelty," Eliot wrote in 1921; "the General Reading Public knows no tradition, and loves staleness."[74]

The claim that one's standards antedate the tastes of the mainstream audience belongs to the antimarket side of the modern ideology of occupation; it is a way of keeping the membership restricted, so to speak. But Eliot's early essays appealed to his generation, we might guess, not only because of their severity, their seductive coldness ("Mr. Eliot is more grudging of praise than blame; often, indeed, he seems to grudge us our enjoyment," complained a reviewer for *TLS;* but others were glad for the chastisement[75]); they were persuasive because they made an argument that their readers already knew. For tradition-making in the late nineteenth and early twentieth centuries was not an activity limited to artists and other professionals. It was the period in Europe and America of what E. J. Hobsbawm has recently called the mass production of traditions, and some of his examples indicate the extraordinary thoroughness of the phenomenon. The late nineteenth century saw the first use of historical postage stamps; the development of modern professional sports, with their annual championships; the creation of much of the ceremonial pageantry that surrounds the British monarch; the institution of public ceremonies such as Bastille Day (1880) and May Day (1890); the founding of the Daughters of the American Revolution (1890); and the invention of the old school tie (1890s).[76] It was a time, that is, when any activity wanting to be perceived as having the status of an institution naturally undertook to make its past visible. So even if Henry Ware Eliot did not consider himself a professional man of business, he might have appreciated the importance Pound attached to the ancient roots of his vocation—and even appreciated a little their obscurity.

The pervasiveness of tradition-making in the early modern period makes for one of the distinctive ironies of modern culture: the modern artist seems to have invented traditions for his work in order to set himself at a distance from a society most of whose "traditions" were in turn invented scarcely a decade or two earlier. For as the self-conception of the nineteenth-century artist, in the way Conrad's story gives such a wonderfully condensed picture of, seems to have been bound up with changes in the nineteenth-century ideology of occupation, the modern artist belongs to the moment when capitalism, entering its corporate phase, provided its professional class with a set of values that present themselves as preindustrial in origin. The cultivation of tastes and principles that seem antagonistic to the capitalist world view, that appear to have derived from the culture of some other, more venerable social formation, is, of course, an activity highly valued in late capitalist society. It is a feature of the life style of those who fill the society's highest-status occupations; it is in fact a feature of their socialization. Noting the irony of this social fact has sometimes seemed to mean disapproving of it, but on what moral ground would the disapprover stand? One of the things that hold our social formation together is the possibility of believing ourselves to be in part the product of traditions that preexist it. Because it helps us to feel that we can criticize our world and therefore change it if we wish, this is a valuable sense to have, and art is one of its sources.

6

"Poetry as Poetry"

Eliot devoted himself in his early critical essays to debunking a good deal more of the nineteenth century than he could reasonably have expected to get along without, which is one of the reasons it is not surprising that many of the celebrated phrases in those essays have been discovered in various nineteenth-century settings. It gives any commentator satisfaction, of course, to be able to produce antecedent versions of a particular aesthetic prescription from the very tradition that prescription was apparently aimed at discrediting—as when, to take an especially well-turned example, something like Eliot's historical theory of the dissociation of sensibility, invented in part to disparage Tennyson, is shown to have once been proposed by Arthur Hallam.[1] And Eliot's polemical overreaching has made him seem an easy target for revisionists bent on exposing his profession of anti-Romanticism as either an avant-garde pose (when the interest is sympathetic) or (when it is not) a piece of protective self-deception.

But revisionism works so well with Eliot because Eliot was a reshaper of attitudes and not, by design, a redefiner of things. His own motto for the essays in *The Sacred Wood* (1920)—"when we are considering poetry we must consider it primarily as poetry and not another thing"[2]—seems an instance of misplaced concreteness (for what *is* poetry apart from what we consider it to be?) because like any ironist Eliot worked best with received ideas. His conception of what literature is as a thing in itself generally coincided with the contemporary conception, and his best-known critical judgments were arrived at by giving a traditional aesthetic vocabulary untraditional jobs to do. Praise for a poet's "direct sensuous apprehension of thought," for instance, is Romantic praise of an unexceptional sort, and would hardly have drawn attention applied (as in fact, in the nineteenth century, it was applied[3]) to Keats. It was not even much worth noticing applied, as Eliot of course did apply it, to Donne. Such things had often been said about the metaphysical poets in the later nineteenth century and had been repeated in Eliot's own time by even so moderate a literary progressive as Rupert Brooke.[4] But the trick of praising Donne in this manner *at the expense of* Keats and the Keatsians was an ingenious feat of critical partisanship, not least because of its willingness to take forensic advantage of the unverifiability of its own aesthetic standard. For once we begin to argue over which poet's thought is in fact "felt thought," we risk exposing the purely rhetorical nature of such judgments.

This was strategy of a kind that seems to have occurred frequently to Eliot, and it is what makes his early critical writing a kind of skeptic's guide to the literary values of early modernism—which is to say in many cases to the literary values, in boiled-down or attenuated forms, of the nineteenth century. There was, of course, another side to Eliot's formulations as well: they were for many of his contemporaries positive articulations of the distinctive aesthetic principles of twentieth-century writing. But these aspects of Eliot's importance as a critic are not unrelated; for the thing that gives a statement prescriptive force for one reader is the same as the thing that gives it ironic force for another—its reliance upon what is already taken for granted. And Eliot was never a writer to pass up the chance to draw upon the authority of what already exists. But to say only this does not do justice to the real character of his genius, for Eliot was also a writer who tended to find his greatest opportunities in ideas whose authority was already slightly discredited or whose applications seemed used up.

Notions very like the one named by the term "objective correlative" have been located in a number of nineteenth-century texts: in Pater's chapter on Botticelli in *The Renaissance;* in the *Lectures on Art* (1850) of the American painter Washington Allston, whose work Coleridge admired and made the occasion for a famous series of essays on aesthetics; in a formulation used by Coleridge himself; and (now we are deep inside the enemy camp) in a letter from Schiller to Goethe.[5] But there is no need to look even as far as Pater for the origins of Eliot's term; it derives from a standard item in contemporary definitions of proper poetic procedure: it is the recipe for an image. Eliot got a spectacular use out of it—one imagines him keeping the formula in his pocket until the most unlikely occasion should present itself—because while the notion of a dramatic image was current when the essay on *Hamlet* was written (1919),[6] no one had quite thought to administer an Imagist test to not merely a line or a scene, but an entire Elizabethan play.

Eliot might have run across the general formulation almost anywhere. Ford, for instance, explained the poems in Pound's *Cathay* (1915) to readers of his column in *The Outlook* by invoking what he called "a theory and practice of poetry that is already old—the theory that poetry consists in so rendering concrete objects that the emotions produced by the objects shall arise in the reader";[7] and Pound, always a great clipper of his own notices, gave Ford's review to Eliot, who dutifully quoted from it in his promotional pamphlet, *Ezra Pound: His Metric and Poetry* (1917). But the same argument appeared wherever Imagist practices needed justification. Richard Aldington, a Pound protégé, in *The Egoist* (1914):

> We convey an emotion by presenting the object and circumstance of that emotion without comment. . . . [W]e make the scene convey the emotion.[8]

John Gould Fletcher, an ally of Amy Lowell, in *The Little Review* (1916):

> The Imagist . . . presents the sum-total of the emotions in any given subject in such a way that the reader experiences the self-same emotions.[9]

And by 1918, the formula had become enough of a fixture in the critical vocabulary of the avant-garde to be relied on to explain artistic activity generally. We find, for instance, Dora Marsden, one of *The Egoist*'s original editors, defining Rebecca West's literary method as "imagism in its widest sense," and her talent as

> the power to sense a complex situation, and to take such an accurate and assured grip of the situation's essential attitude that the mental image of some sense-form embodying the precise attitude would spring into the mind by a simply act of association.[10]

These explanations are floated on the notion that every object has an inherent emotional value, cashable in a work of art by presenting the object as it truly is—a notion whose authority the man who wrote "Experience and the Objects of Knowledge in the Philosophy of F. H. Bradley" would of course hardly have been disposed to respect, for it is empiricism's epistemological equation—the right mix of sensations produces the correct mental picture of the external object—read backward. We are likely to be skeptical as well, to feel that the effectiveness of "In a Station of the Metro" has as little to do with the actual faces Pound saw in the Paris subway as the effectiveness of *In Memoriam* VII's "bald street" has to do with the real Wimpole Street where Arthur Hallam lived. But the formula is a match for the practice it was designed to justify; it is a minimalist theory of the imagination, the sentence that remains after what the twentieth-century theorists of the image regarded as the transcendentalist extravagances of Romantic theories of art has been edited out. "Nature" has been reduced to "objects," and the poet's mind figures as a kind of high-frequency receiver of stimuli.[11] Imagism is a theory that tries not to look theoretical (as an Imagist poem is a work of literature that tries not to look literary), and it poses the reductionist's challenge: if *this* is not acceptable as an explanation of the way art works, what sort of claims can be made for theories that explain art's effect on us by its success at tapping into some more elaborately defined chunk of experience—such as the natural world, whose mode of being art's form imitates; or the moral life, whose values its seriousness preserves; or the vision within, whose lineaments its style evokes? For once we have determined to point to something as the true source of legitimate aesthetic effects, we will end with a reproduction of the Imagist formula: we will have isolated an object and loaded it up with value.

If we want to make good on our skepticism by doing without this theoretical paradigm, however, we will find that we cannot quite say that art works in some entirely different way. We can only say that at a cultural moment when art is understood to get its effects from the objects (however defined) it represents (by whatever means), it will succeed only if it can give the impression of having done so. And Eliot's revision of the conventional prescription does not resist such a gloss:

> The only way of expressing emotion in the form of art is by finding an "objective correlative"; in other words, a set of objects, a situation, a chain of events which shall be the formula of that *particular* emotion;

> such that when the external facts, which must terminate in sensory
> experience, are given, the emotion is immediately evoked.[12]

Eliot has rewritten the Imagist scenario by having the original emotion
appear unaccompanied by any object and then depicting the artist looking about for an object that will do the trick of expressing it. And the
right object, in his version, is the object that works; a more metaphysical criterion is not supplied.

The word "only" is what gives Eliot's formula its prescriptive appearance, and it is a good instance of Eliot's critical manner. It announces a discovery where most writers would be content to state a
preference ("The most efficient way of expressing emotion . . ."), and
thereby places the entire formulation at the brink of tautology. Efforts
to read Eliot's sentence as saying something more specific than "The
emotion expressed by a work of art is the product of the elements of
that work" do not even need to venture into the waters of experience
to spring a leak. Eliot punctures his definition as soon as he provides
an example: "Hamlet (the man)," he explains, "is dominated by an
emotion which is inexpressible, because it is in *excess* of the facts as
they appear."[13] Which leaves, of course, the question, If Hamlet can
be said to feel such an emotion, how did Shakespeare manage to convey it?

Few critics, I suppose, have ever wished to defend Eliot's judgment
of *Hamlet*, but many seem to have been convinced of the usefulness of
Eliot's formula (the success of "Hamlet and His Problems" can be
measured by the number of attempts to prove it in error by asserting
that Shakespeare did in fact create an objective correlative in *Hamlet*).
These critics might want to answer the charge of tautology by suggesting that Eliot (wrong though he may have been in this particular
case) knows that Hamlet is possessed by some emotion only because
Hamlet says he is, or acts as though he is, and that the theory of the
objective correlative requires that the play should not *talk* about an
emotion, but should *present* one. But Eliot states quite explicitly that
this is not the problem: "We find Shakespeare's *Hamlet*," he says, "not
in the action, not in any quotations that we might select, so much as
in an unmistakable tone which is unmistakably not in the earlier play."[14]
Well, it might be argued, this "unmistakable tone" indicates the point
of Eliot's objection: the phrase *"particular* emotion" must mean an emotion we can give a description to, and though Shakespeare did, in Eliot's
view, somehow succeed in whipping up an atmosphere of emotionality,

the specific emotion Hamlet is meant to be in the grip of remains indefinite. To this one can only reply that Eliot claims to know exactly the emotion he understands Hamlet to be feeling: "The intense feeling, ecstatic or terrible, without an object or exceeding its object," he informs us, "is something which every person of sensibility has known; it is doubtless a subject of study for pathologists."[15] The unexpected conclusion appears to be that *Hamlet* expresses a particular emotion well enough—it is just not an emotion that is proper for art.

Coming from another critic, this judgment might seem merely pedantic: the distinction being asserted between what qualifies as a work of art and what does not has not been shown to make a difference to our understanding of the play. Eliot's reading of Hamlet as a man who cannot match up his emotions with the objects his world provides is after all a perfectly standard one; it is the reading that makes, for instance, the scene with the players, Hamlet's leap into Ophelia's grave, and Fortinbras's conquest of Poland aspects of a unified action. If Shakespeare contrived to make his play intelligible to this extent without the benefit of an objective correlative, we might conclude, so much the worse for the formula. But coming from the author of "Prufrock" and the "Preludes," the line of argument is curious to say the least— it seems a sort of self-castigation—and the theory of the objective correlative, from the perspective of those early poems, looks less like a truth about poetic language, or even a principle of decorum, than a complaint about the limitations of art disguised as a compliment. Art is a machine for reproducing with economy and precision emotions blurred and attenuated in experience, is the good news; emotions that cannot be made proportionate to the objects the world provides cannot be satisfactorily expressed in art, is the hidden grievance.

This is a view of art that many poets, in moments of frustration, have no doubt held, but it is not a view one would think any poet could be content to rest with. It implies that the poet's estimate of an object's emotional value must be the world's—that the significance a poem ascribes to the relations among its images is somehow answerable to the significance the world gives to the relations among the objects those images represent—and it makes the artifice poetry has customarily relied on to make its kind of discourse work seem illegitimate, a sort of cheating on behalf of the self against the way things really are. Nothing is more revealing of Eliot's flickering suspicion of poetry's claim to be a privileged way of knowing than his willingness to endow this attitude with the authority of a critical standard. And the theory of the objective correlative is nicely paradigmatic, too, of the way modernism sometimes seems to have been determined to transform poetry, in the name of a purer style, from a manner of speaking to a mode of symptomizing. Eliot had reservations, as we have seen, about the possibility of a purified, non-"literary" style, but he had deeper doubts about the writer's ability to exert control over his own meanings. And these doubts surface in the notion of impersonality.

Eliot offers, in the *Hamlet* essay and elsewhere, a single corollary to his utilitarian proposition about objects and emotions: solving the equation correctly, he suggests, relieves the artist of a psychic distress. Thus the essay makes an identification of Hamlet's feelings with Shakespeare's which would otherwise be insupportable—"Hamlet's bafflement at the absence of objective equivalent to his feelings is a prolongation of the bafflement of his creator in the face of his artistic problem"—and indulges in speculation about the emotional circumstances of Shakespeare's life which would otherwise be pointless—"we should like to know whether, and when, and after or at the same time as what personal experience, he read Montaigne, II. xii., *Apologie de Raimond Sebond.*"[16] This notion of the nature of creativity had a consistent appeal for Eliot—it turns up often in his critical writings, particularly where he is describing his own experience as a poet[17]—and it has the proper Imagist look to it. The writer knows his solution is the right one in the same way that the reader knows the result is a work of art: he tests it on his nerves. But efforts to give Eliot's account of art-making a theoretical shape, and thus an interpretive usefulness, are compelled in the end to make some improvements on the suggestions he provides; for at the same time that he was hypothesizing in *The Athenaeum* about Shakespeare's feelings, Eliot was busy discrediting the traditional justification for such hypotheses in *The Egoist*.

Those hypotheses depend, "Tradition and the Individual Talent" advises, on "the metaphysical theory of the substantial unity of the soul"—the belief that personality is a thing definitive enough to sustain coherent expression. And it is, of course, precisely the point of this most famous of Eliot's arguments that to say that for something to happen aesthetically to the person who reads the poem something must first have happened emotionally to the person who wrote it (which is what Eliot does say) is not the same thing as to say that the successful work of art expresses the inner life of the artist who produced it. For there is, in Eliot's view, nothing that might properly be called an inner life to be expressed. If we could examine the artist's mental contents, we would find simply the usual unorganized assortment of experiential odds and ends, a warehouse of "numberless feelings, phrases, images," uninteresting in themselves and distinguished from the contents of nonartistic minds only by their being less easily effaced (this appears to be the essay's version of the Romantic *agon*) by the ordinary processes of forgetting. To read back, therefore, from the nicely particularized emotion of the finished work of art, firmly grounded in its aesthetic "object," to the untidy mass of sensation in the unstable construct of the artistic self is to undertake a journey with the wrong map; for

> Impressions and experiences which are important for the man may take no place in the poetry, and those which become important in the poetry may play quite a negligible part in the man, the personality.

The essay asks us, in short, to accept the proposition that the reader's experience of a genuine "art emotion" depends on the writer's execution of an authentic escape from some troublesome " 'personal' "[18] emotion, and then to regard the connection as, for all practical purposes, a coincidence.

But it is not a coincidence, of course, or else why require the artist to suffer at all? It plainly does not matter to the notion of the objective correlative in its Aristotelian aspect—the audience derives pleasure from the perception of a fitness between situation and emotion—what the private tribulations were of the artist who managed that effect. The principle presents itself, in the manner of the *Poetics,* as a straightforward deduction from the evidence of art that works. It is the suggestion that for the effect to be what "Tradition and the Individual Talent" calls *"significant"*[19] there *must* have been a tribulation, itself properly managed, that gives the concept its nineteenth-century spin. The emotions of the audience are now tied up to the feelings of the artist. The problem with Eliot's formulation is the problem of how, on a view of the integrity of the subject that had grown increasingly skeptical from Pater to Vorticism to "Tradition and the Individual Talent," the presumption of such a connection can be shown to be necessary—can be shown, that is, to make an interpretive difference.

The difficulty consists in coming up with a description of the relation that is weak enough. For though we may find in the work of art figures of speech, or symbols, or images, it is too ambitious to say that these refer us to anything belonging to the artist, since personality is not to be considered, in Eliot's conception, as a container of things as stable and intelligible as thoughts, or unconscious archetypes, or even recollections of discrete moments of sensory experience—things private and discriminable which might, by the right representational trick, be expressed. We are confronted with a relation that is at every point contiguous but at no point correspondent: we have the work of art, considered in its totality as effective or not, and we have the artist, considered as an undifferentiated state of psychic affairs, in balance or out of it. To say that one refers to the other is no more true or false than to say that rosy cheeks refer to health. If they do, the relation has nothing to do with intention. The artist may or may not say what he means, but he cannot help meaning what he says.[20] The "doctrine of impersonality" is the nineteenth-century doctrine of sincerity at its most extreme stage of attenuation: being has become a physiological condition, and its sentiment a symptom.

Like the formula of the objective correlative, the notion of a necessary but obscure connection between the resolution of an unspecified inner crisis on the part of the artist and the enjoyment of a significant "art emotion" on the part of the audience can be found elsewhere in the period. Clive Bell, for instance, was a writer for whom Eliot seems to have had little respect—he once referred to him as "the *boutonnière* of post-1900 culture"[21]—but the argument of Bell's *Art* (1913) runs along the same lines as Eliot's essay of six years later. What all genuine works of art have in common, Bell proposed, is the ability to produce something called an "aesthetic emotion," and they have this ability because they possess "significant form": "In each, lines and colours combined in a particular way, certain forms and relations of forms, stir our aesthetic emotions."[22] These emotions belong to art alone. They are not copies of what we are evidently to think of as "life emotions": "to appreciate a work of art," Bell explained, "we need bring with us nothing from life, no knowledge of its ideas and affairs, no familiarity with its emotions."[23] This is a journey a good distance in the formalist direction, but Bell did not, it turns out, cut every cord, and one tie to the world remains; he calls it his "Metaphysical Hypothesis":

> That which orders the work of art is, I suggest, the emotion which empowers artists to create significant form. . . . To make the spectator feel, it seems that the creator must feel too.

Still, the self is a muddle, and having made this concession to experience (or borrowed this much from experience to buttress his theory), Bell posted the warning Eliot's essay would make famous: "Let no one imagine that the expression of emotion is the outward and visible sign of a work of art." The critic who heads back from the art to the artist is condemned to wander endlessly: "it is because they [works of art] express an emotion that the artist has felt," Bell concluded, "though I hesitate to make any pronouncement about the nature or object of that emotion."[24] Eliot, too, was not disposed to pronounce on that subject, but he was—as long as the matter was understood to remain ultimately a mystery—highly disposed to speculate, as in the case of the relation between Shakespeare's experiences and *Hamlet*'s failure. His theory was, in fact, the ideal license for such speculation: since nothing can ever really be explained by knowledge of the writer's "personal emotion"—since no coherent knowledge of a "personal emotion" is in fact possible—no damage can be done to the impersonal nature of the "art emotion" by indulging in some suggestive discussion.

We can find the same view of the relation between art and emotion, expressed in a manner even closer to that of "Tradition and the Individual Talent" than Bell's and a year before Eliot's essay, in Dora Marsden's article on Rebecca West:

> . . . when one says that a writer is under the emotional necessity of expressing an experience, one can only mean that the experience has assumed a determining control enabling it to outbalance and command all that remains of the forces of the mind. The emotional part is driving the conscious whole. When, however, in submission to such driving force, the mind takes up its task with the adequate courage and strength, this overbalance in powers at once corrects itself. . . . An overpowering subjective condition has been compelled in fact to shed its subjectivity and become an object: a true entity, capable of being expelled from the exclusiveness of the individual and made current as a universal possession. By making it so intimately personal it has indeed become impersonal. . . . Whatever the condition be, by stating it justly the mind makes an escape from its absolute thrall.[25]

Or, in other words, "only those who have personality and emotions know what it means to want to escape from these things."[26]

We can see how far Eliot's thinking goes in the direction of skepticism about the value of literature as a form of knowledge by comparing his view of art as escape from emotion with one more antecedent—the view offered in Nordau's *Degeneration:*

> Artistic activity . . . satisfied the need of [the artist's] organism to transform its emotions into movement. He creates the work of art, not for its own sake, but to free his nervous system from a tension. The expression, which has become a commonplace, is psycho-physiologically accurate, viz., the artist writes, paints, sings, or dances the burden of some idea or feeling off his mind.[27]

It is one of the ironies of literary history that some twenty-five years after Nordau used this analysis of the artistic process as the basis for an attack on the forerunners of modernism, "Tradition and the Individual Talent" made the same notion of creativity part of an argument that seemed to many readers a defense of art's autonomy and value. And Nordau's evolutionary model of cultural change can be detected in the background of Eliot's theory of the dissociation of sensibility as well—a theory that depends on the hypothesis that literary history can be explained not by changes in literary form or in the things writers become interested in, but by changes in the way the brain works.

The argument for impersonality in "Tradition and the Individual Talent" makes an attractive proposition: in return for giving up the desire to express himself, the poet is offered the chance to express something far greater—the shape the tradition takes as it passes through his time. But the structure of this argument is familiar. For if we open up "Tradition and the Individual Talent" and replace "tradition" with "experience," the sequence of texts with the stream of sensations, we will find ourselves with something very like Pater's essay on "Style"; and we will discover at the center of both arguments a similar model of the mind, one that seems both reductive, because such passivity is ascribed to it, and extravagant, because it is required to generate such an exalted kind of truth. The mental eyeball Pater borrowed from the empiricists to explain how the input of random sense data is corrected against the fixed structure of the "inner vision" reappears in "Tradition and the Individual Talent" as the famous "shred of platinum,"[28] the catalyst that adjusts the experience of the contemporary world to the "ideal order" of tradition and guarantees that the result will be "impersonal."

Making the metaphor mechanical instead of organic is a modernist refinement, one we have noticed already in Pound's "vortex":

> The best artist is the man whose machinery can stand the highest voltage. The better the machinery, the more precise, the stronger, the more exact will be the record of the voltage and of the various currents which have passed through it. [29]

For a theorist interested in an "exact record," a machine (like a shred of platinum) makes a better analogy than an eyeball precisely because it is inhuman. It is not of the same stuff as the material it processes, and it can therefore be expected to distinguish reliably between the real and the merely mutable. The metaphor was also, of course, intended to shock; it is the language of the Futurists, whom the Vorticists publicly despised, but whose controversiality they emulated—Blast was patterned after a Futurist manifesto, Apollinaire's "L'Antitradition Futuriste" (1913)—and some of whose antihumanist postures they found it useful to adopt. Futurism seems to have had for Pound around the time of his Blast manifesto something of the same interest it was having for D. H. Lawrence, who used it to explain to Edward Garnett, in the well-known letter on The Rainbow, his new conception of character: "what is interesting in the laugh of the woman is the same as the binding of the molecules of steel or their action in heat: it is the inhuman will, call it physiology, or like Marinetti—physiology of matter, that fascinates me." [30]

The main "character" in a literary work on the Paterian model is the writer. The danger of the model—as Pound became convinced—was that the chief virtue of literature would be taken to be the expression of the writer's "personality," the assortment of moods, tastes, and opinions that go to make up the conscious self. Pater had taken care to distinguish this type of self-expression from the brand of sincerity he endorsed:

> The style, the manner, would be the man, not in his unreasoned and really uncharacteristic caprices, involuntary or affected, but in absolutely sincere apprehension of what is most real to him. . . .
> If the style be the man, in all the colour and intensity of a veritable apprehension, it will be in a real sense "impersonal." [31]

But there is little in Pater to help us identify the point at which the accident of personality ends and radical individuality begins: in the double vision of the "Conclusion" to The Renaissance, everything is either entirely outside or entirely inside. And since an avant-gardist will need such a distinction to underwrite his claim that the traits conventional opinion prizes as original with the individual are actually surface markings conforming to society's impress, Futurism's description of the mind as a piece of machinery gave some of the modernists a useful notion of how such a thing as the "impersonal" or "pre-personal" self might be conceived: the metaphor rediscovered a structure where all structure had been threatening to dissolve. Thus Lawrence contrived to dispense with the artifice of "the old stable *ego*—of character" in his novel by announcing a prior structure of *real* stability, the trans-individual structure of generation, to which all character could be made relative; and thus the mind figures in Pound's theory of poetry as sheer pattern-producing energy, an autonomous entity whose highest function is to leave a sort of mental fingerprint on experience.

Readers have sometimes complained that much of what is presented as "impersonal" in modernist writing looks like nothing more than the moods, tastes, and opinions of the writer, deliberately fragmented, rearranged, and invested with a metapersonal significance—that what Lawrence's novels take to be elemental in human life is a reflection of their author's special convictions about sexual relations, that the *Cantos'* picture of what is lasting in the history of culture is a mosaic of Pound's aesthetic and political enthusiasms, that *The Waste Land* offers as a report on a general spiritual condition a composition of bits of Eliot's favorite reading that surreptitiously refer to private anxieties about his marriage and career. One can respond to these complaints only by asking what else, given the requirements of a generally diffused aesthetic that condemned the expression of personal "views" but tied the value of a literary work to the intensity of the author's private experience, an "impersonal" work could have looked like.

In giving the self so little to express, in making the literary work the symptom of conditions, inner and outer, for which the writer's pen served only as a kind of unconscious conduit, Eliot gave his criticism a powerful vocabulary for revisionism, since what the writer *intended* to say could now be safely ignored in favor of what he could not *help* saying. The vocabulary might be called a rhetoric of hygiene: the metaphor is sometimes neurological, sometimes psychological, sometimes—as in the case of Henry James's mind—sexual; and the pieces collected in *The Sacred Wood* are filled with critical judgments that turn on this vocabulary's key terms. Thus, Coleridge's "feelings are impure," while Aristotle "had [no] impure desires to satisfy";[32] comparing the *Education Sentimentale* to *Vanity Fair* shows us "that the

labour of the intellect consisted largely in a purification, in keeping
out a great deal that Thackeray allowed to remain in"[33] (the judgment
derives, of course, from Pater's praise of Flaubert in "Style"; but most
of the essays in *The Sacred Wood*—even "The Perfect Critic," which
tries to rescue Arnold from Paterianism—are Paterian[34]); Elizabethan
rhetoric "pervaded the whole organism; the healthy as well as the morbid tissues were built up on it";[35] Swinburne's "intelligence is not
defective, it is impure";[36] and in Massinger we find an unrefined nervous system and the record of "the decay of the senses."[37]

The vocabulary is a nice example of what a sociologist of knowledge
might call a negative ideology—an ideology that avoids declaring itself
by adopting a rhetoric whose notions of good and bad seem unarguable.
Who would be "impure"? Only someone already admitting to being
perverse. Part of the appeal of "pure" and "impure" as terms of judgment perhaps had something to do with their professionalist associations: the professional worker is defined by his ability to keep his researches from adulteration by the corrupting forces of the ideological
marketplace. But the rhetoric was appealing for a more practical reason as well. It seemed to encode a set of judgments on a whole range
of nonliterary matters, and to do so using a framework of values that
appeared to be ideologically neutral. For by describing not only the
writer's physiological condition but the condition of his time—the condition of the time *through* the physiological condition—Eliot's vocabulary made an extraordinarily effective tool for putting cultural history
into whatever order the critic wished or was able to claim for it. The
essay on Massinger in *The Sacred Wood* provided some hints in this
direction by setting a comparison of Jacobean dramatists according to
the development of their nervous systems next to remarks about the
devolution of the Puritan moral system. But the project was most
strikingly carried out in the essays on seventeenth-century poetry Eliot
wrote just after the publication of *The Sacred Wood*.

The three essays eventually published by the Hogarth Press in 1924
as *Homage to John Dryden* were originally written for the *Times Literary
Supplement,* where they appeared in 1921. They are the tours de force
of Eliot's early criticism, for later readers found in them a revaluation
of seventeenth-century poetry, a principled indictment of the poetry
and criticism of the nineteenth century, and the outline of a genealogy
justifying modernism. The most influential of the essays was the one
on "The Metaphysical Poets," and its argument has been made famil-

iar by many retellings: the dramatists of the sixteenth and the poets of the seventeenth centuries "possessed a mechanism of sensibility which could devour any kind of experience"; but at some point in the seventeenth century, "a dissociation of sensibility set in, from which we have never recovered." When, in the eighteenth century, poets "revolted against the ratiocinative," "they thought and felt by fits, unbalanced; they reflected"; and the degeneration culminated in the work of Tennyson and Browning, who "ruminated." But the type of mind for which "a thought . . . was an experience" reemerged in the nineteenth century in the poetry of Baudelaire, Corbière, Laforgue—poets who had "the same essential quality of transmuting ideas into sensations" that Donne had—with the implication that this line is continued in the Anglo-American modernist mode.[38]

We know now, thanks to J. E. Duncan's *The Revival of Metaphysical Poetry* (1959) and Frank Kermode's *Romantic Image* (1957), that Eliot managed, by the remarkable influence of the essays in *Homage to John Dryden,* to receive credit for formulations and critical judgments that were common enough in his own time and that had their roots in the literary values of the century his arguments seemed directed against.[39] And it is not difficult to find further evidence for the thesis that the version of literary history those essays propose would not have struck most of Eliot's contemporaries as particularly iconoclastic. The notion, for instance, hinted at in "The Metaphysical Poets" and elaborated upon elsewhere in Eliot's criticism, that Milton was somehow either the cause or the emblem of a deterioration in the ability of English verse to render complex feeling can be found in an essay by Middleton Murry:

> English blank verse has never recovered from Milton's drastic surgery; he abruptly snapped the true tradition, so that no one, not even Keats, much less Shelley or Swinburne or Browning, has ever been able to pick up the threads again. . . . Read any part of "Paradise Lost" [after reading Shakespeare] . . . and you will discover how much subtlety in the instrument has been lost; in other words, how much capacity to express the finer shades of emotion has been sacrificed.[40]

And the extent to which not only the interest in seventeenth-century poetry, and not only the terms Eliot used to praise that poetry, but even the particular literary genealogy Eliot proposed were things circulating in the contemporary air, is suggested by this passage from a 1919 review by the young Aldous Huxley:

An author must be *passionné* by his subject, must feel, if he is writing
of science or philosophy, that the truths with which he is dealing are
in intimate relation with himself. On the rare occasions when this
happens, the versified exposition of science or philosophy becomes poetry. It seems to have happened with that strange and almost great
poet, Fulke Greville. To him, one feels, the problems of philosophy
and statecraft, which occupied his mind, were of vital interest; these
abstract intellectual ideas touched him as nearly as love or hatred.
. . . Donne, in the same way, felt passionately about abstract ideas;
in Blake, too, thought has the quality of emotion. Oddly enough, when
we come to the nineteenth century, a period which was conscious and
very proud of its scientific achievements, we find no poets who took a
sufficiently passionate interest in the new scientific truths to get them
into poetry. Tennyson wrote a good deal about science; but his tone is
frigid, he was never worked up by it to lyrical fervour. . . .

Perhaps the only poet of the nineteenth century who thoroughly
assimilated the science and philosophy of his time, so that it became
a part of himself, a condition of all his emotions, an accompaniment in
every thought and passion, was Laforgue. Plenty of young men of the
generation that was coming to maturity in the early eighties must have
read Hartmann's philosophy of the Unconscious. But there can have
been few to whom the ideas of Hartmann were such a reality that
they were troubled, even in the midst of an embrace, by thoughts of
the Unconscious; and there was but one, so far as we know, who gave
adequate lyrical utterance to his philosophy-ridden emotions.[41]

The overt argument of Eliot's essay on "The Metaphysical Poets" is
an argument about technique; the seventeenth-century conceit is revealed to be the cousin of the nineteenth-century symbol. But the concerns that led Eliot to write the essay were almost certainly not technical. Eliot himself, on the occasion of its republication in 1924,
suggested dissatisfaction with his own indirectness. His argument, he
explained, properly involved "considerations of politics, education, and
theology," matters "which I no longer care to approach in this way."[42]
But any other way, by requiring him to enter specific judgments on
the issues at hand, would have been less effective. Eliot's theory of
the dissociation of sensibility had an extraordinary run precisely because its implications were largely uncontrolled. Eliot himself might
use it later to support an argument about religious history involving
the English Civil War; but the theory takes on very different permu-
tations when the blame for the dissociation is pinned—as later critics
did pin it—on Bacon, on Descartes, or on the rise of capitalism.[43]

The ideological burden is carried in the original essay not by Eliot's own commentary but by the quotations—which is to say, under cover of darkness, since most readers, presented with a passage said to hold some technical interest, will, if the claim strikes them as plausible, skip over the passage. But when we string together three of the strategically crucial quotations, we find a principle of selection in operation that is not merely technical. Eliot cites a passage from Chapman's *The Revenge of Bussy d'Ambois* (1610):

> in this one thing, all the discipline
> Of manners and of manhood is contained;
> A man to join himself with th'Universe
> In his main sway, and make in all things fit
> One with that All, and go on, round as it;
> Not plucking from the whole his wretched part,
> And into straits, or into nought revert,
> Wishing the complete Universe might be
> Subject to such a rag of it as he;
> But to consider great Necessity.

This is contrasted with "some modern passage"[44]—from Browning's "Bishop Blougram's Apology" (1855):

> No, when the fight begins within himself,
> A man's worth is something. God stoops o'er his head,
> Satan looks up between his feet—both tug—
> He's left, himself, i' the middle; the soul wakes
> And grows. Prolong that battle through his life!

And the last quotation in the essay is given to show the persistence of the metaphysical sensibility in the French tradition (it is from Baudelaire's "Le Voyage" [1861]):

> Pour l'enfant, amoureux de cartes et d'estampes,
> L'univers est égal à son vaste appétit.
> Ah, que le monde est grand à la clarté des lampes!
> Aux yeux du souvenir que le monde est petit!

The significance of the comparisons is clearly more than stylistic. In fact, the stylistic analysis—the analysis of the poetry "as poetry"—that would show how the operation of Chapman's brain is unlike the operation of Browning's but like the operation of Baudelaire's, is entirely missing. But if the passages are read for what they say, rather than how they say it, the point is clear enough. The first passage expresses an anti-individualistic ideal that might fairly be called (though in the language of a secular philosophy) Dantesque—"In His Will is our peace"; the second, from the speech of Browning's worldly bishop, describes a Manichean struggle in which the universe is not "round," like the universe in Chapman's lines, but polar, the setting for the individual soul's discovery of its own will and a place where peace is not the desired end; and the third passage expresses a nostalgia for the world-view of the first. It is the irony of the essay that to have placed these passages in the foreground of the argument, and to have explicated them instead of gesturing toward them vaguely as symptoms of their authors' neurological fitness, would have signaled the abandonment of the literary ideology on which Eliot's historical theory was predicated. For it would have meant that what was significant about these writers was not how their brains worked, but what they actually and consciously thought.

Many of Eliot's remarks about the nature of poetry and the shape of the literary tradition were treated by his admirers as discoveries; since the passing of the New Criticism and the school of Leavis, it has been common to think of those "discoveries" as having been more in the nature of inventions. But the distinction is in the end not a particularly useful one, for one of the things literary history seems to teach us about Eliot's early criticism is that he invented his arguments out of what he discovered, in the thought of his own time, to be already there. And to discover what literature is to one's contemporaries is to discover, to the extent that the phrase can make any practical sense, what literature is. It is also to discover something about the sources and the scope of critical power.

This begins to answer what is perhaps the really interesting question, which is how so reductive a group of critical formulations—formulations belonging to a line of aesthetic theorizing which seemed already fatally attenuated and whose philosophical foundations Eliot himself had demonstrated to be factitious—came to be so persuasive. We might enhance the hypothesis about the "already there" nature of Eliot's critical terms with the suggestion that their effectiveness was in fact inseparable from their reductiveness. For the higher the degree of particularity a theory of art has, the more it exposes itself to critique—and there is really no arguing, when all is said and done, with the notion of the objective correlative. It is part of the peculiar design of Eliot's early criticism that the received language of aesthetic theory is used to make arguments whose theoretical content is practically zero— as much as to say, I offer these explanations for my aesthetic preferences, but I am not (though others may be) ready to claim anything of greater significance for them.

Eliot's was a prototypically twentieth-century kind of irony, the irony that "sees through everything." "[T]here is no method," as he put it in a famous and disarming phrase, "except to be very intelligent."[45] In his early writings, this is a posture that, whatever interests it was calculated to conceal, gave his criticism a wonderful forcefulness. In the later criticism, especially in the sociological writings, Eliot's irony takes on something of the quality of an external agent: he cannot seem to get out of the way of his own arguments, he is so eager to qualify them. In *Notes Towards the Definition of Culture* (1948), for instance, efforts to make a thesis about culture issue in some prescriptive advice struggle against—and are, arguably, defeated by—frequent reminders that, properly conceived, culture is an entity so holistic that it cannot really be prescribed for, or even coherently thought about, at all. But there is a continuity between the early and later Eliots, a connection that has to do with the power Eliot habitually granted to the received idea, and it is a continuity postmodernists might do well to contemplate. We are often eager these days to acknowledge that culture is something we can never get outside, but we tend to forget that by the same token it is also something we can never get entirely inside. Our understanding always seems to miss the mark, so that we perpetually make a different thing of what is there regardless of our intentions. If we assume that we can only say what the culture permits us to say— the assumption the attitude of "seeing through everything" compels— we avoid the risk of ascribing to our understanding an objective force it cannot have; but if we ignore the fact that something about the nature of understanding always does place us in a new position relative to what was there, we run the greater risk of becoming the willing victims of our own enlightenment.

7

The Cultural Critic

The protagonist of this book has been a man who possessed a particular—in many ways, I think, a remarkable—kind of intelligence. I have tried to describe some of the things Eliot's style of thought enabled him to do, and to suggest some of the things it may have prevented him from doing. In the writing Eliot produced after *The Waste Land*, there are few examples of the kind of application of mind to moment that seems to me to characterize the early work. This is not to say that the later literary essays and the social criticism and the postconversion poetry hold no interest, only that the interest they do hold is of a different sort. They seem the products not so much of a different mind as of a mind that has required itself to play by different rules.

Eliot's change of manner after *The Waste Land* was so dramatic—it almost seems possible to date it to within a month or two—that some commentators have suggested that only a single, decisive personal crisis can explain it.[1] This is certainly a plausible thesis (though, like most arguments of the kind, it tends to remain, even after all the evidence has been entered, simply speculative); but cultural phenomena tend to have cultural explanations as well as biographical ones, and in the case of the two Eliots, it might be suggested that one of the reasons the later work was different is because its circumstances were different. After *The Waste Land*, Eliot began to write in a context in which the received conception of literary values was no longer an anonymous cultural given, but was to a considerable extent identifiably his own. The manner in which Eliot adapted himself to this state of affairs is worth looking at, both because it involves the interesting spectacle of Eliot's self-revision and because it represents a more general change in the goals of critical thought.

For a certain kind of reader, there is nothing in the later Eliot to compare with the young man who, between the middle of 1919 (he was not yet thirty-one) and the end of 1921 wrote all of *The Sacred Wood,* the three essays on seventeenth-century poetry collected in *Homage to John Dryden,* and *The Waste Land*—or who, in the second half of 1919 alone, wrote "Gerontion" (May–June) and published "A Cooking Egg" (May), the fourth "Reflections on Contemporary Poetry" (July), "Hamlet and His Problems" (September), and "Tradition and the Individual Talent" (September and December). Nor is a preference for the younger Eliot simply a postmodern taste; the notion of a falling off has attracted adherents ever since the appearance of *The Waste Land.* "A great disappointment," F. W. Bateson remembered feeling about that poem;[2] and he was not the only one to sense that Eliot had suffered a letdown. "To me," wrote Clive Bell in 1923, " 'Prufrock' seemed a minor masterpiece which raised immense and permissible hopes: my opinion has not changed, but my hopes have dwindled. . . . [Eliot's] intelligence and wit are as sharp as ever . . . but he has not improved."[3] J. B. Priestley, two years later, complained that "Mr. Eliot's actual accomplishment in criticism so far is extremely small, and such as it is is something of an anti-climax after his tremendous pronouncements";[4] and in 1926, Middleton Murry, in *The Adelphi,* felt it safe to pronounce *The Waste Land* a "failure."[5]

Each of these writers had his reasons, of course, for suggesting that Eliot had made promises as a young man that his later work did not— or could not—fulfill; it is, in any event, an accusation that arises naturally in the case of a writer who seems to establish his authority overnight. Eliot's conquest of literary London was to many of his contemporaries an astonishing achievement.[6] I have proposed some literary reasons for his success, but it is still, as a social fact, a little hard to account for. His manner of appearing more British than the British scarcely seems, in the beginning at any rate, to have disarmed anyone. "I found him dull, dull, dull," wrote Ottoline Morrell after Eliot's first visit to Garsington in 1916. "He never moves his lips but speaks in an even and monotonous voice, and I felt him monotonous without and within. . . . He is obviously very ignorant of England and imagines that it is essential to be highly polite and conventional and decorous and meticulous."[7] "[O]rdinarily just an Europeanized American," Aldous Huxley described Eliot in the same year, trying to explain his surprise at liking some of the poems, "overwhelmingly cultured, talking about French literature in the most uninspired fashion imaginable."[8] And Lytton Strachey told Carrington, after dining with Eliot in 1919, that he had found him "rather ill and rather American: altogether not quite gay enough for my taste."[9]

But the punctiliousness and erudition his Bloomsbury acquaintances found stultifying may have been among the very qualities that helped Eliot achieve a success in what was perhaps even to him an unexpected quarter—among young academics. Eliot made his mark as a critic even before the appearance of *The Sacred Wood* in December 1920; we find his name in a survey of the important contemporary critics—with the suggestion that he is already one of the small group of "star" critics who "control . . . England's literary output"—significantly earlier.[10] But *The Sacred Wood* made Eliot something more than an arbiter of literary taste; with its publication, he became the hero of university English studies. *The Sacred Wood* was apparently regarded as a kind of holy text by literature-minded undergraduates at Oxford and Cambridge in the 1920s: "The stranger who enters an Anglican church at service time is handed two books, *Hymns Ancient and Modern* and *The Book of Common Prayer*," wrote James Reeves in 1948. "When I went up to Cambridge twenty years ago, I was handed as it were, in much the same spirit, two little books, the one in prose, the other in verse. They were *The Sacred Wood* and *Poems 1909–1925*."[11] And F. W. Bateson reported a similar reverence at Oxford:

> *The Sacred Wood* was almost our sacred book [at Oxford in 1920–1924]. It was Eliot the critic who prepared us to welcome Eliot the poet, and not vice versa as apparently at Cambridge. My friends and I were very much aware of Eliot's articles and reviews then appearing in *The Athenaeum, Art and Letters,* the *Nation,* the Poetry Bookshop's Chapbooks, *The Dial* (New York), and *The Times Literary Supplement.*[12]

I. A. Richards, then teaching at Cambridge, read the poems in *Ara Vos Prec* and sought out their author to ask him to join the faculty.[13] And F. R. Leavis, twenty-five years old and a student at Cambridge, bought a copy of *The Sacred Wood* in 1920 and read it through every year, he says, pencil in hand. The essays showed him, he explained many years later,

> what the disinterested and effective application of intelligence to literature looks like, what is the nature of purity of interest, and what is meant by the principle (as Mr. Eliot himself states it) that "when you judge poetry it is as poetry you must judge it, and not as another thing."[14]

For this audience, Eliot's Americanness—or rather his equivocation about it—appears not to have been an issue; it was even a manner those readers were prepared to learn from. Bateson remembered Eliot lecturing, "without a trace of an American accent," to an Oxford literary society in 1922 and 1923: "Balliol . . . received a lesson on how English should be written and how it should be enunciated."[15]

It may be that Eliot owed his success as a cultural figure in England in part to his arriving at precisely the moment when one style of critical discourse was yielding in importance and authority to another—when the sort of freelance, journal-based literary criticism practiced by the members of the Bloomsbury group was being displaced by a new, university-based type: the criticism of the academic with an interest in the condition of contemporary culture.[16] It cannot really be said, as I have suggested, that the critical vocabulary that came to be so strongly associated with Eliot was his own invention;[17] but it might be said that Eliot did invent, for a common set of terms and judgments, a manner—judgmental, hierarchical, but "scientific"—perfectly suited to the needs of the modern academic critic. And the scholarship that occupies such a conspicuous place on the surface of Eliot's writing—both the criticism and the poetry—and that struck many of Eliot's nonacademic contemporaries as idiosyncratic and excessive, was perhaps also one of the things that made him so valuable to this new audience. Defending Eliot, they seem to have felt, meant defending the right of literary studies to a prominent place in the modern educational program.[18]

We get a sense of the transformation of values this development entailed from the tone of two letters written by Arnold Bennett. Bennett—who was, of course, one of the commanding literary figures of the Edwardian era—was impressed by Eliot's work (evidently some of the quatrain poems) in 1918, and asked him to call. "He came to see me," Bennett reported to a correspondent, "& I was well content."[19] Ten years later, Eliot, now the editor of *The Criterion*, solicited an essay from Bennett. "I would like to send you a contribution," Bennett replied, "but I am really afraid of doing so. I should have to take so much care over it! My articles, especially those about books, are rather slapdash. I am also handicapped by an intense ignorance. Indeed my life-long regret is that I have no exact knowledge on any subject on earth. I always envy scholars."[20]

Max Beerbohm once introduced a collection of essays he had written much earlier in his life with the comment that he had not attempted to revise them, out of respect for the imagined feelings of their author upon hearing that his work was to be fixed up, after he had finished with it, by an older man. In Eliot's case, we might say that the older critic was not especially considerate of the feelings of his younger self. The irony in the story of Eliot's influence on modern criticism is that even as his early judgments were being made the basis for new critical programs and revised literary canons, Eliot was already busy reversing them—so that he was, throughout his later career, frequently cited as an authority for arguments he had either repudiated or lost interest in.

The later manner is perfectly displayed in Eliot's preface to *Homage to John Dryden* (1924), which collected the three essays on seventeenth-century poetry—"John Dryden," "Andrew Marvell," and "The Metaphysical Poets"—that had originally appeared in the *Times Literary Supplement* in 1921. "My intention," Eliot explained by way of apology for the volume's sketchiness, "had been to write a series of papers on the poetry of the seventeenth and eighteenth centuries: beginning with Chapman and Donne, and ending with Johnson."

> This forbidden fruit of impossible leisure might have filled two volumes. At best, it would not have pretended to completeness; the subjects would have been restricted by my own ignorance and caprice, but the series would have included Aurelian Townshend and Bishop King, and the authors of "Cooper's Hill" and "The Vanity of Human Wishes," as well as Swift and Pope. That which dissipation interrupts, the infirmities of age come to terminate. One learns to conduct one's life with greater economy: I have abandoned this design in the pursuit of other policies. I have long felt that the poetry of the seventeenth and eighteenth centuries, even much of that of inferior in-

spiration, possesses an elegance and a dignity absent from the popular and pretentious verse of the Romantic Poets and their successors. To have urged this claim persuasively would have led me indirectly into considerations of politics, education, and theology which I no longer care to approach in this way. I hope that these three papers may in spite of and partly because of their defects preserve in cryptogram certain notions which, if expressed directly, would be destined to immediate obloquy, followed by perpetual oblivion.[21]

What is most noticeable about this passage to a reader fresh from Eliot's early writing is the presence of a figure that has suddenly been thrust into the foreground, a figure that seems to be important to our understanding of what is being said, but whose intentions are almost impossible to decipher. The figure is that of Eliot himself, and it is a baffling one indeed. He appears almost equally determined to put himself forward in all earnestness and, at the same time, to deflect—by any means available—our interest in him: he is by turns the modest layman ("my own ignorance and caprice"), the solemn pedant-in-spite-of-himself ("but the series would in fact have included . . ."), the apologist who scarcely bothers to conceal his disingenuousness (the complaint about "the infirmities of age" comes from a man of thirty-six), the purveyor of a self-deprecating humor that cannot be decoded ("That which dissipation [?] interrupts"), the embattled defender of a firmly held but largely unarticulated ideology ("considerations of politics, education, and theology which I no longer care to approach in this way"), the man who is willing to be the martyr of lost causes just for the sake of having a cause, even if its claims are, if taken literally (and there is no other honorable way to take them), clearly absurd ("certain notions which, if expressed directly . . ."). In short, the Possum.

This persona seemed to sponsor a criticism in which no merely literary position is considered worth preserving against the claims of larger interests—though the precise nature of those greater claims is often left unstated. The praise of Donne, for instance, barely survived the appearance of the essay on "The Metaphysical Poets" in volume form. In 1923, Eliot had begun proposing Donne as a remedy for certain vaguely specified cultural ills:

> The range of [Donne's] feelings was great, but no more remarkable than its unity. He was altogether present in every thought and in every feeling. . . . The dogmatic slumbers of the last hundred years are broken, and the chaos must be faced: we cannot return to sleep

and call it order, and we cannot have any order but our own, but from Donne and his contemporaries we can draw instruction and encouragement.[22]

But when Eliot delivered the Clark lectures at Cambridge in 1926, Donne's significance was reversed. He became there the first instance of the modern sensibility, a disappointed Romantic who exploited ideas for their emotional effects—just as Laforge in those lectures became a writer who consciously divided life into thought and feeling, a writer in whose poetry there is a continuous war, as Eliot put it, between the feelings implied by the ideas and the ideas implied by the feelings.[23] And in a 1931 volume of appreciatory writings on Donne that would perhaps not have been compiled but for Eliot's essays of 1921, Eliot was rather severe with Donne's modern admirers, and gave as his reason this piece of analysis:

> In Donne, there is a manifest fissure between thought and sensibility, a chasm which in his poetry he bridged in his own way, which was not the way of mediaeval poetry. His learning is just information suffused with emotion, or combined with emotion not essentially relevant to it.[24]

Eliot's reversal on Donne was largely ignored, perhaps because the argument that backed it seemed to suggest that there was no writer worthy of unequivocal admiration after Dante. But the habit of turning on the very literary tastes he had instilled did not pass without complaint. "[T]he only instance I know," declared Delmore Schwartz in a survey of Eliot's career to 1949, "where anyone has abdicated and immediately succeeded to his own throne."[25] Eliot's change of heart on the subject of Milton's importance struck many readers as a particularly exasperating exercise in arbitrary critical authority. In 1936, Milton is accused of having been a "bad influence"[26] on the language, and poets are warned against reading him; in 1947, Milton is reinvented as a poet whose achievements are said to be in much the same spirit as those of Mallarmé, and whose prosody can therefore be studied with profit.

"That wealthy investor Mr. Eliot," Northrop Frye complained, "after dumping Milton on the market, is now buying him again";[27] and a number of Eliot's reappraisals seem, as in the case of the two Miltons, to have been motivated by little more than a calculated desire to run against those parts of the original modernist polemic that had by their success become popular prejudice. The 1936 introduction to *Poems of Tennyson*, reprinted as "In Memoriam," manages (as condescending as it is) to suggest that Tennyson has been rather underappreciated. And Kipling did even better by his poor advance publicity. In 1919, Eliot condemned him, along with Swinburne, in a memorable essay for having "an idea to impose; and [imposing] it in the public speaker's way, by turning the idea into sound, and iterating the sound."[28] But we find Eliot explaining in 1928 that though "there is, no doubt, a bit of political jingoism in Kipling . . . it does not affect his best work. The imperialism which is in all of Kipling's work, and in the best of it, is not a political passion at all; it has no practical aim, but is merely the statement of a fact."[29] Somewhat later, even the jingoism disappears: "we must accustom ourselves to recognizing that for Kipling the Empire was not merely an idea, a good idea or a bad one," Eliot advised in 1941; "it was something the reality of which he felt."[30] And in the end (1959), Kipling becomes in fact a modernist, a sort of superior Yeats: "Kipling was not a party man. Nor had he—and this is important—a mind gifted for abstract thought: he thought in images. . . . He seems to me the greatest English man of letters of his generation."[31]

Eliot's reassessments of specific critical judgments are the epiphenomena of what was clearly a thoroughgoing sort of retrenchment. Although those literary revaluations seem to correspond to the kind of poetry Eliot must have been contemplating when he made them—the Tennyson essays of 1936 and 1942, the Yeats essay of 1940, and the Kipling essay of 1941, for instance, all appear to figure in important ways in the composition of *Four Quartets*—it is also, of course, the case that most of Eliot's reconsiderations were inspired by concerns that were not literary at all. Eliot's later critical essays seem, as *criticism*, substantially weaker than his earlier productions in part because they are the work of a man who has decided that literature as an activity in itself—literature considered as literature—is no longer enough.

Eliot gave every indication, after the publication *The Waste Land*, of being eager to dissociate himself from his earlier work. "As for 'The Waste Land,' " he wrote to Richard Aldington in November 1922, "that is a thing of the past so far as I am concerned and I am now feeling toward a new form and style."[32] And when Arnold Bennett

told him, in 1924, that he "couldn't see the point" of *The Waste Land,*
Eliot replied that he didn't mind a bit: "he had definitely given up that
form of writing," he told Bennett, "and was now centred on dramatic
writing."[33] The new note is struck almost immediately in the criticism: "The Function of Criticism" (1923) is severe with the historicist
implications of "Tradition and the Individual Talent";[34] the preface to
Homage to John Dryden explains, as we have seen, that its author no
longer cares to deal with the subject of the difference between seventeenth-century and Romantic poetry in a purely literary way; the second edition of *The Sacred Wood* (published in May 1928) announces
that the line taken in those essays—"that when we are considering
poetry we must consider it primarily as poetry and not another thing"[35]—
can carry us only so far; and in the preface to *For Lancelot Andrewes*
(November 1928), Eliot indicates that he has put the volume together
with a view "to dissociat[ing] myself from certain conclusions which
have been drawn from my volume of essays, *The Sacred Wood.*"[36] "At
the present time," he wrote in a piece for *The Harvard Advocate* in
1934,

> I am not very much interested in the only subject about which I am
> supposed to be qualified to write about: that is, one kind of literary
> criticism. I am not very much interested in literature, except dramatic
> literature; and I am largely interested in subjects which I do not yet
> know very much about: theology, politics, economics, and education.[37]

The most striking display of disaffection with literary values—a performance amounting to an attack on the very idea of literature as a
discrete and distinctive social activity—appears in the work that has
given most readers of the later Eliot trouble, *After Strange Gods* (1934).
Eliot never reprinted the volume, but its argument quite clearly meant
a good deal to him at the time he made it. "[P]ure literary criticism
has ceased to interest me," he confessed in a letter to Paul Elmer
More:

> The subject of "The Uses of Poetry" [the Norton lectures at Har-
> vard, 1933] was undertaken merely because it seemed the one on which
> I could write with the minimum of new reading and thinking; the field
> of "After Strange Gods" was one to which my real interest had turned.
> I therefore felt more regret at the inadequacy of the latter than the
> former.[38]

The nature of that "real interest" is not, of course, mysterious. Stephen Spender, in his critical study of Eliot, tells a story that seems to explain it succinctly:

> Eliot addressed an undergraduate club, The Martlets, at University College, Oxford [in 1928]. He declined to give a lecture, but agreed to answer questions. The question was raised whether there was any ultimate criterion for judging a work of art. How can we be certain that *Antony and Cleopatra* and the Acropolis continue always to be beautiful? T., an undergraduate, . . . said that surely it was impossible to believe in aesthetic values being permanent, unless one believed in God in whose mind beauty existed. Eliot bowed his head in that almost praying attitude which I came to know well, and murmured words to the effect of: "That is what I have come to believe."[39]

After Strange Gods is an effort to establish the value of something Eliot calls "orthodoxy" as a criterion for the evaluation of literature—and not only of literature, evidently, but of all enterprise. The argument belongs to the series of Eliot's continuing efforts to rewrite "Tradition and the Individual Talent." Here, "tradition," though it is necessary, is not enough; it is the name for "good habits," and as such it may develop and decay. But "orthodoxy" exists in spite of the state of human affairs; it exists even in the absence of our knowledge of it.[40] This hypostasization of doctrine is, of course, far from the dialectical and historicist notion of value proposed by "Tradition and the Individual," and it represents, in fact, as William Chace has noted,[41] a radical departure from even the main line of conservative thought; the organicist idea of tradition that figured so prominently in the work of Burke and Coleridge—and in the entire nineteenth-century defense of culture—has been trumped by a category that has the polemical advantage of being immutable, but the practical liability of being, to ordinary knowledge, unrecognizable. For the concept of orthodoxy suffers from the problem common to all transcendental criteria: it cannot be translated into the terms of the activity it is called upon to judge without losing its supernatural status. Thus the remarkable series of literary judgments offered in *After Strange Gods*: if the explanations for them (such as they are) make no sense to us—the reading of Joyce's "The Dead" that seems to take no account of the story's irony is one of the more astonishing—it is because they have ruled the ordinary vocabulary of literary criticism out of bounds.

Different readers will have different responses to Eliot's choice of "permanent" values; but we do not need to take sides on the matter, for the issue that choice raises is one worth contemplating in the abstract. The younger Eliot was not a liberal or a secularist; the author of "Reflections on *vers libre*" and "Tradition and the Individual Talent" and *The Waste Land* did not display markedly different political or religious tendencies from the author of "The Function of Criticism" and *Ash Wednesday*. That younger writer seems simply to have subjected every assumption he could identify and bring to light to the critical force of a relentless irony. It was a manner of mind that proved, in circumstances of accelerated cultural change, extraordinarily effective. It did not—as attractive as it may seem to readers not particularly disposed toward the doctrinalism of the later Eliot—produce a value-neutral kind of writing. It only made a profound skepticism about value its ally. A passage in a book review in *The Criterion* in 1926 states as lucidly as anything in Eliot's later work the habit of mind he gave up after *The Waste Land,* and the habit of mind he hoped to acquire. The importance of Proust, Eliot says, is that he stands

> as a point of demarcation between a generation for whom the dissolution of value had in itself a positive value, and the generation for which the recognition of value is of utmost importance, a generation which is beginning to turn its attention to an athleticism, a *training,* of the soul as severe and ascetic as the training of the body of a runner.[42]

We are today quite eager to acknowledge the part interest plays in our critical judgments and analyses, and it might seem that in abandoning the apparently essentialist assumptions of *The Sacred Wood*— the notion of literature as a thing-in-itself—for the explicitly polemical purposes of the later work, Eliot was freeing his criticism for more practical labors. But the reification of the idea of literature is what had given his earlier writing its remarkable force, and when he repossessed that idea in order to make it serve his own ends, he gave himself nothing to play off against. "Orthodoxy" won't do as an ideological given (as "literature" once did) when it stands for something the majority of one's readers have almost no useful associations with. And Eliot was not a great explainer; he was a master of the uses of that-which-needs-no-explanation. Which is, in its paradoxical way, why the later criticism, when we find ourselves disagreeing with its positions, seems to have so little *but* those positions to offer.

Eliot was right, I think, in identifying his own change of strategy as a generational one. The critical thought of the first half of the twentieth century belongs—as Raymond Williams explains in *Culture and Society* (1958)—to a tradition in which "culture" is required to play the role of the transcendent arbiter of value in a social formation characterized precisely by its inhospitality to transcendental agents.[43] High-culture art had a prominent place in that tradition, and the literary modernism of 1910–1922 belongs to a phase when, in order to preserve its values, literature was itself compelled to undergo a transformation. But 1910–1922 was the end of a phase Williams identifies as a kind of interregnum in the tradition, a period when the emphasis seemed to fall on art's autonomy, its independence of the values of society as a whole. And it gave way, after the First World War, to a renewed effort to assess the progress of modern society by the lights, once again, of a comprehensive notion of culture.[44] The Eliot of *The Sacred Wood* belongs, we might say, to the first of these phases, the phase in which writers attempted to solve a problem with literature's reputation by thinking of it solely as literature, as though it were an activity isolable from the rest of the practices of the group. And the Eliot of *Notes Towards the Definition of Culture* belongs to the second phase. It is somehow fitting that of the many attitudes that Eliot the cultural critic found in need of correction, a few could be traced to the work of his younger self—a writer for whom the notion of prescriptive cultural criticism would have seemed only another opportunity for irony.

Acknowledgments

I have tried to write a book for people who are not particularly sympathetic toward the cultural judgments and values that T. S. Eliot is generally associated with, but who find themselves nonetheless impressed by the manner in which Eliot was able to present his views and to make them prevail. I am such a person, and I hope I have been able to convince others like me of the usefulness of understanding the etiology of Eliot's success.

Eliot is not the easiest company to keep; I have found him an unrelenting and sometimes exhausting challenge. I was assisted in my work by funds provided by the Princeton University Humanities Research Council and the Surdna Foundation, and by a generous amount of leave time granted by Princeton University.

A number of friends and colleagues were kind enough to read portions of the manuscript and suggest improvements. I thank Ross Borden, David Bromwich, Lawrence Danson, Samuel Hynes, Alvin Kernan, Jules Law, and John Rosenberg for their comments. A. Walton Litz has been an extraordinary scholarly resource and an extraordinary friend since the beginning of my work on Eliot, and I am indebted to him for his wisdom and his wonderful sense of proportion.

I know of no way to describe how much I have relied, in the construction of this book as in all other things, on the judgment and the love of my wife, Emily Abrahams.

Notes

INTRODUCTION

1. On the subject of Eliot's relation to the aesthetic ideology of the nineteenth century, Frank Kermode's *Romantic Image* (London: Routledge and Kegan Paul, 1957) remains the standard treatment. The many subsequent works proposing revised understandings of Eliot's affiliations with nineteenth-century literary traditions include C. K. Stead, *The New Poetic* (London: Hutchinson, 1964); George Bornstein, *Transformations of Romanticism in Yeats, Eliot, and Stevens* (Chicago: University of Chicago Press, 1976); Edward Lobb, *T. S. Eliot and the Romantic Critical Tradition* (London, Boston, and Henley: Routledge and Kegan Paul, 1981); David Ned Tobin, *The Presence of the Past: T. S. Eliot's Victorian Inheritance* (Ann Arbor: UMI Research Press, 1983); and Carol T. Christ, *Victorian and Modern Poetics* (Chicago: University of Chicago Press, 1984). Michael H. Levenson's *A Genealogy of Modernism: A Study of English Literary Doctrine 1908–1922* (Cambridge: Cambridge University Press, 1984) seems to me to be one of the few literary histories of the modernist period to assess Eliot's relation to the avant-garde of his time in its real complexity.

2. The pioneering biographical treatment is Lyndall Gordon's *Eliot's Early Years* (Oxford: Oxford University Press, 1977); Peter Ackroyd has recently contributed a more extensive account, in *T. S. Eliot: A Life* (New York: Simon and Schuster, 1984). Among numerous works since the 1971 edition of the *Waste Land* manuscripts to draw on unpublished materials in proposing revised readings of Eliot's work, two comprehensive studies make specific claims for the importance an understanding of Eliot's psychological profile has for an

explanation of his achievement as a cultural figure: A. D. Moody, *Thomas Stearns Eliot: Poet* (Cambridge: Cambridge University Press, 1979), see esp. pp. 283–98; and Ronald Bush, *T. S. Eliot: A Study in Character and Style* (New York: Oxford University Press, 1984), see esp. pp. ix–xiii.

3. Martin D. Armstrong to Conrad Aiden, 11 October 1914, Aiken Collection (AIK 47), Huntington Library. "[B]ut the twirlings," Armstrong added, "are always extremely interesting."

CHAPTER 1

1. Lionel Trilling, *Sincerity and Authenticity* (Cambridge, Mass.: Harvard University Press, 1972), p. 99.

2. Harold Rosenberg, *The Tradition of the New* (New York: McGraw-Hill, 1960), pp. 32–33.

3. See Hallam Tennyson, *Alfred Lord Tennyson: A Memoir by His Son* (New York: Macmillan, 1897), I, 305–6.

4. The poem is in a holograph notebook, titled "Complete Poems of T. S. Eliot," in the Berg Collection, New York Public Library. Quotation from the notebook is not permitted. Its contents are described more fully below; for a complete bibliographic account, see Donald Gallup, "The 'Lost' Manuscripts of T. S. Eliot," *TLS*, 7 November 1968, pp. 1238–40.

5. See, for example, Hugh Kenner, *The Invisible Poet: T. S. Eliot* (New York: McDowell, Obolensky, 1959), p. 150. Eliot himself, later in life, was similarly depreciatory; see "The Frontiers of Criticism" (1956), in *On Poetry and Poets* (New York: Farrar, Straus and Cudahy, 1957), p. 121. The footnotes to *The Waste Land* are discussed further in chapter four herein.

6. Quotations from Eliot's published poetry are from *The Complete Poetry and Plays of T. S. Eliot* (London: Faber and Faber, 1969).

7. See Grover Smith, *T. S. Eliot's Poetry and Plays: A Study in Sources and Meaning*, 2d ed. (Chicago and London: University of Chicago Press, 1974), pp. 20–21.

8. Jules Laforgue, "Twilight," in *Selected Writings of Jules Laforgue*, ed. and trans. William Jay Smith (New York: Grove Press, 1956), p. 204.

9. Quotations from Tennyson's poetry are from *The Poems of Tennyson*, ed. Christopher Ricks (London: Longman, 1969).

10. See, among a number of discussions, S. Musgrove, *T. S. Eliot and Walt Whitman* (Wellington: New Zealand University Press, 1952), pp. 45–46; and Bernard Bergonzi, *T. S. Eliot* (New York: Macmillan, 1972), pp. 19–20. James E. Miller, Jr., cites Eliot's admiration for the "Dark house" stanzas to suggest parallels between *In Memoriam* and *The Waste Land*, in *T. S. Eliot's Personal Waste Land: Exorcism of the Demons* (University Park and London: Pennsylvania State University Press, 1977), pp. 1–6; and A. Walton Litz has juxtaposed *In Memoriam* VII and section 2 of "Little Gidding," in " 'That Strange

Abstraction, "Nature" ': T. S. Eliot's Victorian Inheritance," in *Nature and the Victorian Imagination,* ed. U. C. Knoepflmacher and G. B. Tennyson (Berkeley and Los Angeles: University of California Press, 1977), pp. 482–88.

11. Richard Poirier, "The Difficulties of Modernism and the Modernism of Difficulty," in *Images and Ideas in American Culture: The Functions of Criticism,* ed. Arthur Edelstein (Hanover, N.H.: Brandeis University Press, 1979), p. 136.

12. Arthur Symons, "The Decadent Movement in Literature," *Harper's New Monthly Magazine,* 87 (November 1893), 859.

13. "La sincerité, et, à ses fins, l'impression du moment suivi à la lettre sont ma règle préférée aujourd'hui." Paul Verlaine, "Critiques des *Poèmes Saturniens,*" in *Oeuvres en prose complètes,* ed. Jacques Borel (Paris: Gallimard, 1972), p. 720. Symons quoted the phrase in his chapter on Verlaine in *The Symbolist Movement in Literature* (London: William Heinemann, 1899), p. 88.

14. Arthur Hallam, "On Some of the Characteristics of Modern Poetry and on the Lyrical Poems of Alfred Tennyson," in *The Writings of Arthur Hallam,* ed. T. H. Vail Motter (New York: Modern Language Association of America, 1943), p. 187. Hallam's essay originally appeared in *Englishman's Magazine,* 1 (August 1831), 616–28.

15. William Butler Yeats, *The Trembling of the Veil* (1922), in *The Autobiography of William Butler Yeats* (New York: Macmillan, 1965), p. 229.

16. See, for instance, Arthur Bernard Cook, "Associated Reminiscences," *Classical Review,* 15 (October 1901), 338–45: "It is notorious that a well-read writer constantly reproduces phrases that he has come across elsewhere. But it is not so often remarked that the borrowed phrase has a knack of awakening in his memory some other phrase to be found usually, though not always, in the source from which he is borrowing; and that, when this is the case, the borrower may proceed to utilise the second expression as well as the first. . . . It must be added that the whole process is sometimes conscious, sometimes unconscious: to describe such examples of appropriation as plagiarism is to pronounce a rough and ready verdict on a case that may be extremely complicated" (p. 338). One of Cook's examples is the series of echoes in *In Memoriam* VII of section 9 of Wordsworth's Immortality Ode (see p. 340).

17. See Jephson Huband Smith, *Notes and Marginalia Illustrative of the Public Life and Works of Alfred Tennyson, Poet Laureate* (London: Blackwood, 1873), p. 177–81.

18. John Churton Collins, "A New Study of Tennyson," *Cornhill Magazine,* 41 (January 1880), 37. The article appeared in three parts: 41 (January 1880), 36–50; 42 (July 1880), 17–35; and 44 (July 1881), 87–106. Collins's book on the subject, *Illustrations of Tennyson* (London: Chatto and Windus), was published in 1891. Biographical information about Collins (1848–1908) can be found in the *DNB.* For Tennyson's marginalia on the Collins articles, see H. P. Sucksmith, "Tennyson on the Nature of His Own Poetic Genius," *Renais-*

sance and Modern Studies, 11 (1967), 84–89; Tennyson's reaction to the whole affair is described in Robert Pattison, *Tennyson and Tradition* (Cambridge, Mass., and London: Harvard University Press, 1979), pp. 5–8.

19. A. C. Bradley, *A Commentary on Tennyson's "In Memoriam"* (London: Macmillan, 1901), pp. 72, 71, 75.

20. Bradley, p. 89. Bradley also identified, in later editions of his *Commentary* and citing Cook's article, the Immortality Ode as a possible source of "guilty thing." Wordsworth's poem may, in fact, have been more present to Tennyson's mind when he wrote the phrase than *Hamlet.* What matters in the present discussion is not what Tennyson was likely to have thought, but what Tennyson's readers were likely to have perceived. And this distinction applies to my argument generally: an allusion may be to a phrase or a work that has personal value to the poet irrespective of its public success, but to the extent that an allusion means nothing—is either entirely transparent or entirely opaque—to the reader, it is not, in the sense I am discussing it, a "literary" figure.

21. See John D. Rosenberg, "The Two Kingdoms of *In Memoriam,*" *JEGP,* 58 (1959), 230. The phrase appears, in the King James version, in Matthew 28:6, Mark 16:6, and Luke 24:6.

22. This argument was first made by H. M. McLuhan in "Tennyson and the Picturesque," *Essays in Criticism,* 1 (1950), 262–82 (see also McLuhan's "The Aesthetic Moment in Landscape Poetry," in *English Institute Essays, 1951,* ed. Alan S. Downer [New York: Columbia University Press, 1952], pp. 168–81). It is repeated in W. K. Wimsatt, "*Prufrock* and *Maud:* From Plot to Symbol," in *Hateful Contraries: Studies in Literature and Criticism* (Lexington: University of Kentucky Press, 1966), pp. 201–12; Denis Donoghue, *The Ordinary Universe: Soundings in Modern Literature* (New York: Macmillan, 1968), pp. 90–107; and Donald Davie, "Pound and Eliot: A Distinction," in *Eliot in Perspective,* ed. Graham Martin (London: Macmillan, 1970), pp. 62–82. Hugh Kenner makes a parallel argument in "Some Post-Symbolist Structures," in *Literary Theory and Structure,* ed. Frank Brady, John Palmer, and Martin Price (New Haven and London: Yale University Press, 1973), pp. 379–93.

CHAPTER 2

1. See Ray Frazer, "The Origin of the Term 'Image,' " *ELH,* 27 (1960), 149–62.

2. William Wordsworth, "Preface to *Lyrical Ballads* (1850)," in *The Prose Works of William Wordsworth,* ed. W. J. B. Owen and Jane Worthington Smyser (Oxford: Clarendon Press, 1974), I, 142, 139, 125.

3. Matthew Arnold, "Preface to First Edition of Poems (1853)," in *Irish Essays and Others* (London: Smith, Elder, 1882), p. 292.

4. See Frazer, pp. 151–54, and P. N. Furbank, *Reflections on the Word*

"Image" (London: Secker and Warburg, 1970), pp. 25–34, for discussions of the term's ties to empiricist philosophy.

5. Walter Pater, *The Renaissance: Studies in Art and Poetry,* ed. Donald L. Hill (Berkeley and Los Angeles: University of California Press, 1980), pp. 188, 187. This is the text of the 1893 edition.

6. Walter Pater, *Plato and Platonism* (London: Macmillan, 1893), p. 87.

7. In A. D. Nuttall, *A Common Sky: Philosophy and the Literary Imagination* (London: Chatto and Windus, 1974), pp. 16–20. In the discussion that follows, I am particularly indebted to the critiques of empiricism made by Nuttall in this work; by Ian Hacking in *Why Does Language Matter to Philosophy?* (Cambridge: Cambridge University Press, 1975), pp. 15–53, 163–70; and by Richard Rorty in *Philosophy and the Mirror of Nature* (Princeton: Princeton University Press, 1970); and to Ross Borden, whose conversation and whose work in progress first made me see the explanatory power the empiricist model of the mind holds for an understanding of modern aesthetic theory.

8. See Richard Aldington, *Life for Life's Sake* (New York: Viking, 1941), p. 135; Ezra Pound, *Selected Letters 1907–1941,* ed. D. D. Paige (New York: New Directions, 1950), p. 49 n. 1; Christopher Middleton, "Documents on Imagism from the Papers of F. S. Flint," *The Review* [Oxford] (April 1965), 35–51, where Flint's letter to Pound of 3 July 1915 is quoted; and F. S. Flint, "The History of Imagism," *The Egoist,* 2 (1 May 1915), 70–71. Frost's remark is reported in J. Isaacs, "Best Loved of American Poets," *The Listener,* 51 (1 April 1954), 565.

9. William James, "The Sentiment of Rationality," in *The Will to Believe and Other Essays in Popular Philosophy* (New York: Longmans, Green, 1908), pp. 83–84.

10. Richard Rorty, *Philosophy and the Mirror of Nature,* p. 166. But see Rorty's "Philosophy in America Today," in *Consequences of Pragmatism* (Minneapolis: University of Minnesota Press, 1982), pp. 213–14, where he associates Bergson, Whitehead, and the "metaphysical" parts of Dewey and James with other late-nineteenth-century attempts "to answer 'unscientifically' formulated epistemological questions."

11. T. E. Hulme, "Notes on Bergson," in *Further Speculations by T. E. Hulme,* ed. Sam Hynes (Minneapolis: University of Minnesota Press, 1955), pp. 30, 36, 29–30. The essay first appeared in *The New Age,* 9 (19 and 26 October 1911), 587–88, 610–11.

12. Henri Bergson, *Time and Free Will: An Essay on the Immediate Data of Consciousness,* trans. F. L. Pogson (London: George Allen and Unwin, 1910), pp. xix–xx.

13. Bergson, p. 139.

14. Bergson, p. 129.

15. Bergson, pp. 130–32.

16. Henri Bergson, *An Introduction to Metaphysics,* trans. T. E. Hulme, 2d

ed. (Indianapolis and New York: Bobbs-Merrill, 1955), pp. 21, 23, 27–28. The "Introduction" originally appeared in the *Revue de Métaphysique et de Morale,* January 1903; Hulme's translation was published in London in 1913.

17. Hulme, p. 79.

18. Hulme, p. 10. The essay appeared originally in *The New Age,* 5 (19 August 1909), 315–16.

19. Ezra Pound, "This Hulme Business," *The Townsman,* 2 (1939), 15.

20. For a discussion of the character of Pater's relation to this tradition in Romantic thought, see David Bromwich, "The Genealogy of Disinterestedness," *Raritan,* 1 (Spring 1982), 62–92.

21. Pater, *The Renaissance,* pp. 187–88.

22. Walter Pater, *Miscellaneous Studies* (London: Macmillan, 1895), p. 220.

23. Walter Pater, "Style," in *Appreciations* (London: Macmillan, 1904), p. 31.

24. Pater, *The Renaissance,* p. 188.

25. David Hume, *A Treatise of Human Nature,* ed. L. A. Selby-Bigge, 2d ed. (Oxford: Clarendon Press, 1978), vol. I, part 4, sec. 6, p. 253.

26. Pater, *Appreciations,* pp. 34, 9–10.

27. Hulme, p. 75. Hynes dates the lecture 1908 or 1909 (p. xviii).

28. Ezra Pound, "A Retrospect," in *Literary Essays of Ezra Pound,* ed. T. S. Eliot (New York: New Directions, 1954), p. 9. The sentences first appeared in "Prologomena," *Poetry Review,* 1 (February 1912), 72–76.

29. Ford Madox Ford, "Impressionism—Some Speculations," in *Critical Writings of Ford Madox Ford,* ed. Frank MacShane (Lincoln: University of Nebraska Press, 1964), p. 151. Ford's essay was first published in *Poetry,* 2 (August and September 1913), 177–87, 215–25, and became the introduction to his *Collected Poems* (1913).

30. Richard Aldington, "The Poetry of F. S. Flint," *The Egoist,* 2 (1 May 1915), 80.

31. Ezra Pound, "Vortex. Pound," *Blast,* 1 (20 June 1914), 153, 154.

32. Ezra Pound, "Affirmations: As for Imagisme," in *Selected Prose 1909–1965,* ed. William Cookson (New York: New Directions, 1973), pp. 374–75. First published in *The New Age,* 16 (28 January 1915), 349–50.

33. William Wordsworth, "Preface to *Lyrical Ballads* (1800)," in *The Prose Works of William Wordsworth,* I, 126.

34. Pound, *Selected Prose,* p. 376.

35. Eliot to Ezra Pound, 2 February 1915, Pound Center, Beinecke Library, Yale University. The article was "Vorticism," *Fortnightly Review,* n.s. 96 (1 September 1914), 461–71; it is reprinted in Pound's *Gaudier-Brzeska: A Memoir* (New York: New Directions, 1970), pp. 81–94.

36. Hugh Kenner, *The Invisible Poet: T. S. Eliot* (New York: McDowell, Obolensky, 1959), p. 45; J. Hillis Miller, *Poets of Reality: Six Twentieth-Century Writers* (Cambridge, Mass.: Harvard University Press, 1965), pp. 135, 136;

Lyndall Gordon, *Eliot's Early Years* (Oxford: Oxford University Press, 1977), pp. 53, 52; Walter Benn Michaels, "Philosophy in Kinkanja: Eliot's Pragmatism," *Glyph,* 8 (1981), 170–202.

37. Kenner, p. 45. It should be noted that although he characterizes it in his chapter on Eliot and Bradley, Kenner apparently did not receive permission to examine the dissertation in 1959. See Richard Wollheim, "Eliot and F. H. Bradley," in *On Art and the Mind* (Cambridge, Mass.: Harvard University Press, 1974), p. 221, n. 6.

38. Various arguments have been offered with a view to making Eliot's comments on the notion of immediate experience as compatible with Bradleian doctrine as possible. George Whiteside ("T. S. Eliot's Dissertation," *ELH,* 34 [1967]: 400–424) attributes Eliot's apparent reservations to his inability, despite an intellectual eagerness to subscribe to Bradley's position, to convince himself emotionally that experience can indeed cohere (p. 418). John Soldo ("Knowledge and Experience in the Criticism of T. S. Eliot," *ELH,* 35 [1968]: 284–308) suggests that Eliot improved on Bradley's concept by requiring the "co-presence of thought or consciousness" with feeling in the make-up of immediate experience (p. 287). Lewis Freed simply asserts that the dissertation's use of immediate experience is Bradley's, in *T. S. Eliot: The Critic as Philosopher* (West Lafayette, Ind.: Purdue University Press, 1979), p. 49. See also John F. Lynen, *The Design of the Present* (New Haven: Yale University Press, 1969), p. 366; Piers Gray, *T. S. Eliot's Intellectual and Poetic Development 1909–1922* (Sussex: Harvester Press, 1982), pp. 151–53; and Michael Levenson, *A Genealogy of Modernism: A Study of English Literary Doctrine 1908–1916* (Cambridge: Cambridge University Press, 1984), where it is argued that Eliot in 1915–16 agreed with Bradley that " 'actual' knowledge depends on the immediate and finite experience" (p. 182).

Michaels has an excellent discussion, to which my own is very much indebted, of the difference between Eliot and Bradley on this matter (see Michaels, pp. 173–76); for an account of other points of disagreement between the two, see Wollheim, pp. 228–29.

39. F. H. Bradley, *Appearance and Reality: A Metaphysical Essay,* 2d ed. (London: George Allen and Unwin, 1897), p. 459.

40. F. H. Bradley, *Essays on Truth and Reality* (Oxford: Clarendon Press, 1914), pp. 159–60, 161.

41. Bradley, *Essays on Truth and Reality,* pp. 161, 175, 174.

42. *Knowledge and Experience in the Philosophy of F. H. Bradley* (London: Faber and Faber, 1964), p. 17.

43. *Knowledge and Experience,* p. 18.

44. *Knowledge and Experience,* pp. 83–85.

45. *Knowledge and Experience,* p. 166.

46. *Knowledge and Experience,* pp. 167–68.

47. *The Waste Land,* 1. 415. The full quotation from Bradley's *Appearance*

and Reality (p. 346) reads: "My external sensations are no less private to myself than are my thoughts or my feelings. In either case my experience falls within my own circle, a circle closed on the outside; and, with all its elements alike, every sphere is opaque to the others which surround it. . . . In brief, regarded as an existence which appears in a soul, the whole world for each is peculiar and private to that soul."

48. See Wollheim, pp. 242–43; and Anne C. Bolgan, *What the Thunder Really Said: A Retrospective Essay on the Making of "The Waste Land"* (Montreal and London: McGill-Queen's University Press, 1973), pp. 179–81.

49. "Leibniz' Monads and Bradley's Finite Centres," in *Knowledge and Experience*, p. 204. The essay originally appeared in *The Monist*, 26 (October 1916), 566–76.

50. See *Knowledge and Experience*, pp. 141–42. For Bradley's remarks on solipsism, see *Appearance and Reality*, pp. 247–60, and *Essays on Truth and Reality*, pp. 246–47.

51. *Knowledge and Experience*, p. 202.

52. *Knowledge and Experience*, p. 31. Eliot adds: "That Mr. Bradley himself would accept this interpretation . . . is not to be presumed."

53. Gordon, p. 53.

54. *Knowledge and Experience*, p. 157.

55. *Knowledge and Experience*, pp. 151–52.

56. *Knowledge and Experience*, pp. 153–54.

57. For particular applications, see (among many instances) Lewis Freed, *T. S. Eliot: Aesthetics and History* (LaSalle: Open Court, 1962), pp. 132–67, and *T. S. Eliot: The Critic as Philosopher*, pp. 131–49; Soldo; Bolgan, pp. 139–43; Mowbray Allen, *T. S. Eliot's Impersonal Theory of Poetry* (Lewisburg, Pa.: Bucknell University Press, 1974), pp. 139–40; A. D. Moody, *Thomas Stearns Eliot: Poet* (Cambridge: Cambridge University Press, 1979), pp. 73–76; and Levenson, pp. 186–93.

58. "Swinburne as Poet," in *The Sacred Wood: Essays on Poetry and Criticism*, 2d ed. (London: Methuen, 1928), p. 149. Apart from a "Preface to the 1928 Edition" and the title of one of the essays, the contents of this edition of *The Sacred Wood* are identical to those of the first (1920); but the pagination is different, and since it is the second edition that has been many times reprinted, it is the one cited throughout.

59. Leslie Brisman, "Swinburne's Semiotics," *Georgia Review*, 31 (1977), 579, 597.

60. *Knowledge and Experience*, pp. 132–33.

61. Michaels, pp. 182–83.

62. *Knowledge and Experience*, p. 155.

63. *Knowledge and Experience*, pp. 17–18.

64. *Knowledge and Experience*, p. 21.

65. *Knowledge and Experience*, p. 18; "The Metaphysical Poets," in *Selected*

Essays of T. S. Eliot, new ed. (New York: Harcourt, Brace and World, 1950), p. 247; "Donne in Our Time," in *A Garland for John Donne,* ed. Theodore Spencer (1931; rpt. Gloucester, Mass.: Peter Smith, 1958), p. 8.

CHAPTER 3

1. Ford Madox Ford to Lucy Masterman, 23 January 1912, in *Critical Writings of Ford Madox Ford,* ed. Frank MacShane (Lincoln: University of Nebraska Press, 1964), p. 154.

2. Ezra Pound to Harriet Monroe, January 1915, in Ezra Pound, *Selected Letters 1907–1941,* ed. D. D. Paige (New York: New Directions, 1950), p. 49.

3. See "Literature," in Raymond Williams, *Keywords: A Vocabulary of Culture and Society* (New York: Oxford University Press, 1976). The *OED* dates the first use of "literaryism" as 1879; see also, in the first volume of the *Supplement,* "arty" and "artiness," both 1901. Pejorative senses of aesthetic terms seem somewhat underrepresented in the *OED* for some reason—"poetical," for instance, is not recorded as a term of abuse; but see F. R. Leavis, *New Bearings in English Poetry* (London: Chatto and Windus, 1932), pp. 5–15.

4. Ford Madox Ford, "A Jubilee," *The Outlook,* 36 (10 July 1915), 47.

5. Ford Madox Ford, "Impressionism—Some Speculations" (1913), in *Critical Writings,* p. 145.

6. Ezra Pound, "The Hard and Soft in French Poetry," in *Literary Essays of Ezra Pound,* ed. T. S. Eliot (New York: New Directions, 1954), p. 285. The essay originally appeared in *Poetry,* 11 (February 1918), 264–71.

7. Ezra Pound to James Joyce, 17 March 1917, in *Pound/Joyce,* ed. Forrest Read (New York: New Directions, 1967), p. 102.

8. For a generally appreciative account, see Marjorie Perloff, *The Poetics of Indeterminacy* (Princeton: Princeton University Press, 1981), pp. 155–99. Michael Harper expresses some reservations in "The Revolution of the Word," in *Ezra Pound and William Carlos Williams: The University of Pennsylvania Conference Papers,* ed. Daniel Hoffman (Philadelphia: University of Pennsylvania Press, 1983), pp. 92–94.

9. See Hugh Kenner, *The Pound Era* (Berkeley and Los Angeles: University of California Press, 1971), pp. 488–93.

10. Delmore Schwartz, "Ezra Pound's Very Useful Labors," in *Selected Essays of Delmore Schwartz,* ed. Donald A. Dike and David H. Zucker (Chicago and London: University of Chicago Press, 1970), p. 107n. The essay first appeared in *Poetry,* 51 (March 1938), 324–39.

11. Walter Pater, "Style," in *Appreciations* (London: Macmillan, 1904), p. 36.

12. Edward Thomas, "The Newest Poet," *Daily Chronicle* (London), 23

November 1909, p. 3. A review of Pound's *Exultations;* reprinted in *Ezra Pound: The Critical Heritage,* ed. Eric Homberger (London and Boston: Routledge and Kegan Paul, 1972), pp. 61–62.

13. Harold Monro, *Some Contemporary Poets (1920)* (London: Leonard Parsons, 1920), p. 210.

14. Harold Monro, "The Imagists Discussed," *The Egoist,* 2 (1 May 1915), 79.

15. May Sinclair, "Two Notes," *The Egoist,* 2 (1 June 1915), 88.

16. Pater, *Appreciations,* pp. 19, 18.

17. Pater, *Appreciations,* p. 18.

18. Pater, *Appreciations,* p. 35.

19. Edward Thomas, *Walter Pater: A Critical Study* (London: Martin Secker, 1913), p. 211.

20. Pater, *Appreciations,* p. 19.

21. Thomas, *Walter Pater,* p. 79. See Oscar Wilde, "The Critic as Artist" (1891), in *The Artist as Critic: Critical Writings of Oscar Wilde,* ed. Richard Ellmann (New York: Random House, 1969): "Even the work of Mr. Pater, who is, on the whole, the most perfect master of English prose now creating amongst us, is often far more like a piece of mosaic than a passage in music, and seems, here and there, to lack the true rhythmical life of words and the fine freedom and richness of effect that such rhythmical life produces" (p. 351). Thomas quotes the passage in *Walter Pater,* p. 219.

22. Thomas, *Walter Pater,* p. 202.

23. Pater, *Appreciations,* p. 17.

24. Ezra Pound, "Vortex. Pound," *Blast,* 1 (20 June 1914), 153.

25. Ezra Pound, "How I Began," *T.P.'s Weekly,* 6 June 1913, p. 707.

26. See Ezra Pound, *Gaudier-Brzeska: A Memoir* (New York: New Directions, 1970), p. 89. "Vorticism" first appeared in the *Fortnightly Review,* n.s. 96 (1 September 1914), 461–71.

27. The source seems to be Monro's *Some Contemporary Poets (1920),* p. 93.

28. "Reflections on *vers libre,*" *New Statesman,* 8 (3 March 1917), 518.

29. "Reflections on *vers libre,*" p. 519.

30. *Some Imagist Poets, 1916: An Annual Anthology* (Boston and New York: Houghton Mifflin, 1916), p. ix.

31. *Some Imagist Poets: An Anthology* (Boston and New York: Houghton Mifflin, 1915), pp. vi–vii. This preface, too, was the work of Richard Aldington.

32. *Some Imagist Poets, 1916,* p. xii.

33. "Reflections on *vers libre,*" p. 518.

34. "Reflections on *vers libre,*" p. 519.

35. *Some Imagist Poets (1915),* p. vi. One finds this style of self-presentation everywhere among the modern writers of the period; Pound was perhaps its

master. It is the modesty of the student who got a perfect score on the exam-
ination. He only knows what he is supposed to know, and he assumes that
those who received a lesser score will naturally be eager to learn what it was
they missed.

36. See chapter five herein.

37. Harriet Monroe, *The New Poetry: An Anthology,* ed. Harriet Monroe
and Alice Corbin Henderson (New York: Macmillan, 1917), pp. x–xi, xii.

38. Monroe, p. vi.

39. "The Borderline of Prose," *New Statesman,* 9 (19 May 1917), 158.

40. "The Borderline of Prose," pp. 159, 158.

41. "Reflections on Contemporary Poetry I," *The Egoist,* 4 (September 1917),
118.

42. "Reflections on Contemporary Poetry I," pp. 118–19.

43. See the introduction to *The Sacred Wood: Essays on Poetry and Criticism,*
2d ed. (London: Methuen, 1928), pp. xi–xii. This is the edition cited below.

44. "Reflections on Contemporary Poetry [II]," *The Egoist,* 4 (October 1917),
134.

45. "Reflections on Contemporary Poetry [III]," *The Egoist,* 4 (November
1917), 151.

46. "Whether Rostand Had Something About Him," *The Athenaeum,* 25
July 1919, p. 665.

47. "Reflections on Contemporary Poetry [IV]," *The Egoist,* 6 (July 1919),
39. It is worth putting next to this the relevant passage of Longinus's treatise:

> For many men are carried away by the spirit of others as if inspired, just as it
> is related of the Pythian priestess when she approaches the tripod, where there
> is a rift in the ground which (they say) exhales divine vapour. By heavenly
> power thus communicated she is impregnated and straightway delivers oracles
> in virtue of the afflatus. Similarly from the great natures of the men of old
> there are borne in upon the souls of those who emulate them (as from sacred
> caves) what we may describe as *effluences,* so that even those who seem little
> likely to be possessed are thereby inspired and succumb to the spell of the
> others' greatness. . . . This proceeding is not plagiarism; it is like taking an
> impression from beautiful forms or figures or other works of art. And it seems
> to me that there would not have been so fine a bloom of perfection on Plato's
> philosophical doctrines . . . unless he had with all his heart and mind strug-
> gled with Homer for the primacy. . . . Accordingly it is well that we ourselves
> should shape some idea in our minds as to how perchance Homer would have
> said this very thing . . .

(*On the Sublime,* trans W. Rhys Roberts [Cambridge: Cambridge University
Press, 1899], secs. XIII, XIV, pp. 81–83). Harold Bloom, the contemporary
exponent of Longinus who is also, of course, one of the chief antagonists of
Eliot's version of how literary history is created, has recently cited this passage
from "Reflections on Contemporary Poetry [IV]," with the comment that "I

do not underestimate Eliot here, or elsewhere." Bloom contrasts the "Reflections" with the "official" view of influence presented in "Tradition and the Individual Talent"—official presumably because it was the essay Eliot chose to reprint in *The Sacred Wood;* but there is no evidence that he regarded the "Reflections" as incompatible with the argument of the later essay. See Bloom's *The Breaking of the Vessels* (Chicago and London: University of Chicago Press, 1982), pp. 17–18. There is a distinct echo of "Reflections on Contemporary Poetry [IV]" in Eliot's "Religion and Literature" (1935)—very much an "official"-sounding essay; see Eliot, *Selected Essays,* new ed. (New York: Harcourt, Brace and World, 1950), pp. 348–49.

48. "Reflections on Contemporary Poetry [IV]," p. 39. Eliot's notion of the irruption of the truly original from the mass of tradition is very close to a Longinean conception of sublimity. It reappears in some of the frequently quoted passages of *The Sacred Wood:* "the most individual parts of [the new poet's] work may be those in which the dead poets, his ancestors, assert their immortality most vigorously" ("Tradition and the Individual Talent," p. 48); "Immature poets imitate; mature poets steal" ("Philip Massinger," p. 125; the essay was first published in May 1920). Compare Rupert Brooke: " 'Originality' is only plagiarizing from a great many" ("A Note on John Webster," *Poetry and Drama,* 1 [March 1913]: 29); the similarity of some of Eliot's best-known phrases to the critical observations of his contemporaries is discussed herein in chapter six.

The observations on the nature of poetic composition and the sources of literary excellence that Eliot offered in "Reflections on Contemporary Poetry [IV]" (July 1919) and developed in "Tradition and the Individual Talent" (September and December 1919) may have sprung (for there is nothing quite like them earlier in Eliot's criticism) from some remarks made about the peculiar character of Eliot's own poetry in an anonymous review of his *Poems* (June 1919):

> Mr. Eliot is always quite consciously 'trying for' something, and something which has grown out of and developed beyond all the poems of all the dead poets. Poetry to him seems to be not so much an art as a science, a vast and noble and amusing body of communal feeling upon which the contemporary poet must take a firm stand and then launch himself into the unknown in search of new discoveries. That is the attitude not of the conventional poet, but of the scientist who with the help of working hypotheses hopes to add something, a theory perhaps or a new microbe, to the corpus of human knowledge. . . . The poetry of the dead is in his bones and at the tips of his fingers . . . [a]nd at the same time he is always trying for something new, something which has evolved—one drops instinctively into the scientific terminology—out of the echo or the line, out of the last poem of the last dead poet . . .

("Is This Poetry?" *The Athenaeum,* 20 June 1919, p. 491). Eliot evidently thought Virginia Woolf the author of the review, but it seems that Leonard

Woolf had in fact written these sentences; the Woolfs preferred anonymity because Eliot's *Poems* was a Hogarth Press book. See Virginia Woolf to T. S. Eliot, 28 July 1920, in *The Letters of Virginia Woolf,* ed. Nigel Nicolson and Joanne Trautmann, I (New York and London: Harcourt Brace Jovanovich, 1976), 437.

49. *The Sacred Wood,* p. 51. Part I of "Tradition and the Individual Talent" appeared in *The Egoist,* 6 (September 1919), 54–55; parts II and III in *The Egoist,* 6 (December 1919), 72–73.

50. *The Sacred Wood,* p. 52.

51. Quoted in Arturo Schwarz, *The Complete Works of Marcel Duchamp* (New York: Abrams, n.d.), p. 456. The piece is called "En avance du bras cassé"; it was the first of Duchamp's ready-mades, the most famous of which is the urinal, "Fountain" (1917).

52. Eliot to Charlotte Eliot, 18 December 1919; quoted in *The Waste Land: A Facsimile and Transcript of the Original Drafts,* ed. Valerie Eliot (New York: Harcourt Brace Jovanovich, 1971), p. xviii.

CHAPTER 4

1. The fullest biographical account of the writing of *The Waste Land* is the one provided by Valerie Eliot in the introduction to her edition of *The Waste Land: A Facsimile and Transcript of the Original Drafts* (New York: Harcourt Brace Jovanovich, 1971), pp. ix–xxix. Lyndall Gordon provides a detailed study of the evolution of the manuscript in *Eliot's Early Years* (Oxford: Oxford University Press, 1977), pp. 86–109, 143–46.

2. Conrad Aiken, "An Anatomy of Melancholy," in *T. S. Eliot: The Man and His Work,* ed. Allen Tate (New York: Dell, 1966), p. 195.

3. See Ronald Bush, *T. S. Eliot: A Study in Character and Style* (New York: Oxford University Press, 1984), pp. 67–72.

4. Anthony Cronin, "A Conversation with T. S. Eliot About the Connection Between *Ulysses* and *The Waste Land,*" *The Irish Times,* 16 June 1971, p. 10. The conversation took place in the late 1950s.

5. "Whether Rostand Had Something About Him," *The Athenaeum,* 25 July 1919, p. 665. Eliot was commenting on his sense that the effort to avoid rhetoric had become a rhetoric itself.

6. *Knowledge and Experience in the Philosophy of F. H. Bradley* (London: Faber and Faber, 1964), p. 157. Eliot's dissertation is discussed herein in chapter two.

7. Oscar Wilde, "Mr. Pater's Last Volume," in *The Artist as Critic: Critical Writings of Oscar Wilde,* ed. Richard Ellmann (New York: Random House, 1969), p. 231. Wilde's review first appeared in *Speaker,* 1 (22 March 1890), 319–20.

8. Walter Pater, *The Renaissance: Studies in Art and Poetry*, ed. Donald L. Hill (Berkeley and Los Angeles: University of California Press, 1980), p. 185.

9. Pater, p. 99. For a discussion of Pater's relation to late-nineteenth-century historicism and the development of modern hermeneutics—to the thought of Dilthey, Croce, and Meinecke—see Peter Allan Dale, *The Victorian Critic and the Idea of History: Carlyle, Arnold, Pater* (Cambridge, Mass., and London: Harvard University Press, 1977), pp. 171–205. The co-presence in Pater's writing of two conceptions of the subject—one continuous with outer circumstance (*The Renaissance*), the other a core of individuality radically distinct from everything outside it ("Style")—is noted herein in chapter three, where Pater's troubles with the latter model are discussed.

10. Pater, p. 185.

11. Oscar Wilde, "The Critic as Artist," in *The Artist as Critic*, pp. 382–84.

12. Dale, p. 204.

13. *The Sacred Wood: Essays on Poetry and Criticism*, 2d ed. (London: Methuen, 1928), pp. 49–50. This is the edition cited below.

14. *The Sacred Wood*, pp. 52–53.

15. *The Sacred Wood*, p. 48.

16. Quotations from *The Waste Land* are from the Boni and Liveright edition (1922), reprinted at the end of *The Waste Land: A Facsimile and Transcript of the Original Drafts*, ed. Valerie Eliot.

17. Grover Smith makes this identification in "T. S. Eliot's Lady of the Rocks," *Notes and Queries*, 194 (19 March 1949), 123–25. "The Madonna of the Rocks" is the title given to another Leonardo portrait.

18. Pater, p. 99. Crawling down a wall head first is a habit of vampires, one exhibited by the hero of Bram Stoker's popular *Dracula* (1897). In an earlier version of this passage in *The Waste Land*, the woman gives way first to a vampire, then to a man who wishes not to be reborn, and finally to something like the "diver in deep seas" of Pater's description (see *The Waste Land* facsimile, pp. 113–15).

19. *The Sacred Wood*, p. 52.

20. Wilde, *The Artist as Critic*, p. 398.

21. Wilde, *The Artist as Critic*, pp. 359, 349.

22. Wilde, *The Artist as Critic*, p. 316.

23. J. F. Nisbet, *The Insanity of Genius and the General Inequality of Human Faculty Physiologically Considered*, 6th ed. (New York: Scribner's, 1912), p. 263.

24. Nisbet, pp. xvii, 254, 279; on the elements of literary style, see pp. 254–300.

25. See Allon White, *The Uses of Obscurity: The Fiction of Early Modernism* (London, Boston, and Henley: Routledge and Kegan Paul, 1981), esp. pp. 1–9. White uses the advent of symptomatic reading (the phrase, as he notes, is

borrowed from Althusser) to account for some of the salient characteristics of modernist writing, notably the difficulty it presents to its readers. I am indebted, in this chapter, to his demonstration of the movement's importance.

26. Max Nordau, *Degeneration,* trans. from the 2d German ed. (1895; rpt. New York: Howard Fertig, 1968), p. 17. This is the standard English translation; new editions appeared in 1898, 1913, and 1920.

27. The tendency, that is, to treat the changes that according to evolutionary theory require millennia to produce as though they could happen over the course of a few generations. Ruskin's "The Storm-Cloud of the Nineteenth Century" (1884) is an especially dramatic example of the coloring the Darwinian metaphor could give to the social criticism of modern life. The notion that modernist style was a response to changes in the structure of human consciousness (as opposed, say, to changes in beliefs or social arrangements) belongs to this version of popular Darwinism; it was, of course, an important feature of twentieth-century literary ideology. Virginia Woolf's explanation that "human character changed" in 1910 is a hyperbolic, possibly parodic instance of the mode. Eliot's theory of the dissociation of sensibility (like Ruskin's and Nordau's, and unlike Woolf's, a *de*volutionary account) is discussed as a contribution to this manner of accounting for cultural change in chapter six herein.

28. Nordau, pp. 42, 40, 41.

29. Nordau, p. 27.

30. Nordau, pp. 318–19.

31. Nordau, p. 336.

32. The manuscript of Eliot's paper—usually referred to as "The Interpretation of Primitive Ritual"—is in the Hayward Bequest in the King's College Library, Cambridge. Eliot describes the paper briefly but usefully (and gives it its title) in his introduction to Charlotte Eliot's *Savonarola: A Dramatic Poem* (London: R. Cobden-Sanderson, n.d. [1926]), p. viii. Substantial selections are quoted in Piers Gray, *T. S. Eliot's Intellectual and Poetic Development 1909–1922* (Sussex: Harvester Press, 1982), pp. 108–42. A summary of the paper and the seminar discussion that followed appears in *Josiah Royce's Seminar, 1913–1914: As Recorded in the Notebooks of Harry T. Costello,* ed. Grover Smith (New Brunswick, N.J.: Rutgers University Press, 1963), pp. 72–87. I have generally quoted from Costello's version of Eliot's paper (which Gray reports to be faithful to the substance of the manuscript); quotations of Eliot's remarks to Royce are, of course, from the same source.

33. *Josiah Royce's Seminar,* p. 85. Eliot seems to have been willing, for the purposes of this argument, to regard interpretation in natural science as a nonproblem: "[T]here is a difference," he explained, "between natural and social evolution in that in the former we are able practically to neglect all values that are internal to the process, and consider the process from the point of view of *our* value, wh[ich] is for our purposes conceived of as outside the

process. . . . While to some extent in a social progress, and to a very great extent in religious progress, the internal values are part of the external description" (quoted in Gray, p. 115). But he took a more radical view in his dissertation, where he argued that an external object of any kind is an insupportable abstraction: "in order to conceive the development of the world, in the science of geology, let us say, we have to present it as it would have looked had we, with *our* bodies and our nervous systems, been there to see it. [But] [t]o say that the world was as we describe it, a million years ago, is a statement which overlooks the development of mind" (*Knowledge and Experience*, p. 22). The nature of a rock, that is, depends on the nature of the mind that observes it; we can assume that rocks were different things a million years ago because we assume that minds were different as well.

34. *Josiah Royce's Seminar*, p. 78.

35. *Josiah Royce's Seminar*, p. 76.

36. *Josiah Royce's Seminar*, p. 78.

37. *Josiah Royce's Seminar*, p. 77.

38. It is part of the tradition of *Waste Land* hermeneutics to regard the notes as more or less incidental to the poem proper, and therefore as bits of text that can be treated selectively—some notes may be considered more applicable than others, at the discretion of the commentator—and at face value, as meaning what they say in a way the rest of the poem is assumed not to. (Thus, for instance, the poem has been reprinted in various anthologies, including *The Norton Anthology of English Literature*, with editorial annotations of some lines interspersed among Eliot's own notes.) It is true, of course, that *The Waste Land* was first published without the notes, which Eliot added for the book edition; but they appeared together in every subsequent reprinting. The relevance of Eliot's graduate paper on interpretation alone, not to mention the larger intellectual background I have sketched in, seems enough to justify an approach that considers the notes as part of the poem; but even if Eliot did intend the notes to be straightforward elucidations of the meaning, or some part of the meaning, of his poem, on what hermeneutical grounds can they be considered differently from the rest of the text?

It might be noted that when Arnold Bennett asked Eliot, in 1924, whether the notes to *The Waste Land* were "a skit," Eliot answered that "they were serious, and not more of a skit than some things in the poem itself" (*The Journals of Arnold Bennett*, ed. Newman Flower [London: Cassell, 1933], III, 52; entry for 10 September 1924). For Eliot's own comments on the circumstances of publication that led to the production of the notes, see "The Frontiers of Criticism" (1956), in *On Poetry and Poets* (New York: Farrar, Straus and Cudahy, 1957), pp. 121–22. It is natural (on my view of the poem) that Eliot should generally have disparaged the explanatory (as opposed to the literary) significance of the notes—they are, in any case, fairly self-disparaging as they stand—since their interpretive inadequacy is precisely their point.

39. The conflation, for instance, of the iconography of the Tarot pack, the symbolic figures of Frazer's vegetation rites, and the mythology of Christianity (highlighted by the note to line 46).

40. See A. Walton Litz, "*The Waste Land* Fifty Years After," in *Eliot in His Time*, ed. Litz (Princeton: Princeton University Press, 1973), p. 7.

41. See Edmund Wilson, Jr., "The Poetry of Drouth," *The Dial*, 73 (December 1922), 611–16 ("the very images and the sound of the words—even when we do not know precisely why he has chosen them—are charged with a strange poignancy which seems to bring us into the heart of the singer" [p. 616]); I. A. Richards, *Principles of Literary Criticism*, 2d ed. (1925; rpt. New York and London: Harcourt Brace Jovanovich, n.d.), pp. 289–95 ("the poem still remains to be read. . . . But that is not difficult to those who still know how to give their feelings precedence to their thoughts, who can accept and unify an experience without trying to catch it in an intellectual net or to squeeze out a doctrine. . . . The ideas [in Eliot's poetry] . . . combine into a coherent whole of feeling and attitude" [pp. 292–3]); F. R. Leavis, *New Bearings in English Poetry* (London: Chatto and Windus, 1932), pp. 90–113 ("the unity of *The Waste Land* is no more 'metaphysical' than it is narrative or dramatic. . . . The unity the poem aims at is that of an inclusive consciousness" [p. 103]).

42. See Frank Kermode, "A Babylonish Dialect," in *T. S. Eliot: The Man and His Work*, ed. Tate, p. 240; and Eloise Knapp Hay, *T. S. Eliot's Negative Way* (Cambridge, Mass., and London: Harvard University Press, 1982), p. 48.

43. See A. D. Moody, *Thomas Stearns Eliot: Poet* (Cambridge: Cambridge University Press, 1979), p. 79; and Gordon, *Eliot's Early Years*, p. 110.

44. Virginia Woolf, *The Diary of Virginia Woolf*, ed. Anne Olivier Bell, II (New York and London: Harcourt Brace Jovanovich, 1978), 203. Entry for 26 September 1922.

45. "Contemporary English Prose," *Vanity Fair*, 20 (July 1923), 51. First published, in French, in *Nouvelle Revue Française*, 19 (1 December 1922), pp. 751–56; it was solicited for *Vanity Fair* by the magazine's young managing editor, Edmund Wilson (see Wilson, *Letters on Literature and Politics 1912–1972*, ed. Elena Wilson [New York: Farrar, Straus and Giroux, 1977], p. 103).

46. "The Function of Criticism," *The Criterion*, 2 (October 1923), 40–41, 42.

47. Introduction to *Savonarola*, p. vii.

48. Introduction to *The Wheel of Fire: Essays in Interpretation of Shakespeare's Sombre Tragedies*, by G. Wilson Knight (London: Oxford University Press, 1930), pp. xv–xvi, xix.

49. Joseph H. Summers, *The Heirs of Donne and Johnson* (New York and London: Oxford University Press, 1970), p. 129.

CHAPTER 5

1. Ezra Pound to Henry Ware Eliot, Sr., 28 June 1915, typed transcript of draft, Pound Center, Bienecke Library, Yale University. The passage beginning "Browning in his *Dramatis Personae*" and ending "in their day" is cancelled in the original manuscript.

2. We can say that modernism possesses this ambivalence, I think, because it is part of the way the subject is perceived; a number of recent critical works on modernism seem to have been provoked by an interest in accounting for it. See generally C. K. Stead, *The New Poetic* (London: Hutchinson, 1964); Robert Langbaum, *The Modern Spirit: Essays on the Continuity of Nineteenth and Twentieth Century Literature* (New York: Oxford University Press, 1970); and George Bornstein, *Transformations of Romanticism in Yeats, Eliot, and Stevens* (Chicago: University of Chicago Press, 1976).

3. Joseph Conrad, *Youth and Two Other Stories* (Garden City and New York: Doubleday, Page, 1922), p. 45. Conrad's story first appeared in *Blackwood's Edinburgh Magazine*, February–April 1899; *Youth and Two Other Stories* was published by Blackwood in 1902.

4. Conrad, p. 45.

5. Lionel Trilling, for example, inexplicably assigns several of the narrator's remarks about England to Marlow, in *Sincerity and Authenticity* (Cambridge, Mass.: Harvard University Press, 1972), pp. 108–9.

6. Conrad, p. 48.

7. Conrad, p. 48.

8. Conrad, pp. 153–54.

9. Conrad, pp. 69, 79, 75.

10. Conrad, pp. 73–74.

11. The station manager might be called an instance of brute professionalism. He displays certain underdeveloped attributes of the professional type, which I will discuss more fully later on. He also represents a development in fictional characterization. If he were to appear in a novel by Dickens, he would have a tic to stand for the repressed side of his nature, and the point of Conrad's character is that he has none. The station manager should also be distinguished, of course, from a character type encountered in the novels of Dickens and Lawrence and elsewhere in Conrad's work—the worker who identifies with his job without remainder, so to speak, precisely because it is a source of personal fulfillment.

12. Conrad, p. 79. Ian Watt explains the historical circumstances that led to men like Kurtz being sent to Africa in *Conrad in the Nineteenth Century* (Berkeley and Los Angeles: University of California Press, 1979), pp. 139–40.

13. Conrad, p. 138.

14. Conrad, pp. 137–38.

15. See Jonah Raskin, "*Heart of Darkness*: The Manuscript Revisions," *Re-*

view of English Studies, n.s. 18 (1967), 35. Kurtz's cry in the final version—
" 'Oh, but I will wring your heart yet!' " (p. 148)—is a little more the cry of
a lover, and therefore belongs to another story of the story.

E. J. Hobsbawm observes of the nineteenth-century reputation of the early
industrialist:

> The capitalist manufacturers of the first phase of industrial revolution were—
> or saw themselves as—a pioneering minority seeking to establish an economic
> system in an environment by no means entirely favourable to it: surrounded by
> a population deeply distrustful of their efforts, employing a working-class un-
> accustomed to industrialism and hostile to it, struggling—at least initially—to
> build their factories out of modest capital and ploughed-back profits by absti-
> nence, hard work and grinding the faces of the poor. The epics of the rise of
> the Victorian middle class, as preserved in the works of Samuel Smiles, looked
> back to an often quite mythical era of heroes of self-help, expelled by the stupid
> progress-hating multitude yet returning later in triumph and top hats

(*Industry and Empire* [Harmondsworth: Penguin, 1969], p. 121). It is this my-
thos of early industrialism, and not the historical facts of it, that matters to
my reading of *Heart of Darkness* and to the analysis of the ideology of occupation that follows. It is perhaps worth repeating that the argument of this
chapter is an argument about perception, the perception of literature in the
context of the value attributed to certain kinds of work; it is not an argument
about changes in the things themselves. *Heart of Darkness,* in other words, is
evidence of the way the history of the capitalist enterprise looked in 1899, but
(though it seems to reflect an actual process of economic and social change) it
is not itself a history.

16. This is a thesis, now generally accepted, first put forward by John Gal-
lagher and Ronald Robinson in "The Imperialism of Free Trade," *Economic
History Review,* 2d series 6 (1953), 1–15. An account of the change this article
made in the existing version of economic history can be found in C. C. Eld-
ridge, *Victorian Imperialism* (Atlantic Highlands, N.J.: Humanities Press, 1978),
pp. 5–8. In the discussion that follows, I have relied in part on the extended
and persuasive application of the thesis made in Hobsbawm, pp. 109–53, 172–
93.

17. Hobsbawm, p. 192.

18. The verb is Marlow's (and Conrad's) favorite. "Do you see him?" Marlow asks his companions. "Do you see the story? Do you see anything? . . .
Of course in this you fellows see more than I could then. You see me, whom
you know . . ." (Conrad, pp. 82–83).

19. Conrad, p. 94. On the spirit of British business at the turn of the
century, see D. H. Aldcroft, "The Entrepreneur and the British Economy,
1870–1914," *Economic History Review,* 2d series 17 (1964), 113–34; and
Hobsbawm, pp. 182–85.

20. Conrad, p. 122.

21. Conrad, pp. 55–56.

22. Conrad, pp. 121, 130. On the evidence of the manuscript, Conrad had some trouble deciding whether to call the heads "symbols" or "symbolic" (see Raskin, p. 34). "Symbolist" as a term for contemporary art and literature was in vogue in the 1890s; it was at the same time Conrad was writing *Heart of Darkness* that Arthur Symons was trying to settle—with the assistance of W. B. Yeats—on the best term for the French writers he had discussed in the essays to be collected in *The Symbolist Movement in Literature* (1899) (see Richard Ellmann, "Discovering Symbolism," in *Golden Codgers: Biographical Speculations* [New York and Oxford: Oxford University Press, 1973], pp. 101–12). So Conrad may have had something like the Romantic—and almost certainly had something like the artistic—sense of the word in mind when he called the heads "symbolic."

23. Conrad, p. 134.

24. On the clothing Apollo Korzeniowski dressed his son in, see Zdzisław Najder, *Joseph Conrad: A Chronicle* (New Brunswick, N.J.: Rutgers University Press, 1983), p. 14. It might be noted as well (if we are looking for hints of Conrad himself in the story) that, like the "harlequin," Conrad went to sea to avoid conscription in the Russian army, to which, as a citizen of the Russian empire, he was subject. The harlequin's patchwork suggests, in the context of the map, Conrad's own mixed national identities. Tadeusz Bobrowski's comment is quoted in Najder, p. 102.

25. The notion that exceptional mental ability reflects a physiological condition only marginally different from madness was, as we have seen (chapter four herein) part of the popular psychology of the nineties. It was the suggestion of the works that promoted this view—Nisbet's *The Insanity of Genius* (1891), Nordau's *Degeneration* (1892), Cesare Lombroso's *The Man of Genius* (1891), where genius is defined as "a special morbid condition" ([London: Walter Scott], p. v)—that when to call a certain type of behavior inspired and when to call it demented is a decision that depends on social tastes, not physiological facts, since the physiologies are virtually the same. So Kurtz, whose condition is read by Marlow as authenticity and by the station manager as insanity, fits the contemporary paradigm nicely.

When writers and artists of the 1890s referred to themselves as decadents, they were responding to this Victorian obsession with the dangers of physiological abnormality. Arthur Symons, for example, described decadent literature as "a new and beautiful and interesting disease. Healthy we cannot call it, and healthy it does not wish to be considered" ("The Decadent Movement in Literature," *Harper's New Monthly Magazine*, 87 [November 1893], 859). And Wilde's consistent equation of art and criminality—particularly sexual deviance—plays on Lombroso's and Nordau's diagnosis of the avant-garde artist as a sociopathic type. This is an aspect of late-nineteenth-century culture that is, strictly speaking, outside the context of professionalism, but it should be kept in mind as yet another pressure being exerted on such traditional items in the vocabulary used to characterize literary excellence as "genius," "inspiration," and "originality."

26. See chapter one herein. This use of literary form predates twentieth-century modernism, of course. Joyce's *Dubliners* (1916), with its style of "scrupulous meanness," is a classic example of the technique in its early, Flaubertian mode. But later modernist developments go far beyond Flaubert's manner of generating irony by treating petit-bourgeois manners in a slightly banal, but still correct, classical style.

27. "*Ulysses*, Order and Myth," *The Dial*, 75 (November 1923), 483. Some of the peculiarities of Eliot's doctrine of the objective correlative are discussed herein in chapter six.

28. See Magali Sarfatti Larson, *The Rise of Professionalism: A Sociological Analysis* (Berkeley, Los Angeles, and London: University of California Press, 1977), pp. 53–63. I am particularly indebted to the analyses of the phenomenon of professionalism given in this work and in Burton J. Bledstein's *The Culture of Professionalism: The Middle Class and the Development of Higher Education in America* (New York and London: W. W. Norton, 1976).

29. G. H. Lewes, "The Principles of Success in Literature," *Fortnightly Review*, 1 (15 May 1865), 86. The article was the first in a series; they were collected and published as a book, after Lewes's death, in 1898 (London: Walter Scott).

30. Lewes, pp. 85, 94.

31. Lewes, pp. 86, 87, 89.

32. Lewes, p. 95.

33. *The Three Trials of Oscar Wilde,* ed. H. Montgomery Hyde (New York: New York University Books, 1956), p. 124. The exchange took place during Wilde's first trial (*Reg.* v. *Queensberry*), 3 April 1895.

34. See, for example, Jocelyn Baines, *Joseph Conrad: A Critical Biography* (London: Weidenfeld and Nicolson, 1960), pp. 141–48; and Najder, pp. 170–71.

35. See the *OED*. The dictionary also notes that Mayhew recorded the terms "amateur" and "professional" being applied to prostitutes in London street talk in 1861, which is a nice instance of a middle-class honorific functioning as a working-class sarcasm—a reminder, too, of the fact that (except when there is a Mayhew around) dictionaries only pick up a usage when those who write have coined or caught up with it.

36. See Geoffrey Millerson, *The Qualifying Associations: A Study in Professionalization* (London: Routledge and Kegan Paul, 1964), esp. pp. 183–86; Larson, p. 5; Bledstein, p. 288.

37. See Emile Durkheim, *The Division of Labor in Society,* trans. George Simpson (Glencoe, Ill.: Free Press, 1933), pp. 29–31.

38. Sidney and Beatrice Webb and G. Bernard Shaw, "Special Supplement

on Professional Associations," *The New Statesman*, 9 (21 and 28 April 1917), 48.

39. R. H. Tawney, *The Acquisitive Society* (London: G. Bell and Sons, 1921), pp. 187, 180. A somewhat different version of this work appeared in the United States in 1920.

40. See Bledstein, pp. 85–87. For a full-length study of the case of the social sciences, see Thomas L. Haskell, *The Emergence of Professional Social Science: The American Social Science Association and the Nineteenth-Century Crisis of Authority* (Urbana: University of Illinois Press, 1977); on the professionalization of philosophy, see Bruce Kuklick, *The Rise of American Philosophy: Cambridge, Massachusetts, 1860–1930* (New Haven and London: Yale University Press, 1977).

41. Edward Marsh, "Prefatory Note," *Georgian Poetry 1911–1912* (London: Poetry Bookshop, 1912).

42. Rebecca West, "Imagisme," *The New Freewoman*, 1 (15 August 1913), 86. This manner of presenting its work collectively was one of the things Amy Lowell objected to in Pound's management of the Imagist movement; she made a point of insisting on the independence of the writers represented in *Some Imagist Poets*.

43. Taylor was the author of *The Principles of Scientific Management* (1911), Gilbreth of *A Primer of Scientific Management* (1911). As efficiency engineers, they considered themselves, of course, professionals. Gilbreth organized the Society for the Promotion of the Science of Management, later known as the Taylor Society.

44. See Larson, pp. 4–6.

45. J. M. M[urry], "The Condition of English Poetry," *The Athenaeum*, 5 December 1919, p. 1283 (a review of the fourth volume of *Georgian Poetry* and the fourth "cycle" of *Wheels*). See also Murry's unsigned leader, "Modern Poetry and Modern Society," *The Athenaeum*, 16 May 1919, pp. 325–26. On the general reaction against literary corporatism, see Robert H. Ross, *The Georgian Revolt: The Rise and Fall of a Poetic Ideal, 1910–1922* (Carbondale and Edwardsville: Southern Illinois University Press, 1965), esp. pp. 136–38, 197–200. On Pound's disenchantment with the anti-individualistic flavor of the programmatic literary movement, see Michael H. Levenson, *A Genealogy of Modernism: A Study of English Literary Doctrine 1908–1922* (Cambridge: Cambridge University Press, 1984), pp. 135–36.

46. See Hubert Langerock, "Professionalism: A Study in Professional Deformation," *American Journal of Sociology*, 21 (1915–16), 30–44.

47. See F. H. Hayward, *Professionalism and Originality* (Chicago: Open Court, 1917), pp. 9–106. Hayward saw aestheticism as an example of "the treason of professionalism": "The artist's formula is 'art for art's sake' by which he means that he may set aside morals, etc., in his search for beauty, or even that the

interests of the world as a whole are to be subordinated to the professional ideals of artists" (p. 26).

48. "Professionalism in Art," *Times Literary Supplement,* 31 January 1918, pp. 49–50. The apparent contradiction ("easy difficulties") belongs to the logic of antiprofessionalism: by making tasks appear difficult, professionalism makes it easy for anyone—by dint of application but without inspiration—to perform them. (This was the kind of judgment I have suggested Conrad, for instance, was hoping to avoid.)

49. "Professional, Or . . .," *The Egoist,* 5 (April 1918), 61.

50. "In Memory of Henry James," *The Egoist,* 5 (January 1918), 2.

51. "Turgenev," *The Egoist,* 4 (December 1917), 167.

52. See "In Memory of Henry James": "It is the final perfection, the consummation of an American to become, not an Englishman, but a European— something which no born European, no person of any European nationality, can become" (p. 1).

53. See Larson, p. 4.

54. Marsh's argument for excluding Frost from the second *Georgian Poetry* (see Ross, p. 110). As Ross notes, Marsh had approached Pound for a contribution for the first volume. It may have been the nature of the public reception of that volume, its somewhat patriotic tone, that persuaded Marsh to adopt this policy.

55. "Verse Pleasant and Unpleasant," *The Egoist,* 5 (March 1918), 43.

56. "Observations," *The Egoist,* 5 (May 1918), 69.

57. "Professional, Or . . .," p. 61.

58. "The Perfect Critic," in *The Sacred Wood: Essays on Poetry and Criticism,* 2d ed. (London: Methuen, 1928), p. 1. This is the edition cited below.

59. "Style and Thought," *The Nation,* 22 (23 March 1918), 770.

60. *The Diary of Virginia Woolf,* ed. Anne Olivier Bell, II (New York and London: Harcourt Brace Jovanovich, 1978), 203. Entry for 26 September 1922. See also Eliot's "The Lesson of Baudelaire," *The Tyro,* 1 (Spring 1921): "Tennyson decorated the morality he found in vogue; Browning really approached the problem [of morality], but with too little seriousness, with too much complacency" (p. 4).

61. "The Romantic Generation, If It Existed," *The Athenaeum,* 18 July 1919, p. 616.

62. "London Letter," *The Dial,* 72 (May 1922), 510. See also the letters Eliot contributed to the issues of April 1921, October 1921, and July 1922.

63. "The Lesson of Baudelaire," p. 4. The statement recapitulates the argument—or one side of the argument—of Matthew Arnold's "The Literary Influence of Academies" (1863). Arnold was, of course, useful to Eliot's attack on the Romantic tradition; the charge in "The Function of Criticism at the Present Time" (1864) that the Romantics "did not know enough" is resur-

rected as a piece of unfinished critical business in the introduction to *The Sacred Wood.* It was one of the trickier assignments Eliot faced in his critical writing to enlist Arnold as an authority in the case against Romanticism and at the same time to hold him up as a cautionary example of Romanticism's deleterious effects.

64. "The Three Provincialities," *The Tyro,* 2 (1922), 11–12.

65. See A. C. Bradley, "The Reaction Against Tennyson," in *A Miscellany* (London: Macmillan, 1929), pp. 1–31. Originally delivered as a lecture to the English Association, 1914. He was wrong, of course; the real damage was done in the twenties, by Harold Nicolson's *Tennyson: Aspects of His Life, Character, and Poetry* (1923) and Hugh I'Anson Fausset's *Tennyson: A Modern Portrait* (1923)—books that gave Eliot the chance, in his 1936 essay on *In Memoriam,* to seem even a little iconoclastic by making an unexpected display of sympathy.

66. See Herbert Spencer, *The Principles of Sociology,* III (New York: D.-Appleton, 1896), 179–324.

67. Hayward, p. 3.

68. "The Post-Georgians," *The Athenaeum,* 11 April 1919, p. 172.

69. "A Foreign Mind," *The Athenaeum,* 4 July 1919, p. 533. This was, appropriately, something of a party line on Yeats, which indicates the problems a nineteenth-century reputation could pose in 1919; see J. Middleton Murry's unsigned review of *The Wild Swans at Coole,* "Mr. Yeats' Swan Song," *The Athenaeum,* 4 April 1919, p. 136:

> even when the poet turns from legend and history to create his own myth, he must make one whose validity is visible, if he is not to be condemned to the sterility of a coterie. The lawless and fantastic shapes of his own imagination need, even for their own perfect embodiment, the discipline of the common perception. The phantoms of the individual brain, left to their own waywardness, lose all solidity and become like primary forms of life, instead of the penultimate forms they should be.

70. Clive Bell, "Tradition and Movements,"*The Athenaeum,* 4 April 1919, p. 142.

71. John Drinkwater, "Tradition and Technique," *Poetry Review,* 1 (July 1912), 296, 300. The "danger rarely equalled" is not specified, but it seems to be a purely literary one, apparently the loss of the art of versification.

Compare, with both Drinkwater and Bell, these sentences from "Tradition and the Individual Talent":

> We dwell with satisfaction upon the poet's difference from his predecessors, especially his immediate predecessors; we endeavour to find something that can be isolated in order to be enjoyed. Whereas if we approach a poet without his [sic] prejudice we shall often find that not only the best, but the most individual parts of his work may be those in which the dead poets, his ancestors,

assert their immortality most vigorously. . . . Tradition . . . cannot be inherited, and if you want it you must obtain it by great labour. . . . [The poet] must be aware that the mind of Europe . . . is a mind which changes, and that this change is a development which abandons nothing *en route,* which does not superannuate either Shakespeare, or Homer, or the rock drawing of the Magdalenian draughtsmen. . . . There are many people who can appreciate the expression of sincere emotion in verse, and there is a smaller number of people who can appreciate technical excellence. But very few know when there is expression of *significant* emotion, emotion which has its life in the poem and not in the history of the poet. [Bell: "So, by insisting on the fact that Matisse, Cézanne, Poussin, Piero and Giotto are all in the tradition we insist on the fact that they are all artists. We rob them of their amusing but adscititious qualities; we make them utterly uninteresting to precisely 99.99 per cent. of our fellow creatures; and overselves we make unpopular" (p. 142).] The emotion of art is impersonal. And the poet cannot reach this impersonality without surrendering himself wholly to the work to be done

(*The Sacred Wood,* pp. 48, 49, 51, 59).

72. The extent to which what seems new in Eliot's early criticism can be understood as simply a reinscription of conventional critical notions is discussed herein in chapter six. In the case of "Tradition and the Individual Talent," the last-minute and rather unconvincing effort—mostly rhetorical—to distinguish the essay's account of the process of poetic composition from the Wordsworthian formula of "emotion recollected in tranquillity" (see p. 58) is a good instance in point. One imagines that Eliot began the essay intending in a general way to discredit the valorization of originality popularly associated with Romanticism, and then found unexpectedly and somewhat disconcertingly that he had ended up producing a description of successful literary practice that seemed to echo Wordsworth's.

Inconsistencies in *The Sacred Wood*'s treatment of Romanticism are discussed, though (incorrectly, I think) in disparagement of Eliot, in Ernest J. Lovell, Jr., "The Heretic in the Sacred Wood; Or, the Naked Man, the Tired Man, and the Romantic Aristocrat: William Blake, T. S. Eliot, and George Wyndham," in *Romantic and Victorian: Studies in Memory of William H. Marshall,* ed. W. Paul Elledge and Richard L. Hoffman (Rutherford, N. J.: Fairleigh Dickinson University Press, 1971), pp. 75–94. See also, for a reading of Eliot's remarks about poetic composition in the light of nineteenth-century literary values, Stead, *The New Poetic,* pp. 125–47.

73. "The Perfect Critic," in *The Sacred Wood,* pp. 12–13.

74. "London Letter," *The Dial,* 70 (April 1921), 451.

75. "Poetry and Criticism," *TLS,* 2 December 1920, p. 795 (a review of *The Sacred Wood).* For more enthusiastic responses to the "scientific" quality of Eliot's detachment, see L[eonard] W[oolf], "Back to Aristotle," *The Athenaeum,* 17 December 1920, pp. 834–35; and Marianne Moore, "The Sacred Wood," *The Dial,* 70 (March 1921), 336-39. "It makes some of us feel," wrote

F. R. Leavis some years later about Eliot's criticism, "that we never read criticism before" ("T. S. Eliot—A Reply to the Condescending," *The Cambridge Review*, 8 February 1929, p. 254).

76. See Eric Hobsbawm, "Mass-Producing Traditions: Europe, 1870–1914," in *The Invention of Tradition*, ed. Hobsbawm and Terence Ranger (Cambridge: Cambridge University Press, 1983), pp. 263–307; and also his remarks in *Industry and Empire*, p. 170.

CHAPTER 6

1. See F. N. Lees, "The Dissociation of Sensibility: Arthur Hallam and T. S. Eliot," *Notes and Queries*, n.s. 14 (1967), 308–9; and Carol T. Christ, "T. S. Eliot and the Victorians," *Modern Philology*, 79 (1981), 159–60.

2. "Preface to the 1928 Edition," *The Sacred Wood: Essays on Poetry and Criticism*, 2d ed. (London: Methuen, 1928), p. viii. This is the edition cited below.

3. "The most remarkable property of [Keats's] poetry . . . is the degree in which it combines the sensuous with the ideal. . . .His body seemed to think; and, on the other hand, he sometimes appears hardly to have known whether he possessed aught but body. His whole nature partook of a sensational character in this respect, namely, that every thought and sentiment came upon him with the suddenness, and appealed to him with the reality of a sensation." [Aubrey Thomas de Vere], *Edinburgh Review*, 90 (July–October 1849), 425–26.

4. "[Donne] belonged to an age when men were not afraid to mate their intellects with their emotions." Rupert Brooke, "John Donne, The Elizabethan," *The Nation*, 12 (15 February 1913), 825. See also Brooke's "John Donne," *Poetry and Drama*, 1 (June 1913), 185–88: "The pageant of the outer world of matter and the mid-region of the passions came to Donne through the brain. The whole composition of the man was made up of brain, soul, and heart in a different proportion from the ordinary prescription. This does not mean that he felt less keenly than others; but when passion shook him, and his being ached for utterance, to relieve the stress, expression came through the intellect" (p. 186).

5. See David J. DeLaura, "Pater and Eliot: The Origin of the Objective Correlative," *Modern Language Quarterly*, 26 (1965), 426–31; R. W. Stallman, ed., *The Critic's Notebook* (Minneapolis: University of Minnesota Press, 1950), p. 116; Pasquale DiPasquale, Jr., "Coleridge's Framework of Objectivity and Eliot's Objective Correlative," *Journal of Asethetics and Art History*, 26 (1968), 489–500; and René Wellek, *A History of Modern Criticism: 1750–1950*, I (New Haven: Yale University Press, 1955), 253–54.

6. Pound took Eliot in 1916 to see Yeats's *At the Hawk's Well*, the first of

the Noh-influenced plays. On the Noh plays and Imagism, see Eliot's "The Noh and the Image," *The Egoist*, 4 (August 1917), 102-3; on the possible influence of the Poundian aesthetic on this aspect of Yeats's work, see Francis J. Thompson, "Ezra in Dublin," *University of Toronto Quarterly*, 21 (1951), 64–77.

7. Ford Madox Hueffer, "From China to Peru," *The Outlook*, 35 (19 June 1915), 800.

8. Richard Aldington, "Modern Poetry and the Imagists," *The Egoist*, 1 (1 June 1914), 202.

9. John Gould Fletcher, "Three Imagist Poets," *Little Review*, 3 (May 1916), 30.

10. D[ora] M[arsden], "The Work of Miss Rebecca West," *The Egoist*, 5 (October 1918), 115.

11. The immediate problem, as Pound and Hulme seem to have understood it, was that of distinguishing the Image from the late-nineteenth-century Symbol. We can see the kind of explicit transcendentalism the Imagist formula tries to avoid in, for example, Yeats's essay on "The Symbolism of Poetry" (1900): "All sounds, all colours, all forms, either because of their preordained energies or because of long association, evoke indefinable and yet precise emotions, or, as I prefer to think, call down among us certain disembodied powers, whose footsteps over our hearts we call emotions" (*Essays and Introductions* [New York: Macmillan, 1961], pp. 156–57). See Ezra Pound, "Status Rerum," *Poetry*, 1 (1913), 123–27, for Pound's effort to dissociate his poetic from Yeats's. Frank Kermode weighs the significance of the distinction between the modernist image and the Romantic symbol, and finds it minimal, in his chapter on Hulme in *Romantic Image* (London: Routledge and Kegan Paul, 1957), pp. 119–37. See also Graham Hough, *Image and Experience: Reflections on a Literary Revolution* (Lincoln: University of Nebraska Press, 1960), where Imagism is defined as "roughly Symbolism without the magic" (p. 9); and Ian Fletcher, "Some Anticipations of Imagism," in *A Catalogue of Imagist Poets* (New York: J. Howard Woolman, 1966), pp. 39–53, which offers a similar definition (Poundian Imagism is "Symbolism with its 'magical' components discounted" [p.43]). This conclusion has been disputed: see Donald Davie, *Ezra Pound: Poet as Sculptor* (New York: Oxford University Press, 1964), pp. 65–67; and Herbert N. Schneidau, *Ezra Pound: The Image and the Real* (Baton Rouge: Louisiana State University Press, 1969). For an account of the metamorphosis of the "soft," "subjective" symbol or impression into the "hard," "objective" Vorticist image, see Michael H. Levenson, *A Genealogy of Modernism: A Study of English Literary Doctrine 1908–1922* (Cambridge: Cambridge University Press, 1984), pp. 103–36.

12. "Hamlet and His Problems," in *The Sacred Wood*, p. 100. The essay appeared originally in *The Athenaeum*, 26 September 1919, pp. 940–41; it is

reprinted as "Hamlet" in *Selected Essays,* new ed. (New York: Harcourt, Brace and World, 1950), pp. 121–26. There are slight variations among the three versions.

13. *The Sacred Wood,* p. 101.

14. *The Sacred Wood,* p. 100. *Selected Essays* has 'Shakespeare's Hamlet" (p. 124).

15. *Selected Essays,* p. 126. *The Sacred Wood* (p. 102) and the *Athenaeum* version (p. 941) have "a study to pathologists."

16. *The Sacred Wood,* pp. 101, 102. Eliot's essay on *Hamlet* appeared in September 1919; it is worth noting, in connection with the essay's speculation about the emotional circumstances of Shakespeare's life, that Eliot has already read, in manuscript form, Stephen Dedalus's virtuosic biographical criticism of *Hamlet* in the "Scylla and Charybdis" chapter of *Ulysses*—remarking in a letter to John Quinn, dated 9 July 1919, "I have lived on it ever since I read it." See Robert Adams Day, "Joyce's Waste Land and Eliot's Unknown God," *Wisconsin Literary Monographs,* ed. Eric Rothstein, 4 (Madison, Milwaukee, and London: University of Wisconsin Press, 1971), 180.

17. For instance, in his now well-known remark about *The Waste Land*: "Various critics . . . have considered it, indeed, as an important bit of social criticism. To me it was only the relief of a personal and wholly insignificant grouse against life" (quoted in *The Waste Land: A Facsimile and Transcript of the Original Drafts,* ed. Valerie Eliot [New York: Harcourt Brace Jovanovich, 1971], p. 1); and in his comment, two years before his death, to Herbert Read that his best poetry had cost him dearly in experience (see Peter Ackroyd, *T. S. Eliot: A Life* [New York: Simon and Schuster, 1984], p. 334).

18. "Tradition and the Individual Talent," in *The Sacred Wood,* pp. 56, 55, 56, 57, 58.

19. *The Sacred Wood,* p. 59.

20. The issue of the relation between the poet's experience and the emotional value of the poem was, of course, always a complicated one. The nineteenth-century writer did not consider "sincerity" a purely representational value. When Tennyson insisted that *In Memoriam* was *"not* an actual biography" (Hallam Tennyson, *Alfred Lord Tennyson: A Memoir* [New York: Macmillan, 1897], I, 304), he did not mean to say that it was not sincere. Robert Langbaum discusses the problem of the poetic persona and the requirement of sincerity in *The Poetry of Experience: The Dramatic Monologue in Modern Literary Tradition* ([New York: Random House, 1957], esp. pp. 28–35), where he suggests that *"Insincerity* together with its offshoot in Yeats' *mask,* in fact the whole literary attempt since the late nineteenth century to escape from personality, have created a literature in which sincerity and autobiography are encoded, written backwards" (p. 35). What is remarkable about Eliot's critical prescriptions on the matter is that while he continues to tie the aes-

thetically distinctive character of a given poem to the "real" self of the poet, he has given that self almost nothing to express.

21. "Shorter Notices," *The Egoist,* 5 (June–July 1918), 87. Unsigned.

22. Clive Bell, *Art* (London: Chatto and Windus, 1913), pp 7–8.

23. Bell, p. 25. Compare Eliot's "The Perfect Critic": "a literary critic should have no emotions except those immediately provoked by a work of art—and these (as I have already hinted) are, when valid, perhaps not to be called emotions at all" (*The Sacred Wood,* pp. 12–13); and "Tradition and the Individual Talent": "The effect of a work of art upon the person who enjoys it is an experience different in kind from any experience not of art" (*The Sacred Wood,* p. 54).

24. Bell, pp. 60–61, 61–62, 59.

25. Marsden, p. 118.

26. *The Sacred Wood,* p. 58.

27. Max Nordau, *Degeneration,* trans. from the 2d German ed. (1895; rpt. New York: Howard Fertig, 1968), p. 324.

28. "When the two gases previously mentioned [oxygen and sulphur dioxide] are mixed in the presence of a filament of platinum, they form sulphurous acid. This combination takes place only if the platinum is present; nevertheless the newly formed acid contains no trace of platinum, and the platinum itself is apparently unaffected; has remained inert, neutral, and unchanged. The mind of the poet is the shred of platinum" (*The Sacred Wood,* p. 54).

29. Ezra Pound, "Affirmations: As for Imagisme," in *Selected Prose 1909–1965,* ed. William Cookson (New York: New Directions, 1973), p. 376. First published in *The New Age,* 16 (January 1915), 349–50.

30. D. H. Lawrence to Edward Garnett, 5 June 1914, in *The Letters of D. H. Lawrence,* ed. George Zytaruk and James T. Boulton, II (Cambridge: Cambridge University Press, 1981), 183.

31. Walter Pater, "Style," in *Appreciations* (London: Macmillan, 1904), pp. 36–37. Compare Matthew Arnold's preface to *Poems* (1853): the poet "needs . . . to be perpetually reminded to prefer his action to everything else; so to treat this, as to permit its inherent excellences to develop themselves, without interruption from the intrusion of his personal peculiarities; most fortunate, when he most entirely succeeds in effacing himself, and in enabling a noble action to subsist as it did in nature" ("Preface to First Edition of Poems [1853]," in *Irish Essays and Others* [London: Smith, Elder, 1882], pp. 292–93). Eliot's notion of impersonality seems—somewhat surprisingly, given the self-consciously "classical" character of Arnold's preface—closer to Pater's than to Arnold's.

32. "The Perfect Critic," pp. 13,11.

33. "The Possibility of a Poetic Drama," p. 65.

34. The relations between the author of *The Sacred Wood* and Matthew Arnold on the one hand and Walter Pater on the other are hopelessly tangled.

Most discussions of the lines of filiation between Arnold and Eliot as critics
concentrate on Eliot's later writings (see, for instance, John Henry Raleigh,
Matthew Arnold and American Culture [Berkeley and Los Angeles: University
of California Press, 1961], pp. 193–219; Ian Gregor, "Eliot and Matthew
Arnold," in *Eliot in Perspective: A Symposium,* ed. Graham Martin [New York:
Humanities Press, 1970], pp. 267–78; and Roger Kojecký, *T. S. Eliot's Social
Criticism* [London: Faber and Faber, 1971], esp. pp. 19–34); I discuss Arnold's
presence in *The Sacred Wood* in "The Nineteenth Century in Modernist Crit-
icism," Diss. Columbia University 1980, pp. 73–116.

Echoes of Pater in *The Sacred Wood* are a little more difficult to account
for, given that book's general attack on the "impressionistic criticism" of the
Paterian school. But they are there; compare, for instance, this statement in
Eliot's essay on George Wyndham: "What is permanent and good in Romanticism is curiosity . . . a curiosity which recognizes that any life, if accurately
and profoundly penetrated, is interesting and always strange" ("A Romantic
Aristocrat," p. 31), with Pater's definition in the postscript to *Appreciations:*
"It is the addition of strangeness to beauty, that constitutes the romantic character in art; and the desire of beauty being a fixed element in every artistic
organization, it is the addition of curiosity to this desire of beauty, that constitutes the romantic temper" (p. 246). Compare also this passage in the essay
on Massinger (only a few sentences after English criticism has been de-
nounced for its unscientific character):

> Reading Shakespeare and several of his contemporaries is pleasure enough,
> perhaps all the pleasure possible, for most. But if we wish to consummate and
> refine this pleasure by understanding it, to distil the last drop of it, to press
> and press the essence of each author, to apply exact measurement to our own
> sensations, then we must compare; and we cannot compare without parcelling
> the threads of authorship and influence

("Philip Massinger," p. 124), with Pater's advice in the preface to *The Renaissance:*

> the function of the aesthetic critic is to distinguish, to analyse, and separate
> from its adjuncts, the virtue by which a picture, a landscape, a fair personality
> in life or in a book, produces this special impression of beauty or pleasure, to
> indicate what the source of that impression is, and under what conditions it is
> experienced. His end is reached when he has disengaged that virtue, and noted
> it, as chemist notes some natural element, for himself and others

(*The Renaissance: Studies in Art and Poetry,* ed. Donald L. Hill [Berkeley and
Los Angeles: University of California Press, 1980], pp. xx–xxi). It is hard to
see how Eliot's prescription for "The Perfect Critic," with its motto from
Gourmont, "Eriger en lois ses impressions personnelles, c'est le grand effort
d'un homme s'il est sincère," is in the end different from Pater's—in spite of
the effort of that essay to make a meaningful distinction in favor of Arnold's

"knowing the object as it really is" against Pater's "knowing one's impression as it really is."

But this sort of inconsistency is only another instance of Eliot's general practice of appropriating whatever is available to suit his own uses, which is why Arnold and Pater often reappear as disguised authorities in his essays a few paragraphs after their influence has been deplored.

35. "A Romantic Aristocrat," p. 30.

36. "A Note on the American Critic," p. 39.

37. "Philip Massinger," p. 129.

38. "The Metaphysical Poets," in *Selected Essays*, pp. 247–49.

39. See Joseph E. Duncan, *The Revival of Metaphysical Poetry: The History of a Style, 1800 to the Present* (Minneapolis: University of Minnesota Press, 1959), pp. 118–29; and Frank Kermode, *Romantic Image* (London: Routledge and Kegan Paul, 1957), esp. pp. 138–61. On the Romantic antecedents of Eliot's nominally anti-Romantic critical formulations, see Edward Lobb, *T. S. Eliot and the Romantic Critical Tradition* (London, Boston, and Henley: Routledge and Kegan Paul, 1981), esp. pp. 60–92.

Parts of Eliot's discussion of the metaphysical poets are in fact rather sharply reminiscent of the preface to *Lyrical Ballads*: "A good deal resides in the richness of association," he remarks of some lines by Lord Herbert of Cherbury, ". . . but the meaning is clear, and the language simple and elegant. It is to be observed that the language of these poets is as a rule simple and pure. . . . The *structure* of the sentences, on the other hand, is sometimes far from simple, but this is not a vice; it is a fidelity to thought and feeling. The effect, at its best, is far less artifical than that of an ode by Gray" ("The Metaphysical Poets," in *Selected Essays*, pp. 244–45). Eliot must have had Arnold's essay on Gray (1880), with its attack on the prosaic quality of the poetry of Pope and Dryden, on his mind here, and not Wordsworth's strictures. It might also be remembered that Eliot's definition of Marvellian wit is made to depend on Coleridge's description of the imagination in chapter fourteen of the *Biographia Literaria* (see "Andrew Marvell," in *Selected Essays*, pp. 256–57). But the relation between "The Metaphysical Poets" and English Romanticism, as Kermode has demonstrated, is much more than a matter of common critical phrases.

40. J. Middleton Murry, "Milton or Shakespeare?" *The Nation and the Athenaeum*, 28 (26 March 1921), 916–17. "The Metaphysical Poets" appeared in October 1921. Eliot's comprehensive attack on Milton came in the 1936 essay ("A Note on the Verse of John Milton," in *Essays and Studies by Members of the English Association*, 21 [Oxford: Clarendon Press, 1936], pp. 32–40), which repeats Murry's argument (though it does not mention Murry) about the deleterious effects of Miltonic blank verse. It is typical of Eliot's relations with Murry that when he performed his famous recantation in the *second* Milton essay (1947; first published in *On Poetry and Poets* [1957]), the critic he attacked for having too severe a view of Milton's influence was Middleton Murry.

41. A. L. H[uxley], "Poetry and Science," *The Athenaeum,* 22 August 1919, p. 783. Standing behind Huxley's view of Laforgue (as it certainly stands behind Eliot's) is Remy de Gourmont's essay of 1904: "His [Laforgue's] intelligence was very lively, but closely linked to his sensibility. All original intelligences are so composed—they are the expansion, the flowering, of a physiology. But in the process of living, one acquires the faculty of dissociating intelligence from sensibility" ("The Sensibility of Jules Laforgue," in *Selected Writings,* trans. and ed. Glenn S. Burne [Ann Arbor: University of Michigan Press, 1966], p. 199). The connection between literary style and physiological condition was a preoccupation of Gourmont's ("Style is a physiological product, and one of the most constant," he asserts in *Le Problème du style* [1902] [*Selected Writings,* p. 112]). On what Eliot's terminology owed to Gourmont, and how Eliot put that terminology to uses of his own, see F. W. Bateson, "Dissociation of Sensibility," *Essays in Criticism,* 1 (1951), 302–12.

42. Preface to *Homage to John Dryden* (London: Hogarth Press, 1924), p. 9.

43. See Eliot's "Milton II," in *On Poetry and Poets* (New York: Farrar, Straus and Cudahy, 1957), p. 173; L. C. Knights, "Bacon and the Seventeenth-Century Dissociation of Sensibility," *Scrutiny,* 11 (Summer 1943), 268–85; Basil Willey, *The Seventeenth Century Background* (New York: Columbia University Press, 1958), pp. 86–92; and Jürgen Kramer, "T. S. Eliot's Concept of Tradition: A Revaluation," *New German Critique,* 6 (1975), 20–30.

44. *Selected Essays,* p. 246.

45. "The Perfect Critic," in *The Sacred Wood,* p. 11.

CHAPTER 7

1. See, in particular, F. W. Bateson, "Criticism's Lost Leader," in *The Literary Criticism of T. S. Eliot: New Essays,* ed. David Newton-DeMolina (London: Athlone Press, 1977), pp. 1–19; and Ronald Bush, *T. S. Eliot: A Study in Character and Style* (New York: Oxford University Press, 1984), esp. pp. 72–78, 102–6.

2. Bateson, p. 8.

3. Clive Bell, "T. S. Eliot," *The Nation and the Athenaeum,* 33 (22 September 1923), 772.

4. J. B. Priestley, "Contemporary Criticism: A Note," *London Mercury,* 11 (March 1925), 500.

5. John Middleton Murry, "The 'Classical' Revival," *The Adelphi,* 3 (February 1926), 590.

6. See, for example, Richard Aldington, *Life for Life's Sake* (New York: Viking, 1941): "Tom Eliot's career in England has been exactly the reverse of Ezra's. Ezra started out in a time of peace and prosperity with everything in his favour, and muffed his chances of becoming literary dictator of London— to which he undoubtedly aspired—by his own conceit, folly, and bad manners.

Eliot started in the enormous confusion of war and post-war England, handicapped in every way. Yet by merit, tact, prudence, and pertinacity he succeeded in doing what no other American has ever done—imposing his personality, tastes, and even many of his opinions on literary England" (p. 217).

7. Ottoline Morrell, *Ottoline at Garsington: Memoirs of Lady Ottoline Morrell 1915–1918*, ed. Robert Gathorne-Hardy (London: Faber and Faber, 1974), pp. 101–2. She and Eliot later became quite close.

8. Aldous Huxley to Julian Huxley, 29 December 1916, in *The Letters of Aldous Huxley*, ed. Grover Smith (London: Chatto and Windus, 1969), p. 117.

9. Lytton Strachey to Dora Carrington, 14 May 1919, quoted in Michael Holroyd, *Lytton Strachey: A Critical Biography* (New York: Holt, Rinehart and Winston, 1968), II, 364.

10. Douglas Goldring, "Modern Critical Prose," *The Chapbook*, 2 (February 1920), 12–13. Eliot, said Goldring, "has undoubtedly one of the most distinguished critical minds of our time" (p. 11).

11. James Reeves, "Cambridge Twenty Years Ago," in *T. S. Eliot: A Symposium*, ed. Tambimuttu and Richard March (New York: Tambimuttu and Mass, 1948), p. 38.

12. F. W. Bateson, "T. S. Eliot: 'Impersonality Fifty Years After,' " *Southern Review*, n.s. 3 (1969), 637.

13. See I. A. Richards, "On TSE," in *T. S. Eliot: The Man and His Work*, ed. Allen Tate (New York: Dell, 1966), pp. 2–6.

14. F. R. Leavis, "Approaches to T. S. Eliot," in *The Common Pursuit* (London: Chatto and Windus, 1952), p. 280. First published in *Scrutiny*, 15 (December 1947), 56–67.

15. Bateson, "T. S. Eliot: 'Impersonality Fifty Years After,' " p. 638.

16. For a recent discussion of the rise of academic English studies, see Francis Mulhern, *The Moment of "Scrutiny"* (London: NLB, 1979), pp. 3–34; on the demise of the extra-academic critical tradition, see, generally, John Gross, *The Rise and Fall of the Man of Letters: A Study of the Idiosyncratic and the Humane in Modern Literature* (New York: Macmillan, 1969).

17. See chapter six, herein.

18. For no critic was this more true, of course, than for F. R. Leavis. The first phase of his career was devoted in large part to showing the academic relevance of Eliot's early work—as subsequent phases were devoted to undoing the influence of Eliot's later critical positions; see, for Leavis's own summary of the situation, "A Retrospect 1950," in *New Bearings in English Poetry* (Ann Arbor: University of Michigan Press, 1960), pp. 215–38.

Eliot's American influence was scarcely limited to the Southern New Critics; F. O. Matthiessen's *The Achievement of T. S. Eliot* (Boston and New York: Houghton Mifflin, 1935) is a good instance of another style of appreciation (Matthiessen thought Leavis's defensive posture somewhat supererogatory [see p. 45]). Edmund Wilson commented in 1931 on Eliot's general eminence as a critic in *Axel's Castle: A Study in the Imaginative Literature of 1870–1930* (New York: Scribner's, 1931), pp. 114–24. Wilson was himself an early admirer of *The Sacred Wood;* see Wilson, "America and Other Tragedies," *Vanity Fair,* 20 (August 1923), 6: "T. S. Eliot's *The Sacred Wood . . .* contained an intellectual current sufficient to reduce to a flimsy cinder most of the literary journalism of the new regime."

19. Arnold Bennett to Elsie Herzog, 7 September 1918, in *The Letters of Arnold Bennett,* ed. James Hepburn (London: Oxford University Press, 1970), III, 68.

20. Arnold Bennett to T. S. Eliot, 3 June 1927, in *The Letters of Arnold Bennett,* III, 286. Bennett felt similarly about Virgina Woolf: "She is the queen of the high-brows," he wrote of her, and he came to regard their quarrel about the novel as a quarrel between popular and mandarin art (see Samuel Hynes, introduction to *The Author's Craft and Other Critical Writings of Arnold Bennett,* ed. Hynes [Lincoln: University of Nebraska Press, 1968], p. xvii). Another figure (though Bennett's junior) who felt himself displaced in this way was Frank Swinnerton, who associated Eliot's success with the advent of a "new academicism" (see Swinnerton, *The Georgian Scene: A Literary Panorama* [New York: Farrar and Rinehart, 1934], pp. 485–95).

21. Preface to *Homage to John Dryden* (London: Hogarth Press, 1924), p. 9.

22. "John Donne," *The Nation and the Athenaeum,* 33 (9 June 1923), 332.

23. The lectures are in the Hayward Bequest at King's College, Cambridge. Their argument is summarized, and selections are quoted, in Edward Lobb, *T. S. Eliot and the Romantic Critical Tradition* (London, Boston, and Henley: Routledge and Kegan Paul, 1981), pp. 15–59. The third lecture was published, in French translation, as "Deux attitudes mystiques: Dante et Donne," *Chroniques,* 3 (1927), 149–73.

24. "Donne in Our Time," in *A Garland for John Donne,* ed. Theodore Spencer (1931; rpt. Gloucester, Mass.: Peter Smith, 1958), p. 8.

25. Delmore Schwartz, "The Literary Dictatorship of T. S. Eliot," *Partisan Review,* 16 (February 1949), 120.

26. "Milton I," in *On Poetry and Poets* (New York: Farrar, Straus and Cudahy, 1957), p. 156. "Milton II" is in the same volume, pp. 165–83.

27. *Anatomy of Criticism: Four Essays* (Princeton: Princeton University Press, 1957), p. 18.

28. "Kipling Redivivus," *The Athenaeum,* 9 May 1919, p. 297. Compare Eliot's remarks on Swinburne in this essay with Hart Crane, "Joyce and Ethics," *The Little Review,* 5 (July 1918), 65 (on "Swinburne's instability in criticism and every form of literature that did not depend almost exclusively on sound for effect").

29. "The Idealism of Julien Benda," *The New Republic,* 57 (12 December 1928), 106.

30. "Rudyard Kipling," in *On Poetry and Poets,* p. 284. Originally published

in Eliot's selection, *A Choice of Kipling's Verse* (London: Faber and Faber, 1941), pp. 5–36.

31. "The Unfading Genius of Rudyard Kipling," *The Kipling Journal*, 26 (March 1959), 11–12.

32. Eliot to Richard Aldington, 15 November 1922, quoted in *An Exhibition of Manuscripts and First Editions of T. S. Eliot* (Humanities Research Center, University of Texas [Austin], 1961), p. 8.

33. Arnold Bennett, *The Journals of Arnold Bennett*, ed. Newman Flower (London: Cassell, 1933), III, 52. Entry for 10 September 1924. For further statements of Eliot's expressing disillusionment with the poem, see Lyndall Gordon, *Eliot's Early Years* (Oxford: Oxford University Press, 1977), pp. 118–19.

34. The subject is discussed in detail in chapter four herein.

35. Preface to *The Sacred Wood: Essays on Poetry and Criticism*, 2d ed. (London: Methuen, 1928), p. viii.

36. Preface to *For Lancelot Andrews* (London: Faber and Faber, 1928), p. 7.

37. "The Problem of Education," *The Harvard Advocate*, 121 (September 1934), 11.

38. Eliot to Paul Elmer More, 20 June 1934, quoted in Roger Kojecký, *T. S. Eliot's Social Criticism* (London: Faber and Faber, 1971), p. 78.

39. Stephen Spender, *T. S. Eliot* (New York: Viking, 1975), pp. 133–34.

40. *After Strange Gods: A Primer of Modern Heresy* (New York: Harcourt, Brace, 1934), pp. 31–32.

41. See William Chace, *The Political Identities of Ezra Pound and T. S. Eliot* (Stanford: Stanford University Press, 1973), pp. 160–61.

42. "Mr. Read and Mr. Fernandez," *The New Criterion*, 4 (October 1926), 752–53. The magazine bore this title during its brief existence as a monthly.

43. Williams's work on this subject seems to me not to have been superseded. For recent discussion of the nineteenth-century notion of culture with reference to *Culture and Society*, see Gerald L. Bruns, "The Formal Nature of Victorian Thinking," *PMLA*, 90 (1975), 904–18; and Michael Timko, "The Victorianism of Victorian Literature," *New Literary History*, 6 (1975), 609–28, esp. pp. 620–21.

44. See Raymond Williams, *Culture and Society 1780–1950* (New York: Columbia University Press, 1958), pp. 295–97.

Index